# The Illustrated Encyclopedia of
# TECHNOLOGY

Marshall Cavendish

**Academic Advisors:**
Professor John Taylor, M.A., Ph.D.,
Professor of Mathematics,
King's College,
University of London.

**Editors:**
Michael Bisacre
Richard Carlisle
Deborah Robertson
John Ruck

Published by Marshall Cavendish Books Limited
58 Old Compton Street,
London W1V 5PA.

© Marshall Cavendish Limited 1975—84

Printed and bound in Italy by New Interlitho SpA.

ISBN 0 86307 197 X

This volume is not to be sold in Australia, New Zealand,
the United States of America or its Territories.

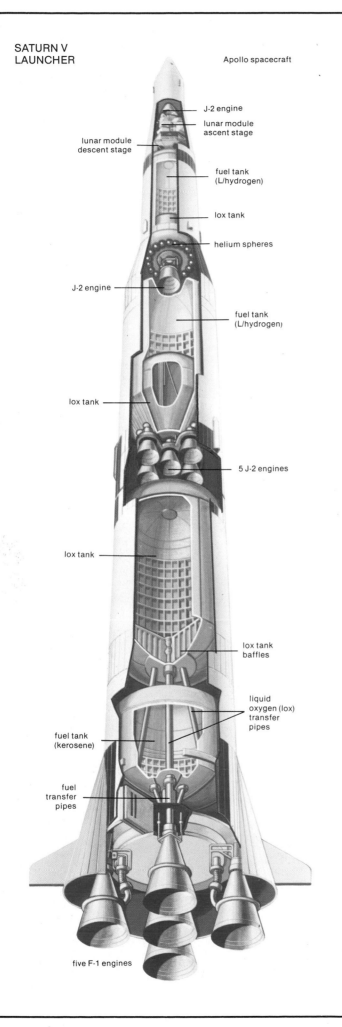

SATURN V
LAUNCHER

Apollo spacecraft

J-2 engine

lunar module
ascent stage

lunar module
descent stage

fuel tank
(L/hydrogen)

lox tank

helium spheres

J-2 engine

fuel tank
(L/hydrogen)

lox tank

5 J-2 engines

lox tank

lox tank
baffles

liquid
oxygen (lox)
transfer
pipes

fuel tank
(kerosene)

fuel
transfer
pipes

five F-1 engines

# Contents

## Consumer and Service Technology

| | |
|---|---|
| Dairy Products | 2 |
| Food Processing | 6 |
| Beers, Wines and Spirits | 10 |
| Farm Technology | 14 |
| Domestic Appliances | 19 |
| Electricity Supply | 22 |
| Water Supply | 26 |

## Building Technology

| | |
|---|---|
| Road Building | 32 |
| Tunnels | 37 |
| Bridges | 40 |

## Transport Technology

| | |
|---|---|
| Aircraft | 48 |
| Helicopters and Autogyros | 52 |
| Hovercraft and Hydrofoils | 56 |
| Bicycles and Motorcycles | 60 |
| Cars, Trucks and Buses | 64 |
| Railways | 68 |

## Military and Space Technology

| | |
|---|---|
| Guns | 74 |
| Explosives | 80 |
| Warships and Submarines | 84 |
| Rockets and Missiles | 90 |
| Spaceflight | 94 |

## Applied Technology

| | |
|---|---|
| Mechanics | 102 |
| Machine Tools | 106 |
| Welding | 109 |
| Telephone and Telegraph | 112 |
| Radio | 118 |
| Cameras and Film | 122 |
| Sound Recording | 126 |
| Sound Reproduction | 130 |
| Cinema | 136 |
| Calculators | 141 |

# Consumer
# and
# Service Technology

# Dairy Products

Dairying, the rearing of animals for their milk and the use of this milk for drinking, or for making milk products such as butter, cheese and yogurt, probably originated in south-west Asia at the end of the Stone Age. Since these early beginnings, when most of the milk was obtained from sheep and goats, the dairy industry has become a major source of food, particularly in Western countries. Although the cow is the chief source of milk in developed countries, this is not always the case in less developed areas where the climate may not be suitable for cattle rearing. Other animals used as sources of milk include sheep, goats, buffalo, reindeer and camels.

Milk is the only natural food which contains, to a greater or lesser extent, most of the essential nutrients. Proteins, principally *casein* (which gives milk its characteristic white colour), *lactalbumin* and *lactoglobulin*, account for about 3.75 per cent of the weight of milk. Fats, in the form of tiny globules which are lighter than the water in the milk and so float to the top as cream, constitute about 3 to 5 per cent of milk.

Another constituent of milk is the carbohydrate *lactose* or milk sugar. Lactose, which accounts for about 4.75 per cent of the weight of milk, is easily digested by most people, and in addition to its value as an energy source it also promotes the growth of *Lactobacillus* bacteria in the intestines. The lactobacillus bacteria create acidic conditions in the intestines, and this inhibits the growth of certain harmful bacteria there.

Calcium is one of the most important minerals contained in milk, whose mineral content is about 0.75 per cent by weight. Other important minerals in milk are phosphorus and potassium, and small amounts of iron are also present. The principal vitamins in milk are vitamin A (*retinol*) and vitamin B$_2$ (*riboflavin*), plus some vitamin C (*ascorbic acid*) and vitamin D (*calciferol*).

## Milk production

One of the most important advances in dairy farming was the invention of the milking machine, which allowed large herds to be milked quickly, hygienically, and with a minimum of labour. The forerunners of today's machines appeared in the late nineteenth century, and all the basic features had been established by the 1920s. The vacuum-operated milking machine uses a combination of sucking and squeezing on the cow's teats to make the milk flow, and the milk is drawn into a calibrated container so that the yield from the cow can be measured and recorded. A good cow on a modern farm may yield as much as 4,100 litres (900 gal) of milk per year.

When the milk has been collected, it must be cooled to below 10°C (50°F) to inhibit the growth of the bacteria which are found in fresh 'raw' milk. The traditional way of storing the milk for collection and delivery to the dairy is by putting it into metal churns, but many farms are now equipped with refrigerated milk tanks. These tanks cool the milk to 4.4°C (40°F) and keep it at that temper-

ature, until it is collected by a refrigerated milk tanker.

## Milk processing

Nearly all the milk sold to the public has undergone some form of processing to destroy the bacteria which cause souring by converting the lactose into *lactic acid*. This processing is designed to extend the keeping life of the milk. One of the commonest forms of treatment is *pasteurization*, named after the French chemist and bacteriologist Louis Pasteur (1822-95) whose work led to the development of the process.

Pasteurization is carried out prior to bottling, and most dairies now use the HTST (high temperature, short time) process. This is a continuous process, in which the milk is heated to over 72°C (161°F) for at least 15 seconds, then cooled rapidly to about 3°C (38°F) and bottled. Pasteurized milk will keep well in a refrigerator for about three days, but then it begins to go off because of the action of *proteolytic* bacteria which attack the milk proteins.

These proteolytic bacteria can be destroyed by *sterilization*. The milk is first pasteurized, and then *homogenized* by forcing it through very small openings so that the fat globules are broken up. The fat then remains thoroughly dispersed throughout the milk and does not separate out and float to the top. Pasteurized milk is often homogenized before bottling, and sold as pasteurized homogenized milk.

In the sterilization process itself, the pasteurized, homogenized milk is bottled and then steam-heated for between 20 and 30 minutes at least at 100°C (212°F). Sterilized milk will keep well, even without refrigeration, for several weeks.

The most effective form of milk treatment is the UHT (ultra heat treatment) process, of which there are several versions. In one of these, milk is preheated to 75 to 80°C (165 to 175°F). Then steam is injected into it to raise its temperature rapidly to about 150°C (300°F) and keep it at that temperature for about three seconds to kill off all the bacteria and mould spores present. The milk is then passed into a vacuum chamber, where the water which condensed into it from the steam evaporates again and cools the milk as it does so. The milk is then homogenized, and packed into sterile, foil-lined cartons. It will keep for several months without refrigeration.

Two other forms of liquid milk which

**Above left: Milking a cow by hand. Cows begin producing milk when they have calves, at about 2 years old, and to ensure a regular supply of milk they are usually mated or artificially inseminated about every 12 months. This means that they can be milked for about 9 or 10 months in each year.**

**Above: Cows being milked by machine in a modern *rotary herringbone* milking parlour. The milking stalls are arranged in a herringbone pattern around a platform which rotates around the operator's work area, so that, for example, up to 180 cows can be milked in an hour by only two operators.**

**Above: The traditional way of taking milk from the farm to the dairy is in churns, which are collected from the farm and taken to the dairy by truck. This picture shows samples of milk being taken for quality checks after delivery to a French dairy. France has the largest dairy industry in Europe.**

**Below: The pasteurization section of an automated dairy. Milk is delivered to the dairy by tanker, tested for quality, then passed through the pasteurization plant and filled into bottles or cartons. Strict standards of quality and hygiene are maintained throughout the process.**

# DAIRY PROCESSES

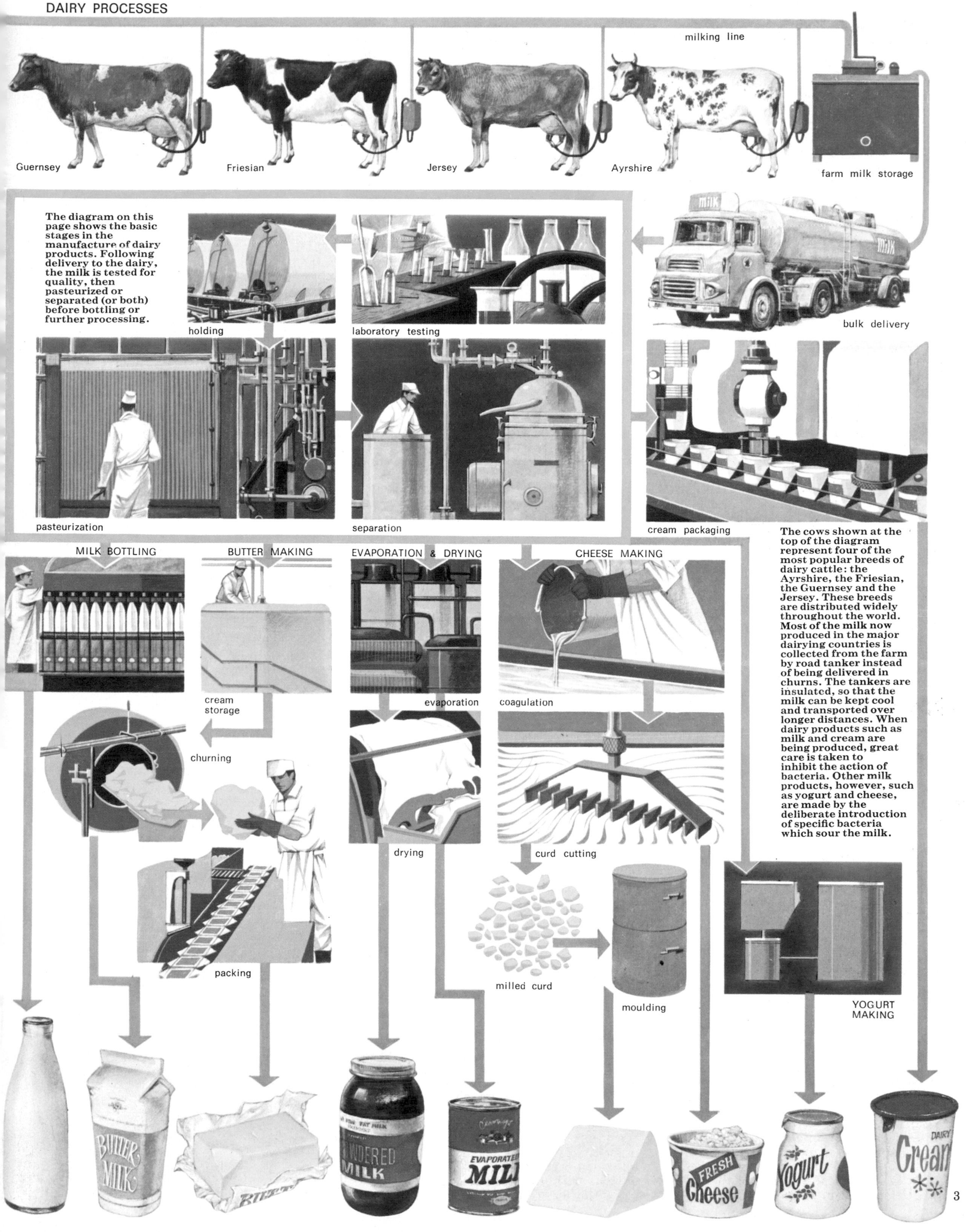

Guernsey

Friesian

Jersey

Ayrshire

milking line

farm milk storage

The diagram on this page shows the basic stages in the manufacture of dairy products. Following delivery to the dairy, the milk is tested for quality, then pasteurized or separated (or both) before bottling or further processing.

holding

laboratory testing

bulk delivery

pasteurization

separation

cream packaging

MILK BOTTLING

BUTTER MAKING

EVAPORATION & DRYING

CHEESE MAKING

The cows shown at the top of the diagram represent four of the most popular breeds of dairy cattle: the Ayrshire, the Friesian, the Guernsey and the Jersey. These breeds are distributed widely throughout the world. Most of the milk now produced in the major dairying countries is collected from the farm by road tanker instead of being delivered in churns. The tankers are insulated, so that the milk can be kept cool and transported over longer distances. When dairy products such as milk and cream are being produced, great care is taken to inhibit the action of bacteria. Other milk products, however, such as yogurt and cheese, are made by the deliberate introduction of specific bacteria which sour the milk.

cream storage

evaporation

coagulation

churning

drying

curd cutting

milled curd

moulding

YOGURT MAKING

packing

BUTTER MILK

POWDERED MILK

EVAPORATED MILK

FRESH Cheese

Yogurt

DAIRY Cream

3

Edouard Rousseau/Snark

Right: Removing butter from a churn at an automated butter factory in New Zealand. The butter produced in New Zealand is made from pasteurized cream and it is salted. This means it has good keeping properties under refrigeration, which is an advantage because most of New Zealand's butter has to be shipped long distances to overseas customers such as the United Kingdom.

Below: Blocks of Cheddar cheese ready to be cut, weighed and packed. Cheddar cheese, made from pasteurized milk, is ripened for up to 9 months at a temperature of about 10°C (50°F) and a relative humidity of 80 to 90 per cent.

Unigate

keep well for long periods are *condensed* milk and *evaporated* milk. Both of these products are basically milk which has been concentrated by having the water removed from it by evaporation in a vacuum. The temperature at which water boils is reduced when the surrounding air pressure is low, and so when milk is heated in a vacuum the water will boil away at less than 54°C (130°F). At such temperatures, the nutritious constituents of the milk are practically unaffected, whereas they would be if the milk were concentrated by prolonged boiling at 100°C (212°F).

### Dried milk
Dried milk may be made either from whole fresh milk or from *skim milk*, milk from which most of the cream has been separated. Most dried milk is made by *spray drying*, although milk intended for use as baby food may be dried by passing it over heated rollers. Milk to be spray dried is first concentrated by vacuum evaporation to reduce its water content to about 60 per cent. It is then preheated to about 65°C (150°F), and sprayed into a large chamber into which air at a temperature of about 190°C (375°F) is blown. The water is driven out of the milk droplets, leaving particles of dried milk solids which contain less than 5 per cent moisture.

### Butter and cream
The simplest way of separating cream from milk is simply to leave the milk to stand undisturbed, so that the cream floats to the top and can be merely skimmed off. A quicker and more effective method is to heat the milk to about 49°C (120°F), and pass it through a *centrifuge*. The centrifuge is basically a rapidly-rotating bowl, and when the warm milk is put into it the heavier part of it, the skim milk is flung out to the edge by centrifugal force. The lighter part, the cream, remains near the centre of the bowl, and the skim milk and cream are discharged from the centrifuge through separate outlets.

Above: One of the causes of milk spoilage is the action of *proteolytic* bacteria which attack the milk proteins. These bacteria can be destroyed by sterilization. In this process, pasteurized, homogenized milk is bottled and then steam-heated to 100°C (212°F) for up to 30 minutes.

Below: Rows of Emmenthal cheeses ripening under conditions of controlled temperature and humidity. The length of the ripening time depends upon the type of cheese. Many soft cheeses need no ripening, but hard cheeses may require months of ripening before they mature.

New Zealand Dairy Board

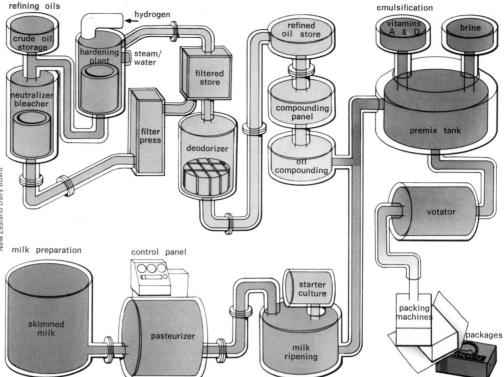

Diagram labels: refining oils, crude oil storage, hardening plant, steam/water, hydrogen, neutralizer bleacher, filter press, filtered store, deodorizer, refined oil store, compounding panel, oil compounding, emulsification, vitamins A & D, brine, premix tank, votator, packing machines, packages, milk preparation, control panel, skimmed milk, pasteurizer, starter culture, milk ripening

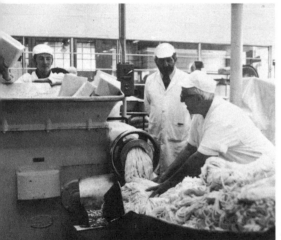

Unigate

**Above:** The first stage in the manufacture of processed cheese is to extrude a hard cheese, such as Cheddar, into this spaghetti-like form. It is then emulsified with salts (such as citrates or phosphates), water and whey powder, and heated and mixed to give it the required consistency.

**Below:** Yogurt is made from whole, evaporated, partly skimmed or dried milk, to which is added a 'culture' containing bacteria which converts the lactose to lactic acid. In this picture, a culture is being prepared from a 'mother culture'. One type of bacteria commonly used is *Lactobacillus bulgaricus*.

**Above:** Ordinary margarine is made by emulsifying blended vegetable and animal oils with ripened skimmed milk. The oils used, which include palm, sunflower, coconut and groundnut oils, fish oils, and animal fats such as lard, are bleached, hardened and deodorized and then blended before entering the premix tank. In the premix tank the blended oils are mixed with the milk which has been ripened to give it flavour and acidity, and vitamins are added. This mixture is solidified in a machine called a *votator*, which chills and mixes it to produce the required texture and consistency.

Alfa-Laval

Dairies produce many types and grades of cream. In Britain they range from *half cream*, which must contain at least 12 per cent milk fat (also known as *butterfat*), to *clotted cream*, which has a minimum fat content of 55 per cent. Creams may be pasteurized, sterilized or ultra heat treated, and some are also homogenized. A small amount of untreated cream is also produced.

Butter may be made either from plain pasteurized cream, known as 'sweet cream', or from cream which has been 'ripened' by bacteria cultures such as *Streptococcus paracitrovorus* to enhance its flavour. Sweet cream butter, such as New Zealand butter, has very good keeping qualities. Butter is made in large churns, stainless steel barrels which are rotated mechanically so that the butterfat particles in the cream cling together to form grains of butter. The churning continues until the butter grains are approximately pea-sized, then the liquid residue or *buttermilk* is removed.

Next, the butter is rinsed with water, and if a salted butter is to be produced the salt, up to about 5 per cent of the butter weight, is added at this stage. Salting gives the butter a stronger flavour and prolongs its storage life. The churning is then continued to work the butter into a single mass of the required consistency and to remove excess moisture. Finally, the butter is removed from the churn and packed.

## Cheese

There are hundreds of different types of cheese produced throughout the world, but they can be divided roughly into two groups, 'hard' cheeses and 'soft' cheeses.

Hard cheeses, such as Cheddar, are made from pasteurized whole milk which has been ripened with a culture of lactic acid bacteria, which converts some of the lactose into lactic acid.

The milk proteins are then coagulated into a *curd* by the addition of *rennet*, a substance containing the enzymes *rennin* and *pepsin* which is obtained from the stomachs of young calves. The curd is next cut into cubes to allow the liquid residue or *whey* to separate out. The curd is heated to 38°C (100°F) to drive out the whey, which is drained off, and then cut into blocks which are pressed to remove the last of the whey.

The blocks of dry curd are *milled* (cut into small pieces) and then salt is added to improve the flavour and act as a preservative. The final cheese is produced by pressing the salted curd in moulds for about 48 hours, then ripening it under conditions of controlled temperature and humidity for three to six months. The ripening is a result of bacterial and enzyme action.

Soft cheeses are made in a similar way, except that the whey is left to drain from the curd by gravity, without the application of pressure or heat. The resulting cheese has a high moisture content, between 50 and 70 per cent, and so has a soft texture. Certain soft cheeses are inoculated with mould cultures that excrete enzymes which give them characteristic flavours. Camembert, for example, is treated with *Penicillium camemberti*, and blue-veined cheeses are pierced with wires to allow air into the interior so that the growth of the mould used, *Penicillium roqueforti*, is encouraged along the wire holes.

Lactic acid cheeses are produced by the action of lactic acid on the milk protein. The acid coagulates the protein into a soft curd, which is then simply drained of whey and salted. Cottage cheese is made in a similar way, but it is made from pasteurized fat-free milk and the curd is washed with skim milk, often containing skim milk powder, to give it its characteristic texture.

# Food Processing

Techniques of food preservation derive from the historical need for man to preserve surplus food produce in times of plenty to allow for seasonal variations and famines. When plant or animal tissue is harvested, the food immediately becomes subject to spoilage attack by enzymes, bacteria, moulds and yeasts.

*Enzymes* are proteins which catalyze biochemical reactions within the food tissue. The browning of apples, for example, is caused by the oxidation of the amino acid *tyrosine* by the enzyme *phenolase*. Enzymes in harvested fruits and vegetables are normally made harmless by steam or water blanching at temperatures from 90 °C to 100 °C (194 to 212 °F) for 3 to 5 minutes.

*Bacteria* are micro-organisms varying in size from 0.001 mm to 0.003 mm. Frequently, bacteria cause only food spoilage, as in the case of the lactic acid bacteria which sour milk. But much more serious are the bacteria which excrete a toxin—a type of spoilage termed *pathogenic*. The best-known pathogenic bacteria is *Clostridium botulinum* and it has been estimated that one teaspoon of the toxin from this micro-organism would be sufficient to poison a large urban water supply. To destroy the spores of a pure culture of *Cl. botulinum* requires 2.5 minutes at 121.1 °C (250 °F), and canning processes are always designed so that all the food within the can has adequate heat treatment to kill this and other pathogenic organisms. Equivalent processing times at 121.1 °C are sometimes of the order of 10 minutes to take account of the thermal protection afforded to the micro-organisms by the food.

*Moulds* are filamentous micro-organisms. *Byssochlamys fulva* is a particularly heat-resistant variety which attacks the *pectin* in the tissue cell walls of fruit, causing disintegration, for example, of canned strawberries. It can be inactivated by heat treatment at 91 °C (196 °F). *Yeasts* have a low heat resistance and can be eliminated by a few minutes' exposure at 74 °C (165 °F).

An important parameter determining the susceptibility of a processed food to spoilage is its *water activity*. This is the ratio of the pressure of the water vapour in the food to the vapour pressure of pure water at the same temperature. Most foods will be free from spoilage at a water activity below 0.62. It is this principle that gives the long shelf life of comparatively moist foods such as dried fruits (15-20 per cent moisture) and cakes.

Additives such as glycerol and salt are frequently used in small quantities (such as 0.5 per cent salt and 1.6 per cent glycerol) to lower the water activity of cakes and thus extend their shelf life. These additives, or *humectants*, are frequently employed because there is a limit to the amount of moisture which can be removed from a cake without significantly altering its freshness and 'mouthfeel'.

## Low temperature processing

Low temperature food processing can be divided into two main categories: *chilling* and *freezing*. Chilling does not involve crystallization of the water in the food,

Above: Salting cod. The fish is split, headed and cleaned, then packed between layers of pure salt. Eventually, the salt content of the fish reaches a concentration of about 18 % of the weight of the fish, and then the surplus is washed off and the fish is dried to reduce its moisture content to less than 15 %, which prevents mould growth.

Right: Gherkins are pickled in brine, which reduces their moisture content and creates a chemical environment which inhibits the growth of decay-producing organisms. Here, Polish gherkins are being pickled in barrels of brine kept in pools of slightly salted water.

and occurs within the temperature range 0 °C (32 °F) to 8 °C (46 °F), the upper figure being typical of a domestic refrigerator. Fruits such as apples and pears, for example, can be preserved for about one year by storage at temperatures of between 1.5 °C and 3.0 °C (35 and 37 °F).

The preservation of meat involves both chilling and freezing. Typically, a 164 kg (360 lb) carcass of high-quality beef is chilled to 12 °C (54 °F) in 25 hours using air at −1 °C (30.2 °F) circulated in the chiller at a speed of 2 m/sec (6.7 ft/sec). Further chilling and freezing is then completed by using air at −10 °C (14 °F). Both stages of the operation are completed within approximately 5½ days of slaughter.

The rate of beef freezing can be increased by butchering it into smaller portions and *blast freezing* it. For example, beef quarters can be frozen to −20 °C (−4 °F) in 21 hours by passing the meat from the slaughtering and dressing line into an air-blast freezing tunnel. Within the tunnel, fans circulate the air at 5.1 m/sec (16.7 ft/sec) at −40 °C (−40 °F).

*Fluidized bed freezing* is a method which can be applied to small food particles such as peas. Air at −23 °C (−9.4 °F) is blown through the underside of a continuous stainless steel mesh belt so that the peas become suspended in the air and the mixture of peas and air behaves rather like a fluid. The *Reynolds Number* (air density x pea diameter x air velocity/air viscosity) has to be greater than 100 for this fluidization to occur. Peas can be frozen in three minutes in this type of unit. Hygienic standards are met by passing the steel belt through a sanitizer and a water wash spray before it returns to the freezer to be loaded with more peas.

*Liquid nitrogen spray freezing* is now being more widely adopted in the food industry. Higher priced commodities such as scampi and pre-cooked dishes are ideal for this method. The boiling point of liquid nitrogen is −196 °C (−321 °F) and, since the nitrogen gas that is formed when the liquid vaporizes as it is sprayed on to the food is also initially at −196 °C, it is used to pre-cool the food material on entry to the freezing tunnel. In this way, maximum utilization of liquid nitrogen is achieved and thermal stresses within the food, which could easily cause cracking, are minimized. The manufacture of frozen foods is now a major industry producing an enormous range of goods.

Erich Hartmann/John Hillelson Agency

Interpress/John Watney

Left: Burning the bristles from a pig carcass after slaughtering. An alternative method of removing the bristles is to pass the carcass through a tank of water at 60°C (140°F), which loosens the bristles, and then through a machine which removes them mechanically.

Right: This sequence of four pictures shows some of the stages in the production of canned processed peas. The first picture is of the soaking tanks in which dried peas are rehydrated before being put into storage tanks to await processing. From the storage tanks, the peas pass along a conveyer belt where they are inspected visually and any bad ones are removed (second picture). The third picture shows the filler heads which fill the sterile cans with peas and brine. The cans are then sealed and conveyed into the oven, shown in the fourth picture, where they are cooked for over twenty minutes. After they have cooled, the cans are labelled and then packed for delivery.

Interpress/John Watney

## TYPICAL SORPTION ISOTHERMS

beef
potato
peach
green pepper

moisture content (weight %)

water activity

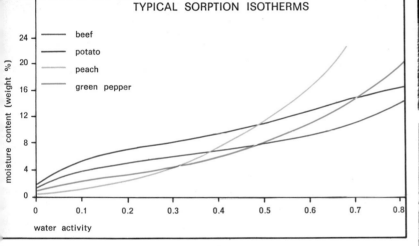

Batchelors

Batchelors

Above: This diagram shows the *sorption isotherms* for some popular foods. The isotherms show the relationship between the moisture content and the water activity of the foods. This type of graph is used to determine to what level the moisture content of a food must be reduced in order to bring its water activity to below that at which it will be free from spoilage: most foods will be free from spoilage below a water activity of about 0.62. Thus beef, for example, could be free from spoilage if its moisture content were reduced to below about 10 per cent.

Left: A cold storage warehouse containing meat and poultry. These warehouses are designed for storing frozen food for long periods, and are rather like enormous refrigerators. They are heavily insulated, and designed in such a way as to avoid heat entering through the doors. The temperature inside cold stores is usually maintained at less than —18°C (0°F) to minimize any deterioration of the stored food.

Imperial Foods Ltd

Batchelors

1    2    3    4    5    6    7    8    9

Heinz

Food Industries Ltd

**Left:** The production control room at a modern soup factory. In this factory, the production process is controlled by a computer, which selects the raw materials for 40 different soups from stocks of 44 separate ingredients. The computer selects the required quantities of ingredients for each type of soup and controls their delivery to the production lines, which can produce up to 68,000 litres (15,000 gallons) of soup per hour.

**Right:** The food industry uses a wide range of flavourings and colourings, particularly in the manufacture of convenience foods such as desserts and savoury snacks. Although there are many synthetic flavourings in use, a large proportion of the flavourings used are concentrated from natural sources.

**Below:** This chart shows the effects of the main food preservation methods on the various organisms and chemical conditions which cause food spoilage.

## High temperature processing

There are three main categories of high temperature processing: *pasteurization* at temperatures below 100°C (212°F); *steam retorting* (after canning) at 121.1°C (250°F); and *ultra heat treatment*, also called ultra high temperature (UHT) processing in the region of 180°C (356°F).

Most canned fruits can be preserved by pasteurizing between 90°C (194°F) and 100°C (212°F) because their pH (a measure of their acidity) is in the range 3 to 4. This is a sufficiently low pH (high acidity) to prevent the growth of pathogenic organisms. Grapefruit segments can be prepared by removing the outer membrane in a 2 per cent sodium hydroxide solution at 98°C (208°F) with a 10-second immersion time. The sodium hydroxide is neutralized by a further immersion in citric acid, and then the peeled segments are pasteurized at 100°C for 20 minutes in a can containing a sucrose syrup of 30 per cent weight concentration.

Food commodities of lower acidity (higher pH) such as soups, meat, fish and vegetable products require a more severe heat treatment. An example of this type of food is canned baked beans, a popular commodity consisting of pea or navy beans in tomato sauce.

The dried beans are first sieved to grade them for size, and any discoloured beans are removed by a photo-electric sorter. Other foreign material sinks out when the beans are *flumed* over a series of waterfalls. Moisture is re-absorbed by the beans by soaking in cold water for 12 to 18 hours, and the enzymes are destroyed by blanching at 88°C to 99°C (190°F to 210°F). At this stage the beans have approximately

Courtesy of Courtaulds Ltd

|  | enzymes | bacteria | fungi | oxygen | water | ph control | ionic |
|---|---|---|---|---|---|---|---|
| cooking | destroys above 80°C | most destroyed | some destroyed |  |  |  |  |
| gas & vacuum packing |  | prevents growth | inhibits | removes or excludes |  |  |  |
| canning or bottling | destroys | destroys | some destroyed | removes and excludes |  |  |  |
| chilling | slows up | inhibits |  |  |  |  |  |
| freezing | lowers reaction | kills 50-80% | inhibits |  | removes |  |  |
| dehydration | destroys | inhibits | inhibits |  | removes |  |  |
| curing | inhibits | inhibits | inhibits | partly replaced by $CO_2$ |  |  | alters |
| pickling | inactivates | inactivates | inhibits |  |  | reduces | alters |
| irradiation |  | destroys | destroys |  |  |  |  |

**Right:** Spaghetti is a form of *pasta*, which is made of durum semolina (which comes from a variety of hard wheat) and water, often with other ingredients such as eggs or spinach. The ingredients are mixed into a dough, which is extruded through a die to form long strands of spaghetti that are then cut into lengths and dried.

**Below:** The principal stages in the making of Kesp, a textured vegetable protein meat substitute made from soybeans. The beans are processed into isolated soya protein, which is then mixed with oils, flavourings and colourings before being spun, formed into shape, dehydrated and packed.

### KESP TEXTURED VEGETABLE PROTEIN PRODUCTION

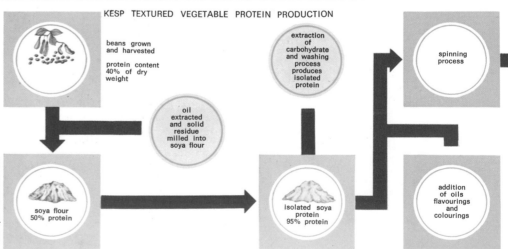

beans grown and harvested

protein content 40% of dry weight

oil extracted and solid residue milled into soya flour

soya flour 50% protein

extraction of carbohydrate and washing process produces isolated protein

isolated soya protein 95% protein

addition of oils flavourings and colourings

spinning process

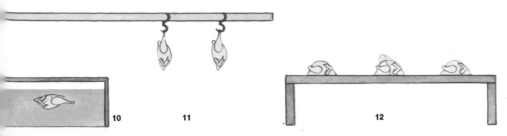

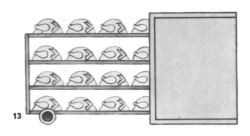

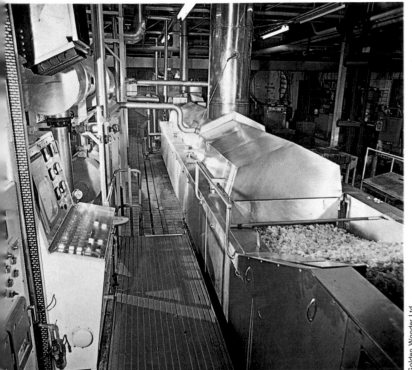

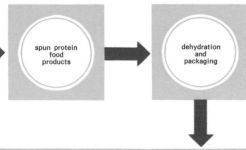

Above: This diagram shows how frozen chickens are produced. The live chickens (1) are stunned electrically (2) then killed by having their throats cut (3). The carcasses, drained of blood, are scalded to loosen the feathers (4) and then passed through machines which pull out the quills (5) and feathers (6). The feet, innards and heads are then removed (7, 8 and 9) before the carcasses are chilled (10), dried (11), trussed and vacuum-packed (12), and finally frozen (13).

Left: Potato crisps emerging from the cooker. To make potato crisps, the potatoes are first put into a machine which peels and washes them. They are then graded for size and inspected for blemishes, and passed through machines which cut them into slices about 1.4 mm (0.056 in) thick. After washing to remove the surface starch, the slices are drained of excess moisture and cooked in hot groundnut oil, then sprinkled with salt or flavourings such as 'cheese and onion' or 'salt and vinegar'.

doubled their original dry weight and are ready for canning after a short oven bake.

The beans and sauce (containing tomato puree, sugar, salt, flour and spices) are machine-filled into cans. The filling temperature must be about 80°C (176°F) in order to give a high final vacuum in the can after closure and retorting. The vacuum is necessary because the product is corrosive and a significant amount of oxygen in the head-space of the can (between the product and the lid) would cause extensive damage to the tin-plate walls of the container. The ends of the can are made from lacquered tin-plate and, after filling and seaming on the lid, the cans are processed in steam retorts at 115°C (240°F). Since the product is viscous, the rate of heat penetration would normally be very slow and result in overcooking. Therefore, it is the usual practice to agitate the cans in a rotary steam retort, particularly when large catering packs are being processed.

With the UHT process, the destruction of micro-organisms in milk is accomplished in approximately three seconds. The familiar tetrahedral and brick-shaped packs are constructed from an aluminium foil-lined waxed sheet which is sterilized by passing it through a solution of hydrogen peroxide ($H_2O_2$) before filling it with the heat-treated milk. This technique of sterilizing the food and container separately is known as *aseptic processing*. It has also been applied to yogurts, fruit purees and baby foods.

### Dehydration processing
Peas can be dried by a *fluidized-bed* technique. Before drying they are washed, graded for size, and then pricked with

needles on a rotating drum so that the rate of rehydration in subsequent home preparation is improved. The enzyme *peroxidase* is inactivated by blanching at about 95°C (203°F), and then the peas are treated with a sodium bicarbonate solution to retain their colour and improve their tenderness. A dilute sodium metabisulphite ($Na_2S_2O_2$) solution is used to inhibit non-enzymic browning and prolong the storage life of the peas.

The first stage of drying is carried out in a series of seven fluidized-bed dryers throughout which the air temperature is gradually raised from 40°C (104°F) to 55°C (131°F). The temperature is lower in the first bed because the moisture evaporates rapidly from the surface of the peas and too high a temperature would cause the sugars to ooze out of them, forming a sticky skin on the surface. Higher temperatures are needed in the later stages of fluidization because moisture is now migrating from the interior of the pea against a greater resistance to drying. By the time the last stage of fluidization is completed, the moisture content has fallen from 80 to 50 per cent by weight.

The second stage of drying reduces the moisture content to 20 per cent, but the drying rate is so slow that fluidization offers no advantage, and so the air velocity is reduced to give thorough drying with a minimum of fluidization. A final moisture content of 5 per cent is achieved in bin dryers after a total drying time of about 16 hours. The peas are packaged inside a plastic laminate to prevent oxidation of the fat content and the absorption of moisture.

*Freeze drying* is a process in which the food is frozen at —18°C (0°F), or lower, and then placed in a vacuum chamber at a pressure of 0.0025 bar (0.036 psi). Under these conditions the ice into which the moisture in the food has turned reverts directly to water vapour, which is condensed out on to the coils of a refrigerator.

Powdered foods are frequently prepared by *spray drying*. The sprays are formed either by a high pressure nozzle or by a vaned-disc atomizer rotating at speeds of up to 40,000 rpm. A unique method for producing dried tomato powder has been developed, in which tomato paste (containing 33 per cent tomato solids) is pumped through a vaned-disc atomizer into a drying chamber fed with filtered air at 80°C (176°F). Nodules of dry powder are formed on the sloping walls of the chamber. Because tomato powder is hygroscopic (water-absorbing) it is packaged in a room of low relative humidity (approximately 60 per cent RH) to prevent the absorption of moisture from the air.

Another product commonly made by spray drying is instant coffee. Coffee is brewed from roasted, ground coffee beans and then sprayed into a chamber through which hot air is blown. The hot air turns the coffee into powder.

spun protein food products

dehydration and packaging

beef flavoured chunks

beef flavoured mince

chicken flavoured chunks

9

# Beers, Wines and Spirits

The production of alcoholic drinks is a craft as old as civilization itself. Archaeological evidence suggests that winemaking began in the Middle East over 10,000 years ago, and gradually spread westward to the Mediterranean countries then up into Europe. Ancient Egyptian wall paintings depict the harvesting of grapes and the making of wine, and also show small stills which indicate that the art of distillation was known to the Egyptians.

Beer is known to have been made by the Egyptians and the Babylonians at least 6,000 years ago, and there is evidence that barley, the raw material for beer, was cultivated in Britain and northern Europe some 5,000 years ago. There is every likelihood that these early Europeans were capable of making the barley into a fermented drink.

Wines can be made from a wide range of fruits and vegetables, but true wine is made from grapes. The juice of the grape is mostly water, but it also contains sugar, fruit acids, and many trace elements which contribute to the distinctive flavour of the final wine. On the outside of the grape skin are millions of tiny living organisms, primarily yeasts, but including a number of moulds and bacteria which are of little importance to the winemaking process.

It is the yeasts on the skin of the grape which, having been brought into contact with the juice when the grapes are crushed, are responsible for the chemical reactions which turn the juice into wine. The yeasts contain enzymes which break down the molecular structure of the grape sugar (mainly *dextrose*, $C_6H_{12}O_6 + H_2O$) and re-arrange the atoms into molecules of alcohol (principally *ethyl alcohol*, $C_2H_5OH$) and carbon dioxide gas ($CO_2$). During this fermentation process the grape juice loses some or all of its sweetness as its sugar is turned into alcohol, and becomes wine, with an alcohol content in the region of 10 to 14 per cent. The rest of the wine consists of water containing traces of acids, sugar and other substances which give it its flavour and colour.

The vines which provide the grapes are hardy, long-living and fast-growing plants which fruit once each year, in the autumn. For commercial wine production, the vine plant is pruned back to little more than a bush, and its life span limited to about 30 years. The vine is best suited to the temperate zones between latitudes of approximately 30 and 50°, both north and south of the equator. Within these zones it does best where the soil and the local climatic conditions most suit it.

The nature of the soil is very important. It should be well drained and never waterlogged; some of the finest wines are produced from grapes grown on poor, stony, chalky soils. The local mini- or micro-climate also influences the growth of the vines, and those grown on slopes which face the sun do better than those grown on slopes which receive less direct sunlight.

The variety of vine predominant in a

Above: A vineyard in the famous French wine region of Burgundy. This region, which produces a wide range of fine red and white wines including Chablis, Beaujolais, Mâcon and Nuits St George, is situated in eastern central France to the south of Champagne, another famous wine region.

Above right: Bottles of Champagne are stored for two or three months as the sediment settles. The bottles are initially stored on their sides, then every day they are given a light shake and twisted slightly. They are gradually moved into an upright position so that the sediment settles on to the cork.

wine-producing region depends on the prevailing soil and climate conditions. Thus the Riesling grape does well in Germany, the Cabernet grape thrives in Bordeaux, and the Pinot grape is widely grown in Burgundy.

The colouring matter that gives red wine its colour is contained in the skins of black grapes, and so to make a red wine it is necessary that the fermentation takes place with the skins still in the grape juice. White wine, on the other hand, can be made from either black or white grapes as the juice is white in both varieties. Providing that fermentation takes place in the absence of the skins, white wine can be made from black grapes.

Champagne, and some other sparkling wines, are made by the *méthode champenoise*. The wines are given a second fermentation in the bottle by the addition of a little sugar and yeast, and the bottles are stored upside down so that the sediment produced settles on the cork. The carbon dioxide formed during the fermentation dissolves into the wine, giving it its sparkle, and when the fermentation is complete the necks of the bottles are frozen, so that the sediment freezes on to the corks and can be removed by drawing the corks. Some sugar is added to give the wine the required sweetness, then the bottles are re-corked.

In the *transfer method* of making sparkling wines, the wine is removed from the bottles after the second fermentation and put into a large vat. It is then filtered to remove the sediment, and re-bottled. Sparkling wines can also be made by the *cuve close* method, in which the second fermentation takes place in a

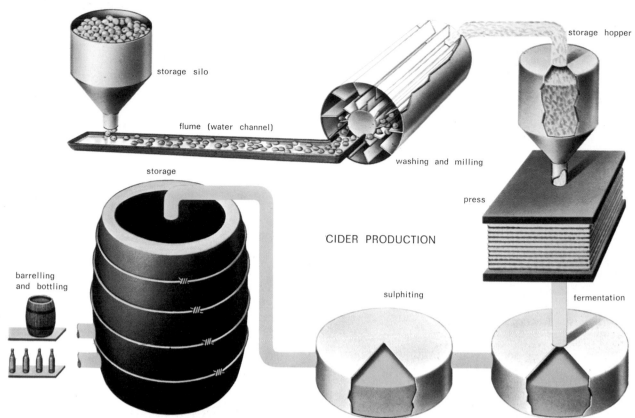

CIDER PRODUCTION

storage silo

flume (water channel)

storage hopper

washing and milling

press

barrelling and bottling

storage

sulphiting

fermentation

Left: Malt whisky is made by distilling the alcoholic liquid obtained by fermenting malt sugar. This sugar is produced by the action of enzymes on the starch in barley, these enzymes being formed in the barley when it is malted. Here, malted barley is being spread in a kiln for drying.

Below left: The alcohol content of a drink is generally expressed in terms of *degrees proof*. There are three main proof scales in use: the Gay-Lussac scale, used on the European continent (which directly indicates the percentage of alcohol in the drink), the US proof scale, and the British (Sikes) scale.

Above: Cider is made by fermenting apple juice. The apples are washed and milled, then the juice is pressed out of the pulp and fermented. The sulphiting process kills off the yeasts to prevent any secondary fermentation. Cider must be matured for about 6 months before it is ready for consumption.

Below: A *spirit still* at a malt whisky distillery, in which the second stage of the distillation is carried out. In the first stage, the 'wash' of fermented malt sugar is distilled in a *wash still*. The distillate obtained is then put into the spirit still for a second distillation.

| Gay-Lussac (% alchohol by volume) | °proof UK | °proof US |
|---|---|---|
| | 175 | 100 | 200 |
| pure alchohol | 160 | 90 | 180 |
| | 140 | 80 | 160 |
| | 120 | 70 | 140 |
| | 100 | 60 | 120 |
| | | 50 | 100 |
| spirits | 80 | 40 | 80 |
| | 60 | 30 | 60 |
| fortified wines | 40 | 20 | 40 |
| beverage wines | 20 | 10 | 20 |
| pure water | 0 | 0 | 0 |

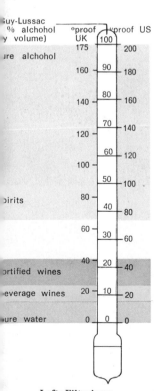

Left: Filtering a sample of the alcoholic wash produced by the fermentation of malt sugar during whisky production. The *specific gravity* of the sample, the weight of a given volume of it compared with that of an equal volume of water, indicates the amount of alcohol being produced.

vat and the wine is filtered before bottling. The cheapest method of making sparkling wine is to inject carbon dioxide gas into chilled wine and bottle it under pressure so that the gas dissolves into the wine, but sparkling wines made by this *carbonation* method soon go 'flat' after the bottle is uncorked as the gas rapidly bubbles out.

Another important group are the *fortified* wines. These include port, sherry and madeira, and are fortified by the addition of extra alcohol, usually in the form of brandy, which gives them an alcohol content of between about 16 and 24 per cent. The extra alcohol inhibits further fermentation, and so these wines usually have a comparatively high sugar content and are thus sweeter than non-fortified wines.

**Spirits**

Spirits are made by the distillation of alcohol which has been produced by a fermentation process. True brandy, for example, such as Cognac, is made by the distillation of wine made from grape juice. The wine is heated in a *still*, and the alcohol which evaporates out of it is condensed and collected. Alcohol has a lower boiling point than water, about 78.4°C 173.12°F) as opposed to 100°C (212°F), and so if the still is heated to just over the boiling point of alcohol, the alcohol will evaporate out leaving most of the water behind (some of the water will evaporate out, even at this temperature).

Apart from alcohol, other substances are given off during distillation, and many of these are poisonous and must be removed. The initial flow of condensed liquid from the still contains the more volatile of these substances, those such as *acetaldehyde* ($CH_3CHO$) which have a lower boiling point than alcohol. This initial flow is collected in a separate tank from that into which the purer alcohol will be run when it starts to flow from the still.

Towards the end of the distillation, other impurities begin to appear in the alcohol as those with higher boiling points begin to evaporate. These include

11

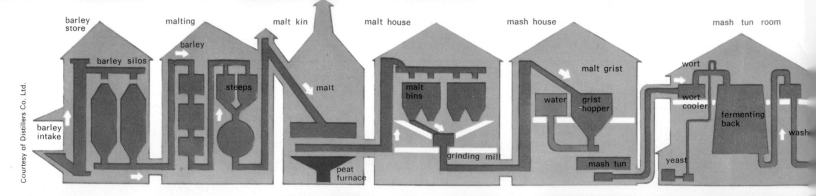

barley store — malting — malt kin — malt house — mash house — mash tun room

barley silos — barley — steeps — malt — malt bins — grinding mill — peat furnace — water — grist-hopper — malt grist — grinding mill — mash tun — yeast — wort — wort cooler — fermenting back — wash — barley intake

**Below:** Most whiskies sold are blends of many different 'single' whiskies, and the blender assesses each sample by its aroma, not its flavour. Malt whiskies are made from malted barley, and grain whiskies from malted barley plus unmalted barley and maize. Both are used in blended whiskies.

ZEFA

**Above:** The part of the hop used in brewing is the female flower cone. It contains oils and resins which impart flavour to the beer and act as preservatives, and tannin which precipitates protein matter out of the wort during boiling and so helps to clarify the beer. The spent hops are sold as fertilizer.

**Right:** One of the first stages in the brewing of beer is the mashing of the malted barley. After the barley has been milled, it is put into one of these *mash tuns* where it is mixed with hot water. This activates the enzymes in the barley that turn the starch into sugar, which dissolves in the water.

*fusel oils*, which consist mainly of *amyl alcohol* and *isoamyl alcohol*, and when these appear in the distillate the flow is diverted once more into the tank containing the impurities given off in the beginning.

Spirit distillation is usually done in two or more stages, and some spirits may be re-distilled to make them more pure. The flavour of a spirit is derived from substances formed during the original fermentation which are retained in the spirit during the distillation process, or from flavourings added after distillation.

An enormous range of spirits are produced from many different source materials. Whiskies are made from grains such as barley, rye and corn (maize); rum is made from molasses, a syrup obtained from cane sugar; brandies can be made from virtually any fermentable sweet fruit (for example Kirsch is made from cherries and Slivovitz from plums). Tequila, the strong Mexican spirit, is made from a form of cactus.

Gin, which originated in Holland, is usually made from grain or molasses spirits flavoured with juniper berries, and often other ingredients such as coriander, orange peel, liquorice and anise.

Liqueurs can be made from any spirit by the addition of flavourings and sweetenings. Cherry brandy, for example, is not a brandy made from cherries (as is Kirsch), but a blend of brandy, cherry essence and sugar. Many other fruits, as well as chocolate, coffee and mint, are used in making liqueurs.

Some of the most famous liqueurs, such as Drambuie, Benedictine and Chartreuse, are blended from spirits and mixtures of herbs and essences whose ingredients are

BREWING

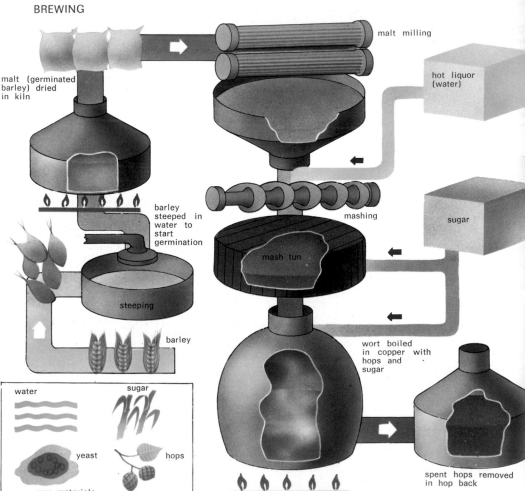

malt milling

malt (germinated barley) dried in kiln

hot liquor (water)

barley steeped in water to start germination

mashing

sugar

steeping

mash tun

barley

wort boiled in copper with hops and sugar

water — sugar — yeast — hops — raw materials

spent hops removed in hop back

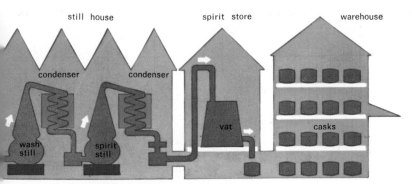

condenser     condenser          vat        casks

wash still     spirit still

**Left: This diagram shows how malt whisky is produced.** The barley is malted by soaking it in water and then allowing it to germinate in a warm, damp atmosphere. After the barley has germinated, further growth is stopped by drying it in a peat-fired kiln, the smoke from which contributes much to the flavour of the whisky. The malt is ground and mixed with warm water to make a sugary solution (wort) which is cooled and mixed with yeast in a vessel called a *fermenting back*, where the yeast converts the sugar to alcohol. The resulting wash is distilled in a copper *pot still* known as the *wash still*, and the distillate is given a second distillation in another pot still, the *spirit still*. The spirit is diluted in the spirit store vat, then put into oak casks to mature for several years. The spirit from the still is colourless and harsh-tasting, and during maturation it absorbs flavour and colour from the casks, which are often casks that have previously contained sherry.

**Left: The traditional type of vessel used for fermenting beer is a large, fairly shallow vat, but many modern breweries use large cylindrical fermenting vessels such as those shown here.**

Bass Worthington

**Below: Filling barrels with beer, an operation which is known as 'racking'.**

closely-guarded secrets. Benedictine, for instance, is still made to a secret recipe invented by a Benedictine monk, Dom Bernardo Vincelli, at the abbey at Fécamp, France, in the early sixteenth century.

## Beer

Beer is usually made from barley (although other grains can be used), hops, yeast and sugar. The barley corns consist largely of starch, which will not ferment, and so it must first be converted into sugar, which ferments readily. This is brought about by *malting* the barley. During the malting process, the barley is soaked and then kept in a warm atmosphere so that it begins to germinate. As the barley germinates, it produces an enzyme called *diastase* which will convert the starch into malt sugars (chiefly *maltose*, $C_{12}H_{22}O_{11} + H_2O$), which in turn are then converted to alcohol by the yeast enzymes during the brewing.

After malting, the barley is milled and then mashed together with hot water and sugar. The resulting liquid, known as *wort* (pronounced 'wert'), is pumped into large copper vessels where it is boiled with hops and sugar. The hops act both as a flavouring and as a preservative. Next, the spent hops are separated from the boiled wort, which is cooled and put into the fermenting vessels. The yeast is now added, and fermentation begins.

British beers begin fermentation at a temperature of about 15.6°C (60°F), and fermentation takes from five to seven days. These beers are top-fermented, that is, the type of yeast used floats on the top of the liquid. The beer, after fermentation, is drawn off into settling tanks where any residual yeast is removed, and then stored for a time (from a few days to a few weeks, depending on the type of beer) at around 0°C (32°F) to allow it to mature before it is *racked* (filled) into casks, bottles or cans.

Lager beers are bottom-fermented, the yeast used settling at the bottom of the vessels during fermentation, which begins at a temperature of from 6 to 10°C (43-50°F) and takes about eight days. Lager beers are matured for up to three months at 0°C (32°F) before racking (the name 'lager' is the German word for 'store'). During the maturation period a second fermentation takes place which clears the beer and improves its flavour and strength.

The term 'ale' originally applied to un-hopped beers, but it is now widely used as a general name for top-fermented beers. The amount of hops used depends upon the type of beer being produced. A strong top-fermented beer may be made with about eight times the amount of hops used in making a light lager.

Another factor which varies according to the type of beer being produced is the malting process. For example, the barley for a top-fermented beer may be germinated for 11 days and then dried at 107°C (225°F) for three or four days, but barley for a lager may only be germinated for seven or eight days and then dried at a temperature of about 55°C (130°F). When dark beers such as brown ales and stouts are to be made, the barley is also highly roasted. The rootlets which sprout from the barley during germination shrivel and drop off when it is dried, and they are usually collected and sold for use in animal feeds.

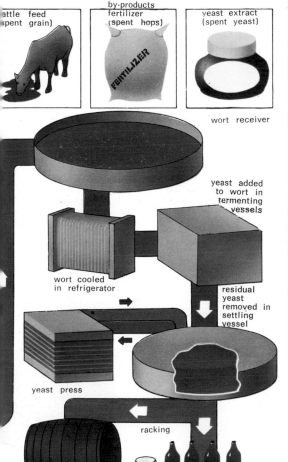

by-products
cattle feed (spent grain)     fertilizer (spent hops)     yeast extract (spent yeast)

FERTILIZER

wort receiver

yeast added to wort in fermenting vessels

wort cooled in refrigerator

residual yeast removed in settling vessel

yeast press

racking

**Left: A typical brewing process.** Milled malted barley, hot liquor (water) and sugar are mixed in the *mash tun*, to produce the sugary liquid known as *wort*. The wort, plus hops and sugar, is boiled in a large 'copper', then discharged into the *hop back* where the spent hops are extracted from it. The wort is cooled and put into the fermenting tanks, where the yeast is added and the sugar is converted into alcohol. Fresh beer from the fermenting tanks is put into settling vessels, where the residual yeast is removed and pressed dry. After a period of storage, the beer is put into barrels or bottles.

Youngs Brewery

13

# Farm Technology

Modern agriculture makes extensive use of many forms of technology, and the wide range of machines that till the soil, plant the seeds and harvest the crops make a vital contribution to the production of the world's food supplies. With the aid of these machines, one man can do as much work in one day as a team of men could do in a week before the introduction of mechanization.

The best-known piece of farm equipment is probably the tractor, first developed around the turn of the century as a replacement for the horse. Tractor design has improved considerably since the 1950s, not only in performance but also in the amount of comfort and safety provided for the driver.

The early tractors gave the driver no protection from the weather, and the only concessions to comfort were footrests and a hard metal seat. The next step was to mount the seat on springs, and to provide crude mudguards to give the driver a certain amount of protection from the mud, dust or water thrown up by the large driving wheels. One result of this lack of attention to the driver's comfort was that tractor drivers were liable to back injuries and a variety of muscular ailments because of having to spend so much of their working lives being bumped around in the cold and wet. In addition, the drivers obtained less output from the

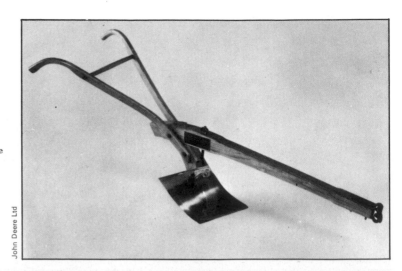

Right: The steel plough invented in the US by John Deere (1804–1886) in 1837. This one was tougher than the iron or iron-faced wooden ploughs then available, and it made an important contribution to the development of agriculture on the American prairies.

Below: A replica of the reaper designed by Cyrus McCormick in the US in 1831. The reaper cut the crop and laid it on the ground, and then it was tied into bundles by hand and taken away for threshing (separating the grains from the stalks). Reapers were succeeded by reaper-threshers, the forerunners of the combine harvester.

John Deere Ltd

International Harvester

Massey Ferguson

Left: A Massey-Ferguson MF 1505 tractor pulling an MF 23 cultivator. The tractor is a large, four-wheel-drive machine, powered by a 134 kW (180 bhp), 10.4 litre V-8 diesel engine, and the cultivator is a heavy-duty model designed for clearing stubble after harvesting and for deep seed bed preparation.

Right: A twenty-row seed drill, the International 511. This machine can sow a wide variety of crop seeds, such as grass or wheat, planting twenty rows at a time at a constant, pre-set depth and depositing the seeds at pre-determined intervals to obtain uniform spacing between the plants.

International Harvester

tractors than they were capable of giving because they drove them relatively slowly to minimize the discomfort.

Another danger faced by the driver was that of being killed or severely injured if the tractor overturned when working on sloping ground or by the side of a ditch.

In the early 1960s, cushioned seats and rudimentary 'weather cabs' were fitted to tractors to improve the comfort and weather protection. These early cabs, however, gave rise to another form of discomfort—noise. The sheet-metal panelling acted as a soundbox, amplifying the noise from the engine, gearbox and hydraulic system so much that the drivers were exposed to damaging levels of noise.

A British survey in the 1960s showed that potential increases in productivity due to improved driver comfort had been offset by losses due to noise. Instead of slowing their tractors to speeds that their bodies could stand, drivers now had to slow them to keep the noise down to a level that their ears could tolerate. The survey estimated that this slowing down reduced output by about 20 per cent.

Since then, tractor cab design has been greatly improved, and the latest cabs give complete protection against the weather, overturning, and noise. Nearly all modern cabs are fitted on rubber mountings to insulate the driver from vibration, and they incorporate sound insulation, comfortable seating, heating and ventilation systems, windscreen wipers and washers, and power-assisted controls.

Most tractors are constructed so that the engine and transmission form a rigid backbone for the whole machine, so that a separate chassis is not needed. Engine powers range from about 15 kW (20 bhp) for small horticultural machines up to 186 kW (250 bhp) or more for the largest heavy-duty models, but most general-purpose farm tractors use engines delivering between about 22 kW (30 bhp) and 89 kW (120 bhp).

The engines themselves are usually diesels, driving the rear wheels or, on some models, all four wheels. The engines also drive the power take-off shafts which provide the drive for implements towed by or mounted on the tractor, and the hydraulic systems which are used for controlling these implements.

## Ploughing and seeding

The plough is the most basic tool of agriculture, and it has been in use in one

# COMBINE HARVESTER

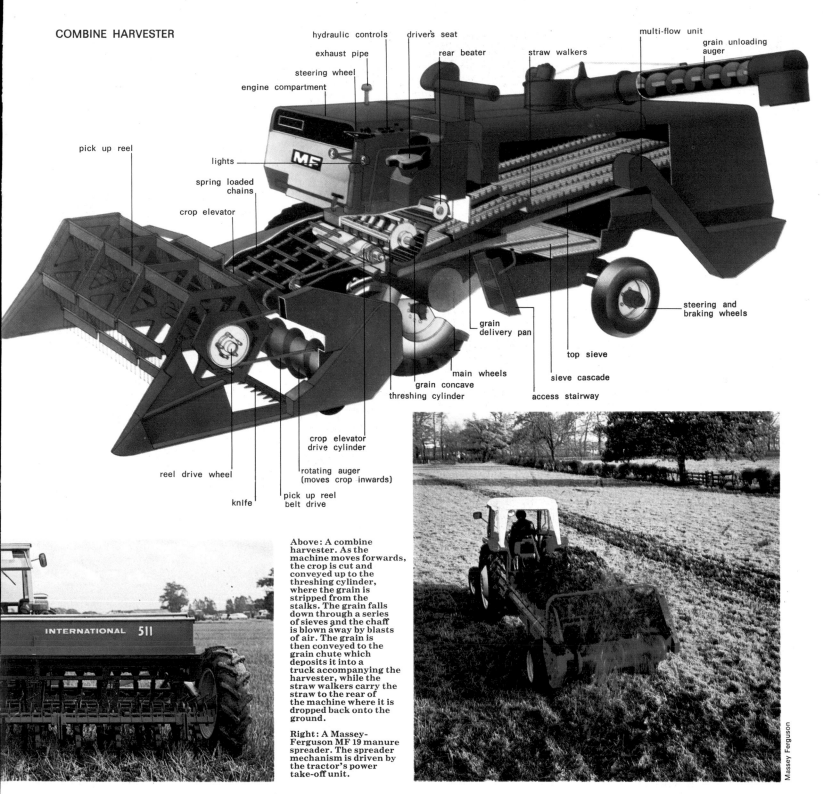

pick up reel

lights

spring loaded chains

crop elevator

engine compartment

steering wheel

exhaust pipe

hydraulic controls

driver's seat

rear beater

straw walkers

multi-flow unit

grain unloading auger

M.F.

reel drive wheel

knife

pick up reel belt drive

rotating auger (moves crop inwards)

crop elevator drive cylinder

threshing cylinder

grain concave

main wheels

grain delivery pan

access stairway

sieve cascade

top sieve

steering and braking wheels

INTERNATIONAL 511

Above: A combine harvester. As the machine moves forwards, the crop is cut and conveyed up to the threshing cylinder, where the grain is stripped from the stalks. The grain falls down through a series of sieves and the chaff is blown away by blasts of air. The grain is then conveyed to the grain chute which deposits it into a truck accompanying the harvester, while the straw walkers carry the straw to the rear of the machine where it is dropped back onto the ground.

Right: A Massey-Ferguson MF 19 manure spreader. The spreader mechanism is driven by the tractor's power take-off unit.

Massey Ferguson

form or another since Neolithic times. Its function is similar in many ways to that of a spade—it turns the topsoil over, loosening it and breaking it up and at the same time burying any trash and weeds. In modern mechanized farming the plough, like many other agricultural implements, is pulled by tractor, although simple ploughs pulled by animals such as horses or oxen are still in use in many countries.

Before crops can be planted in ploughed land, a certain amount of final ground preparation is usually necessary. Just as the gardener uses a rake to prepare soil for planting, the farmer uses a tractor-drawn harrow to level the ploughed soil and destroy any new weeds that may have started to grow. Another type of machine used for soil preparation and weed destruction is the *cultivator*, which uses steel spikes or blades to break up the soil. *Rotary cultivators*, which use spikes or blades mounted on a revolving, power-driven shaft, can often be used to prepare ground that has not previously been ploughed.

The planting of many crops can now be carried out mechanically, using machines which open up the ground, deposit the seeds at pre-determined intervals and depths, then cover them over. Such machines plant a number of rows at a time, and many also apply fertilizer as they plant the seeds.

## Harvesting machinery
A wide range of crops, including root crops such as potatoes, and fruits such as grapes and cider apples, are now harvested by machines. One of the first and most important of these machines was the *combine harvester*, used for grain crops such as wheat. The combine is a self-propelled machine which cuts the crop, separates the grain from the straw and removes the husks, transfers the grain into an accompanying truck, and deposits the straw on to the ground for later collection.

Until recently, straw was regarded mainly as a waste product, useful at best only as bedding for cattle or for providing some roughage in their feed. Consequently, little effort has been put into removing it from the field, especially by arable farmers; it is often simply burnt away. A new process is being developed, however, which may enable straw to be converted economically into animal feed.

15

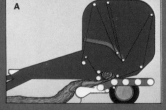

**A** Baler picks up hay and draws it into baling chamber

**B** Hay rolled into bale.

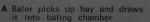

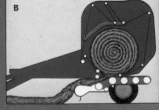

**C** Completed bale bound with twine prior to ejection from machine

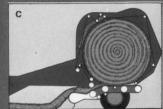

International Harvester

Above: The International 241 big roll baler. The mown hay is collected by the white-painted unit just in front of the baler's wheels.

Below: Potatoes, like any other crop, are susceptible to attack by insects and fungus diseases, and potato fields need to be kept free of weeds which could hinder the growth of the plants. This diagram shows the types of pest likely to afflict potatoes, and some of the chemicals used to combat them: herbicides to kill the weeds without harming the potatoes, and insecticides and fungicides to kill the insects and fungi. The fertilizers enrich the soil and promote the growth of the potatoes.

Novosti

Left: Kolos combine harvesters being built at the Taganrog works, Rostov, Russia. The Soviet Union produces about one sixth of the world's total cereal output, and plans to have its annual output running at over 235 million tonnes in the early 1980s. Output in 1976 was more than 220 million tonnes.

Above: These three diagrams show the way that round 'big bales' of hay are produced. After the grass has been mown, the baler, drawn by the tractor, picks up the crop and feeds it back into the baling chamber where it is rolled into a bale. When the bale is complete it is bound with twine and ejected.

## CHEMICALS USED FOR PROTECTION OF POTATO CROPS

**HERBICIDES:**

couch: dalapon, EPTC, TCA
wild oat: EPTC
other weeds: EPTC; ametryne,
chlorbromuron, cyanazine, dimexan,
dinoseb, linuron, metobromuron,
metribuzin monolinuron,
terbutryne, trietazine

**FUNGICIDES**

leaft blight: captafol, copper
cutraneb, fenfin, mancozeb, maneb
manganese/zinc dithiocarbamate,
nabam, propinab, zineb
leafroll and mosaic virus:
aphicides.
tuber diseases:
2-aminobutane

**INSECTICIDES**

slugs and leatherjackets:
metaldehyde
aphids: aphicides such as aldicarb
demephion, disulfoton, formothion
malathion, phorate, thiometon
eelworm: aldicarb, dichloropropene
colorado beetle: azinphos-methyl,
carboryl, endosulfan.

BLACK BINDWEED

ANNUAL MEADOW GRASS

CHICKWEED

COUCH

CHARLOCK

WILD OAT

BLIGHT

LEAFROLL

SEVERE MOSAIC VIRUS

BLIGHT

SLUG

LEATHERJACKET

EEL WORM

COLORADO BEETLE

APHID

FERTILIZERS
nitrogen, phosphorus
potash, magnesium

Above: One of the many types of harvesting machine now in use. This one is harvesting spinach in Sweden. The tractor-drawn harvester picks the crop and conveys it through a delivery chute into the trailer travelling alongside.

Right: Spraying a field of wheat with Calixin, a brand of *tridemorph* fungicide used to combat the fungus disease known as 'mildew' which affects cereal crops. Mildew in cereals is caused by the fungus *Erysiphe graminis*, which attacks the leaves and root system of a plant. This results in a reduced grain yield, which may be as much as 40% below normal in severe cases of infection.

Above: Good drainage and irrigation are essential to agriculture. This picture shows a crawler tractor fitted with a pipe-laying plough which opens up the ground and lays continuous flexible piping. The tractor is guided along the required route by a laser beam system.

Right: Harvesting tea on a plantation in Georgia, where 96% of the Soviet Union's tea is grown. The machines straddle the rows of tea bushes, and travel along trimming off the outermost leaves and sucking them back into hoppers. Most of the world's tea, however, is still picked by hand.

One of the main constituents of straw is cellulose, which can be used as a food by ruminant (cud-chewing) animals such as cows. The cellulose in straw, however, is enclosed in an indigestible substance called lignin, which must be removed before the straw can be used as feed. The German chemist Ernst Otto Beckmann (1853-1923) developed, during the First World War, a method of soaking straw in caustic soda (sodium hydroxide, NaOH) to dissolve away the lignin. Beckmann's process needed about 50 cubic metres of water per tonne of straw to wash away the dissolved lignin and any excess soda, and this washing also removed all the water-soluble substances from the straw. Without these water-soluble substances, the food value of the straw was considerably reduced, and so the process was never adopted.

In the latest version of the Beckmann process, the straw is first chopped into pieces about 3.75 cm long. A controlled amount of caustic soda solution, about 90 litres per tonne of straw, is then sprayed on as a fine mist and the straw is tumbled around by augers and paddles to ensure that every piece is evenly coated with soda.

The treated straw is then blown into a heap and left for three days, during which time it 'cooks' as the chemical reactions take place between the soda and the lignin. The straw heats up slowly to about 90°C within about 20 hours, and then slowly cools again. During this time the lignin is dissolved away, leaving the cellulose and the water-soluble substances available for cattle feed.

Cattle are usually fed considerable quantities of rolled or crushed barley, but with the high price of cereals this is increasingly regarded as wasteful, particularly when these cereals could be processed directly into human food at a lower cost than is involved in converting them into meat by feeding them to cattle. The chemically-processed straw has about two thirds of the food value of barley, and so it could replace the barley constituents in cattle feed, thus releasing the barley for human consumption.

## Balers

Straw, the stalks of grain crops such as wheat, and hay, grass which is cut and stored for cattle feed, are usually packed into bales for transport and storage. This baling is done by *balers*, tractor-drawn machines which pick up the straw left by the combines or the hay left on the ground by mowers and compress it into bales bound with twine.

One of the biggest revolutions in materials handling on the farm in recent years has been the 'big bale', which weighs about half a tonne whereas the conventional bale weighs only about 27 to 30 kg. Conventional bales measure about 1 m x 45 cm x 35 cm, and after baling they are left in the field in stacks of eight, which in turn are loaded on to trailers and taken to the storage building. All this is wasteful of effort because the bales are handled several times before they reach their destination.

With half-tonne packages there are only about seven bales per hectare of field, compared with about 138 small bales. Consequently there is far less handling involved and the time taken to collect and transport the bales to the store is halved. The cost of the twine

17

Above: The greenhouse of the herbicide laboratory at the BASF research station at Limburgerhof, Germany. The research station develops and tests a wide range of pesticides and fertilizers.

Left and below: The *nutrient film technique* is a new method of rearing crops without soil. The plants are grown, either outdoors or in greenhouses, by planting them in plastic gullies through which a nutrient solution is circulated. The technique was developed by the Glasshouse Crops Research Institute in Surrey, England, and is now being used successfully in many parts of the world.

Dr. A. Cooper/G.C.R.I.

BASF

## NUTRIENT FILM TECHNIQUE

flow pipe

nutrient flow

plug

pump

plants supported by gullies

nutrient feed from flow pipe

nutrient

nutrient solution trench lined with polythene film

needed for tying the bales is also reduced.

Big bales come in two shapes, oblong and round. Oblong bales measure 1.5 x 1.5 x 2.4 m, and bale density is about 64 kg per cubic metre. The bales are made in the same way as conventional bales; the baler collects the crop and pushes it into a chamber the same shape as the bale. Once the correct size has been reached, the twine is tied round the bale and it is ejected into the field.

Round bales are about 1.2 m in diameter and 1.8 m wide, and are made by a machine that rolls the crop between belts until the density is about 144 kg per cubic metre. Their main advantage over oblong bales is that they can be stored in the open without serious deterioration. Because of their formation, the outer layers of round bales act like the thatch on a thatched roof, and rain water runs off them, being able to penetrate, and so damage, only the outer five centimetres of the straw.

Rain will penetrate both the oblong big bale and the conventional bale, and reduce them to waste material within a few weeks. The water-repellent outer layer of the round bale means that it does not need to be stored in a barn; instead, it can be stored in the field in long lines, thus reducing storage costs and eliminating the risk of losing a whole crop of hay or straw, plus a barn, because of fire.

### Crop handling

After a crop has been harvested, more equipment is needed for handling and storing it before it goes to market. This equipment includes items such as trailers, fork lift trucks and conveyers, but a number of rather more sophisticated devices are coming into use on the modern farm.

One example of this type of equipment is the device used for separating soil and stones from harvested potatoes. Potatoes are often harvested when the ground is wet, and if the crop is grown on stony land, quantities of stone and soil may be collected with the potatoes. Wet soil can cause rotting, and stones can cut, scuff and bruise the potatoes. Soil and stones must therefore be removed from the crop to prevent damage to the potatoes.

Soil can be separated from potatoes by passing them over a sieve and letting the soil fall through, but separating stones is more difficult. It can be done by having several pickers standing at either side of a conveyer belt and removing the stones by hand as the crop passes by them, but this is expensive in terms of labour and time. One solution is to use X-rays to differentiate between the stones and potatoes. The crop passes along a conveyer and falls off the end through a series of X-ray beams.

The beams detect the difference in density between a stone and the potatoes, and when a stone has been detected, rubber-coated fingers flick out to remove it while allowing potatoes to fall through. The fingers are operated by compressed air, and the system is about 95 per cent accurate. There is no radiation danger from the X-ray units as they are totally enclosed.

The X-ray sorter has yet to gain widespread acceptance on farms, mainly because of its cost compared to other systems, but as labour costs increase and labour becomes more difficult to recruit for farm work, it is likely to become much more common.

# Domestic Appliances

The tremendous growth in the production and use of domestic appliances has been one of the characteristic features of industrialized societies in the twentieth century. Although their impact on society is, perhaps, more subtle than that of some other forms of modern technology—motor vehicles, aircraft, radio and tv for instance—they have had a significant effect on daily life, and what were once luxury goods are increasingly being regarded as essentials. To people accustomed to the convenience of, for example, refrigerators, vacuum cleaners and washing machines, the prospect of having to go without them is not a pleasant one.

The variety of domestic equipment now produced is enormous, ranging from the large appliances such as cookers and freezers to the small ones such as irons, toasters, electric kettles and the more exotic gadgets like egg boilers and shoe polishers.

## Cookers

The earliest method of cooking food was to heat or roast it over an open fire, and the first ovens and stoves were heated by burning solid fuels. Solid fuel cookers are still available today, but the majority of cookers are now gas or electric. The commonest types of cooker have an oven, hob (gas burners or electric hotplates or radiant rings) and grill incorporated in a single, free-standing unit, but an increasing number of manufacturers are offering these as separate components which can be built-in to the kitchen furniture.

This arrangement, apart from providing greater flexibility in the positioning of the equipment, also makes it easier to use a gas hob in conjunction with an electric oven. This combination offers the controllability and economy of the gas hob with the even heating of the electric oven, particularly when it is fitted with a fan that circulates the warm air so that the whole of the oven is kept at the desired temperature.

When a fan is not used, there may be differences in temperature between the top, middle and bottom parts of the oven, the middle section being at the temperature set on the thermostat control while the top and bottom sections are hotter and cooler respectively.

'Self-cleaning' ovens work on either the *catalytic* or the *pyrolytic* principle. Catalytic ovens have their internal panels coated with a special enamel which encourages any splashes of fat or food that fall on it during cooking to vaporize away. Any splashes not vaporized away during the cooking can be removed simply by wiping with a damp cloth, or by leaving the oven on until they are vaporized.

The pyrolytic ovens clean themselves by burning away the dirt. This process is carried out at a very high temperature, much higher than the highest cooking temperature, and the dirt is reduced to a small amount of ash which can be brushed out later.

## Refrigerators

The basic principle behind refrigeration is that a fluid absorbs heat when it changes from a liquid to a gas, and releases this heat when it changes back from a gas to a liquid. In a refrigerator a fluid, the *refrigerant*, is passed through an *evaporator* placed within the refrigerated compartment. As it enters the evaporator its pressure is reduced and it evaporates from a liquid to a gas, absorbing heat from the refrigerated compartment in the process.

The gas then passes to a *condenser* situated outside the refrigerated compartment, where it condenses back into a liquid and gives off its heat to the atmosphere. The liquid refrigerant from the condenser, having given up the heat it absorbed from the refrigerated compartment, then returns to the evaporator to continue the cycle.

In a typical domestic refrigerator the

Ronan

*Above right: A late nineteenth century dishwasher. The dishes were placed in the machine together with hot, soapy water, and when the handle was turned the water was flung against the dishes by the paddles.*

*Right: In a modern dishwasher, very hot water containing detergent is sprayed on to the dishes by sets of rotating and fixed spray jets. The spray angles and pressures are designed so that all parts of the load are cleaned, and even microscopically small particles of food are removed. On the machine shown here, the temperature and pressure of the water can be varied to suit the type and number of dishes to be washed and their level of soiling.*

*Below: The first electric vacuum cleaners were large machines mounted on horse-drawn carts. They were parked outside the building in which the cleaning was to be done, and the suction hoses were led into the building through doors and windows. This one is in Paris in 1904.*

Robert Bosch Ltd

Ronan

*Below: The cleaning action of an 'upright' vacuum cleaner. The agitator loosens the dirt in the carpet and sweeps it back into the machine, where the* suction created by a fan draws it into the dustbag.

*Right: A modern upright cleaner which works on this principle.*

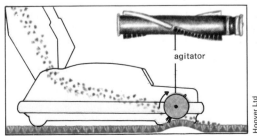

agitator

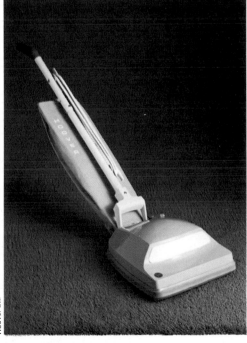

Hoover Ltd

refrigerant is pumped around the system by a motor-driven compressor, which draws the low-pressure gas from the evaporator and passes it at high pressure into the condenser. The refrigerant is usually one of the halogenated hydrocarbons known as *Freons*, such as Freon-12 (dichlorodifluoromethane, $CCl_2F_2$) and Freon-114 (dichlorotetrafluoroethane, $C_2Cl_2F_4$). Carbon dioxide ($CO_2$) and sulphur dioxide ($SO_2$) can also be used as refrigerants.

An alternative to this compression system is the *ammonia absorption system*. In this system there are no moving mechanical parts, the cycle being maintained by heat from an electric element or from a gas or oil burner. There are four main components in this system: an evaporator, which is within the refrigerated area, and a condenser, a *boiler* and an *absorber*, which are all outside it. A strong solution of ammonia ($NH_3$) in water is heated in the boiler so that it gives off ammonia vapour.

As the pressure of this ammonia vapour builds up it is driven into the condenser, where it condenses into a liquid. This liquid passes into the evaporator, where it evaporates and absorbs heat. From the evaporator, the ammonia vapour passes down into the absorber where it is absorbed by a trickle of weak ammonia solution produced in the boiler when the ammonia is driven out of the strong solution. The resulting solution produced in the absorber returns to the boiler to continue the cycle.

Hydrogen gas circulates through the absorber and the evaporator at a lower pressure than that at which the ammonia condenses in the condenser. This means that when the liquid ammonia enters the evaporator it has to evaporate to make up the difference between these two pressures. By using hydrogen in this manner the need for an expansion valve in the evaporator is eliminated, and as the total gas pressure remains effectively constant throughout the system there is no need for pressure reduction valves.

### Freezers

Freezers operate on the compression system, but their cabinet temperatures are much lower than those of refrigerators, having a maximum temperature of $-18°C$ ($0°F$) as opposed to the usual refrigerator main cabinet temperature of between 0 and $7°C$ (32 and $45°F$). In addition, freezers must be capable of freezing fresh food or cooked food rapidly

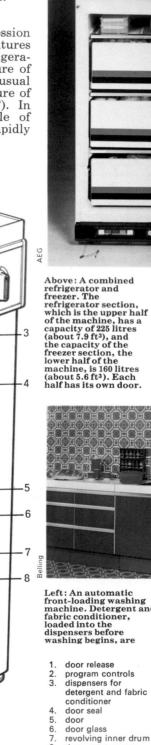

Above: A combined refrigerator and freezer. The refrigerator section, which is the upper half of the machine, has a capacity of 225 litres (about 7.9 ft³), and the capacity of the freezer section, the lower half of the machine, is 160 litres (about 5.6 ft³). Each half has its own door.

Below: Built-in electric oven, grill and hob units. The oven unit has a large fan-assisted oven, with a smaller combined oven and grill beneath it. The hob unit, to the left of the oven, has four rings, and when not in use it can be retracted below the working surface and covered with a lid.

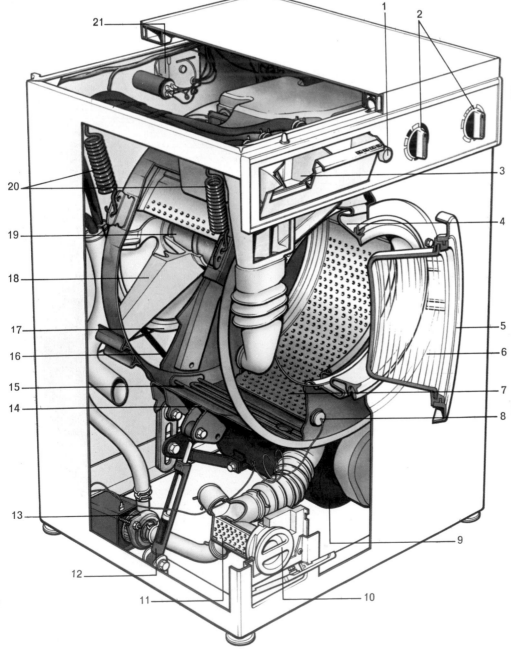

Left: An automatic front-loading washing machine. Detergent and fabric conditioner, loaded into the dispensers before washing begins, are automatically drawn into the drum when required. Ten different programs can be selected to suit various types and colours of fabrics.

1. door release
2. program controls
3. dispensers for detergent and fabric conditioner
4. door seal
5. door
6. door glass
7. revolving inner drum
8. thermostat sensor
9. motor
10. filter access panel
11. lint filter
12. shock absorber
13. drain pump
14. fixed outer drum
15. 3 kW heater
16. drive belt
17. drum pulley
18. drum support
19. drum bearings
20. outer drum suspension springs
21. control circuits

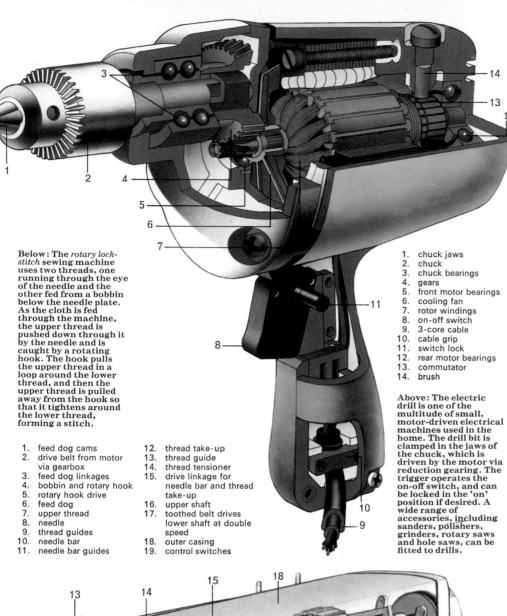

so that its quality and flavour are maintained. This can be done by setting the cabinet temperature to a much lower level than that used simply for storage, but many models have one or more separate fast-freeze compartments, operating at temperatures down to about −35°C (−31°F), in which food can be frozen rapidly.

Good cabinet insulation is essential for freezers, and this is usually provided by a layer of polyurethane a few centimetres thick, equivalent in insulating value to about 5 m (16 ft) of concrete. This level of insulation enables a freezer to maintain its low temperature for more than 24 hours in the event of a power failure.

## Washing machines

Washing machines range broadly from the basic single-tub machines, controlled by simple timer and temperature controls, to the automatic machines controlled by programming units, which perform the entire wash/rinse/spin-dry sequence completely automatically. Most washing machines use one of three types of washing action: *agitator, pulsator* or *tumble* action. The agitator and the pulsator are both used in conjunction with vertical washing tubs, whereas tumble action requires a horizontal drum.

The agitator, which is mounted in the centre of the bottom of the tub and projects upwards towards the top, swirls the clothes back and forth in the water. The pulsator, mounted on the side or bottom of the tub, is a ridged disc which rotates at several hundred rpm to create a vigorous turbulence in the water. Machines using agitators or pulsators are *top-loaders*, that is, the clothes are loaded into the vertical tub through a lid on the top of the machine.

Tumble-action machines, on the other hand, are *front-loaders*. The clothes are loaded through a watertight door, usually circular with a glass window set into it, in the front of the machine. The drum of a front-loader is made of perforated enamelled or stainless steel, and it rotates within an outer, unperforated steel container. During washing, the drum rotates at about 50-55 rpm, tumbling clothes around in the water. On many models the rotation of the drum is reversed at intervals to give a more thorough washing action and prevent tangling of the clothes.

Automatic machines wash the clothes, then discharge the dirty water and rinse the clothes with clean water one or more times. When the rinsing is completed and the last of the rinsing water has been discharged by the drain pump, the machine spin-dries the clothes. The tub or drum rotates at high speed, usually 800-1,000 rpm, so that centrifugal force throws the clothes against the walls of the drum and draws most of the water out of them.

After spin-drying, the clothes can be air-dried, or dried in a *tumble-dryer*, a machine similar in appearance to a front-loader, in which the clothes are tumbled around in a perforated steel drum through which hot air is blown.

Spin-dryers, for drying clothes not washed in an automatic machine, are available as separate units. *Twin-tub* washing machines, having a vertical wash tub and a spin dryer mounted side by side, are another popular type of washing machine.

**Below:** The *rotary lock-stitch* sewing machine uses two threads, one running through the eye of the needle and the other fed from a bobbin below the needle plate. As the cloth is fed through the machine, the upper thread is pushed down through it by the needle and is caught by a rotating hook. The hook pulls the upper thread in a loop around the lower thread, and then the upper thread is pulled away from the hook so that it tightens around the lower thread, forming a stitch.

1. feed dog cams
2. drive belt from motor via gearbox
3. feed dog linkages
4. bobbin and rotary hook
5. rotary hook drive
6. feed dog
7. upper thread
8. needle
9. thread guides
10. needle bar
11. needle bar guides
12. thread take-up
13. thread guide
14. thread tensioner
15. drive linkage for needle bar and thread take-up
16. upper shaft
17. toothed belt drives lower shaft at double speed
18. outer casing
19. control switches

1. chuck jaws
2. chuck
3. chuck bearings
4. gears
5. front motor bearings
6. cooling fan
7. rotor windings
8. on-off switch
9. 3-core cable
10. cable grip
11. switch lock
12. rear motor bearings
13. commutator
14. brush

**Above:** The electric drill is one of the multitude of small, motor-driven electrical machines used in the home. The drill bit is clamped in the jaws of the chuck, which is driven by the motor via reduction gearing. The trigger operates the on-off switch, and can be locked in the 'on' position if desired. A wide range of accessories, including sanders, polishers, grinders, rotary saws and hole saws, can be fitted to drills.

21

# Electricity Supply

The first public electricity supply systems came into operation in the late nineteenth century. They were owned and operated by private companies or by local authorities such as city councils. There was little co-ordination between these individual undertakings; inter-connection between these many different systems was often economically impractical because they operated not only at different voltages but also at different alternating current (ac) frequencies, and in fact many were direct current (dc) systems.

As the use of electricity grew, it became obvious that voltages and frequencies should be standardized on a national level. This would not only permit the easy transmission of power from one part of a country to another, but it would also simplify the design and construction of electrical equipment. With a wide range of supply voltages in use, any electrical apparatus had to incorporate circuitry which enabled it to be adjusted to accept as many different supply voltages as possible.

In many countries, such as Britain and France, the establishment of national supply networks was followed by state ownership of the supply companies. In others, for example the USA and Switzerland, the national network interconnects a mixture of private and public systems.

The largest power system under centralized control anywhere in the world is in England and Wales. Operated by the Central Electricity Generating Board, this system supplies power to local Electricity Boards who in turn supply nearly 21 million consumers.

The system now comprises around 168 power stations with a total of 785 generators, which are able to meet a simultaneous demand of 58,523 MW (millions of watts). These are all interconnected by means of nearly 18,000 kilometres (over 11,000 miles) of high voltage transmission lines—the Grid system.

Power is transmitted over the Grid at three different voltages. More than 4,350 km of transmission lines operate at 400 kV, over 2,300 km at 275 kV and nearly 11,000 km at 132 kV. The 400/275 kV network, often referred to as the Supergrid, will remain adequate for system loads up to at least 110,000 MW, that is, roughly to the end of the century.

Using high voltages for power transmission has two advantages: firstly it reduces the power loss along the cables, and secondly it increases the amount of power that a given size of conductor can carry. For example, a 400 kV line has three times the power-carrying capacity of a 275 kV line and eighteen times the capacity of a 132 kV line.

## Circuit breakers

Three-phase electricity is usually produced in the stator windings of large modern generators at up to about 25 kV, and this is directly connected by heavy cables to a generator transformer in the adjoining main Grid substation. This steps up the voltage to 132 kV, 275 kV or 400 kV. From here conductors carry it to

Above: A diagram showing how electricity is brought from the power station to the consumer. The windings of the power station alternators are arranged so that they produce three separate alternating voltages, which are out of step with each other by 120° of rotation of the alternator rotor. One end of each of these phase windings is connected to a common point, the neutral point, which is connected to earth. The voltage between any two of the phases is about 1.73 times the voltage between any one of them and earth. Large consumers are provided with a three phase supply, but small ones, such as houses, are supplied with one phase and a neutral line. This carries the return current to the substation where the transformer secondary windings have an earthed neutral point. In this diagram, these local low-voltage systems provide 415 V phase to phase, and 240 V phase to neutral or earth.

Right: An 18/400 kV transformer at a power station in Venezuela.

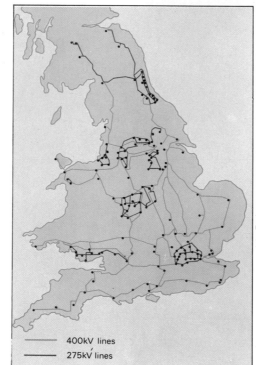

Above: The 400–275 kV main transmission network operated by the CEGB in England and Wales. The CEGB generates power and transmits it over 400 kV, 275 kV and some 132 kV circuits to the 12 Area Electricity Boards. It is then distributed to the consumers at voltages down to 415/240 V.

400kV lines
275kV lines

Above right: The cable ship Dame Caroline Haslett laying the cable which links the CEGB network with that of Electricité de France.

Right: The approximate route of the ±100 kVdc submarine cable which can transfer up to 160 MW of power either way between England and France.

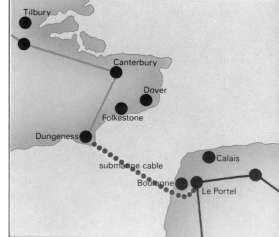

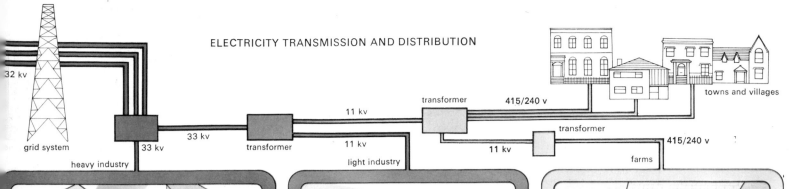

32 kv

grid system

33 kv

heavy industry

33 kv

transformer

11 kv

light industry

11 kv

transformer

11 kv

farms

transformer

415/240 v

transformer

415/240 v

towns and villages

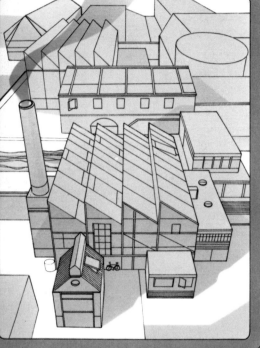

Paul Brierley

CEGB

**Above: 275 kV oil filled circuit breakers in the switching compound of a large power station.**

**Above left: Many circuit breakers can be isolated from the supply by lowering them so that they 'unplug' from the circuit. This picture shows the spiked connectors on the top of a circuit breaker, and the sockets they plug into. The breaker can only be isolated after it has switched off the circuit it controls.**

**Left: The control room of the CEGB's National Control Centre in London. This control centre supervises the seven Area Control Centres of England and Wales, and plans the transfer of power from one area to another.**

CEGB

a series of three switches, comprising an *isolator*, a *circuit-breaker* and another isolator, which are used to connect or disconnect the transformer with the transmission lines. There are three groups of such switches for each generator transformer—one for each of the three phases of the power supply.

The circuit-breaker is a heavy-duty switch capable of operating in a fraction of a second, and is used to switch off the current flowing to the transmission lines. Once the current has been interrupted the isolators can be opened. These isolate the circuit-breaker from all outside electrical sources, so that there is no chance of any high voltages being applied to its terminals. Maintenance or repair work can then be carried out in safety.

From the circuit-breaker the current is taken to the *busbars*—conductors which run the length of the switching compound —and then to another circuit-breaker with its associated isolators before being fed to the Grid. Each generator in a power station has its own transformer, circuit-breaker and isolators but the electricity generated is fed onto a common set of busbars.

Circuit-breakers work like combined switches and fuses, but they have certain special features and are very different from domestic switches and fuses. When electrical current is switched off by separating two contacts, an arc is created between them. At the voltage used in the home, this arc is very small, and only lasts for a fraction of a second. At the very high voltages used for transmission, however, the size and power of the arc is considerable and it must be quickly quenched to prevent damage.

23

One type of circuit-breaker has its contacts immersed in insulating oil so that when the switch is opened, either by powerful electromagnetic coils or mechanically by springs, the arc is quickly extinguished by the oil. Another type works by compressed air which operates the switch and at the same time 'blows out' the arc. These *air-blast* circuit-breakers are almost universally employed on 275 and 400 kV circuits.

## Control centres

Power stations generate electricity most economically when they operate 24 hours a day, but as the demand for electricity is never constant, changes in consumption have to be balanced by starting or shutting down some of the generators in the power stations. The cost of generation is the main factor that guides the control engineers in deciding which power stations to operate. Large modern stations have the lowest running costs, while the older, smaller ones away from fuel sources are the most expensive to operate.

The operation of power stations must therefore be co-ordinated on both a regional and a national basis. In England and Wales there are seven areas, each with its own control centre, which are co-ordinated by the National Control Centre in London. These control centres, in conjunction with the engineers in the power stations, are also responsible for ensuring that the supply frequency, which is 50 Hz in Britain, is maintained at all times.

## Distribution

The main 400/275 kV transmission system of the CEGB is connected to a total of 190 *grid sub-stations*, which together accommodate 519 transformers and associated switchgear. These, in turn, are connected via 132 kV lines to more than 750 *bulk supply points*, large substations again incorporating transformers and switchgear. From these substations, bulk supplies of electricity at 33 kV are taken for primary distribution in the towns and to industrial areas, groups of villages and similar concentrations of consumers. The lines are fed into numerous intermediate substations where transformers reduce the voltage to 11 kV.

The transformers in these substations are usually equipped with automatic or remotely operated *tap changing* gear to ensure that consumers always have the correct supply voltage, within the statutory limits of plus or minus 6%. As the load on the system increases, the voltage tends to drop. The tap changers compensate for this by changing the ratio between the primary and secondary transformer windings to keep the supplied voltages within the legal limits.

Secondary distribution lines radiating from these substations carry the power into the areas to be supplied, and terminate at local distribution substations. Here the voltage is reduced to its final level of 415 V three phase (the voltage between any two phase lines) and 240 V single phase (the voltage between a single phase and earth) for use in small factories, shops, offices, schools and homes.

Some consumers use electricity in such large quantities that they are supplied at a higher voltage than that used in the home. Heavy industries may have their own connections direct to the grid, taking power at 33kV or even higher,

Picturepoint

**Above: The copper conductors which route the power around this 400/275 kV substation are hollow tubes. There is no need for them to be solid, because at these voltages electromagnetic effects cause the current to flow near the surface of a round conductor, and very little flows through the centre.**

**Right: The demand for electricity varies throughout the day, and the year. This graph shows the average demands during winter and summer in England and Wales, plus the days of maximum and minimum demand during 1974. Peak daily demand in summer is at about 9 am, and in winter at about 6 pm.**

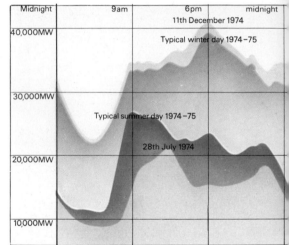

| Midnight | 9am | 6pm | midnight |
|---|---|---|---|
| | | 11th December 1974 | |
| 40,000MW | | Typical winter day 1974–75 | |
| 30,000MW | | | |
| | Typical summer day 1974–75 | | |
| | | 28th July 1974 | |
| 20,000MW | | | |
| 10,000MW | | | |

CEGB

**Above: To avoid any interruption of electricity supplies a great deal of repair work and routine maintenance is carried out without switching off the power. This picture shows men working on a live high voltage line, using insulated glass fibre equipment to handle the conductors.**

**Right: Live line repairs can be carried out on lines operating at as much as 400 kV. The linesman wears an electrically conducting protective suit, which dissipates any electric charges, such as static electricity, which may occur. The sling carrying him is insulated from the tower.**

CEGB

24

Above: This local
substation consists of a
transformer, switchgear
and fuses, enclosed in a
module of aluminium
slats coated with
coloured pvc. This type
of substation is an
alternative to the
ordinary 'outdoor'
substation, which has
the equipment mounted
on a concrete plinth and
surrounded by a fence.

Right: Pole-mounted
transformers are widely
used on overhead
distribution systems.
They are connected to
the high voltage lines,
and the low voltage
supply to the consumers
is taken from them
either by overhead lines
or underground cables.
Fuses and isolators may
also be mounted on
poles.

SWEB

Picturepoint

Paul Brierley

Above: This old type of
underground power
cable has conductors
made of copper wire,
with rubber insulation.
Rubber has been replaced
by special oil-
impregnated paper on
modern cables. These are
often enclosed in a lead
sheath, protected by
steel wire or tape and
a canvas outer layer
impregnated with pitch.

Below: Copper wire
conductors are not
always used on modern
cables. This one has
solid aluminium
conductors, which are
lighter and cheaper than
copper although they
have to be larger in
cross-section to provide
the same current-
carrying capacity. This
one uses a plastic
insulating material.

Paul Brierley

while hospitals, factories and large office
buildings are often supplied directly from
intermediate substations at 11 kV.

Railways have special substations
alongside the tracks, drawing electricity
directly from the Grid; the latest rail
electrification schemes work at 25 kV.

Where existing power stations are
already close to consumers, as in London,
the power is often fed into the local
primary distribution network at 66 kV or
33 kV, connections to the Grid system
also being made in case of breakdown

The distribution of electricity is
arranged so that, as far as is practicable,
supplies are not interrupted if there is a
fault in one section of the system. In a
typical case this is done by running
separate 33 kV lines from the Grid supply
point to the intermediate substation
feeding the town and the substation
serving heavy industry. A further 33 kV
line connects these two points together
to form a ring so that if the direct connection to either substation breaks down,
supplies can still be maintained through
this connecting link. This arrangement
for ensuring the security of supplies is in
widespread use throughout all transmission and distribution networks.

There is no fixed pattern for local
distribution, the arrangement of substations and transmission lines being
developed as a result of the particular
requirements of the area. Sometimes an
intermediate substation may be built
alongside a bulk supply point, and
occasionally, even the bulk supply point
may be in the town centre.

The above survey necessarily presents
a rather simplified view of the power
distribution system. As can be imagined

an enormous amount of equipment and
resources are employed to ensure that a
reliable supply of electricity is available
to all consumers. At present, the final
distribution network operated by the
Electricity Boards in England and Wales
comprises no less than 390,000 substations
and well over half a million kilometres of
mains. These mains are operated at
voltages ranging from 132 kV down to the
415/240 V of the local low-voltage
distribution networks.

The whole network is fully protected by
automatic circuit breakers, lightning
arresters, fuses and other devices to
prevent overloads damaging the system.
In the event of a fault, the line or equipment concerned can usually be isolated
and power routed over alternative lines,
so that interruptions to consumers are
kept to the minimum.

This vast network of overhead and
underground cables, substations, transformers and switchgear represents a
considerable financial investment and it
must all be kept in working order to
ensure continuity of supply. At the same
time, modifications are continuously
being made to reinforce supplies to
particular areas, such as new housing
estates, office buildings, and expanding
or new factories. All this must be done
with the minimum of interruption to
supplies.

In fact, a great deal of work is carried
out without switching off the power.
Techniques of live-line working using
special insulated tools have been
developed in recent years which enable
modifications, repairs and connections to
be made to overhead lines while they are
on load.

# Water Supply

As soon as men began to settle into large communities they were faced with the problems of ensuring an adequate fresh water supply. The small settlements of the Neolithic age had successfully relied on natural springs and simple wells, but such sources were simply not capable of satisfying the towns and cities which began to develop about 4000 BC. At first, as in the cities of Mesopotamia, open conduits were used to channel water from distant springs and lakes. The ruins of Mohenjo-Daro in the Indus Valley, which date from about 2500 BC, boast the earliest known enclosed system.

The ancient Greeks made considerable use of conduits, pipes and tunnels to supply water to their cities, and their techniques were refined and developed by the Romans. Imperial Rome enjoyed a water system unrivalled at the time and unsurpassed for many centuries after. It has been estimated that enough was supplied by the Roman systems to give every urban inhabitant some 225 litres (50 gallons) per day. This is as much as many modern municipalities provide.

## Water quality

Groundwater sources are usually less contaminated than surface waters because they have had less contact with possible impurities. Surface water may have flowed through hundreds of kilometres of stream and river before it reaches the lake or reservoir from which a public supply is taken. In the course of its journey it will have picked up a quantity of minerals, some of which may be poisonous industrial waste, and an assortment of plant and animal matter, including sewage, in various states of decomposition. In addition, lakes may become infested with algae, which give the water an unpleasant taste and smell.

A water treatment works aims to supply water that is safe and pleasant to drink. A number of simple tests are performed on the treated water to ensure that this is the case. Perhaps the most important of these is the *coliform bacteria count*. Coliforms, such as *Escherichia coli*, which is also widely cultivated for use in research, live naturally in human intestines and are excreted in large quantities into sewage. In themselves they are harmless, but the presence of such bacteria in a water sample indicates that other, more dangerous bacteria and viruses may also be present.

The *biochemical oxygen demand* (BOD) test is a useful measure of the amount of decomposing organic material present. Decomposition uses up oxygen, and the BOD test measures the amount of oxygen used up in this way by a sample of water which is maintained at 20°C (68°F) for five days.

The total amount of solid matter suspended in a water sample, which also includes inorganic matter such as clay, can be estimated by measuring the *turbidity* (cloudiness) of a sample. This can be done quite simply by shining light through the water and measuring the proportion of light scattered by the suspended particles.

The presence of an appreciable quantity of nitrogen in water is a good indica-

Above: A Roman aqueduct at Segovia in Spain, built during the reign of the Emperor Trajan (53-117 AD) and still in use today. It carries water from the Rio Frio for about 823 m (2,700 ft) to the old town, its maximum height being about 28.5 m (93.5 ft).

Above right: Laying a pipeline to carry water from a reservoir to a treatment works. The pipes are made of iron lined with concrete.

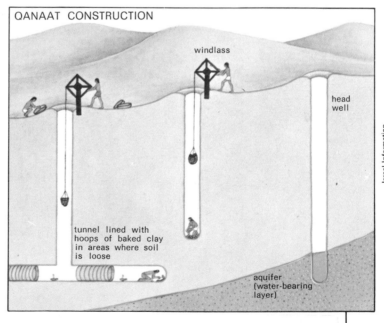

QANAAT CONSTRUCTION

windlass

head well

tunnel lined with hoops of baked clay in areas where soil is loose

aquifer (water-bearing layer)

*Qanaats*, widely used in Iran and other Middle Eastern countries, are inclined irrigation tunnels which carry mountain groundwater to arid plains.

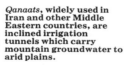

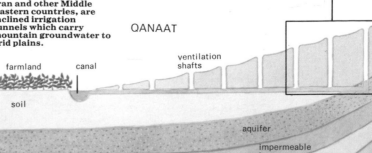

QANAAT

farmland    canal    ventilation shafts

soil

aquifer

impermeable layer

rock

water intake area

Left: The first step in building a qanaat is the digging of a head well down into the water-bearing strata in the hills, and then the tunnel is dug from the downhill end up to the head well. Ventilation shafts are dug at intervals of about 50 m, and the total tunnel length is usually about 10 to 16 km (6-10 mi).

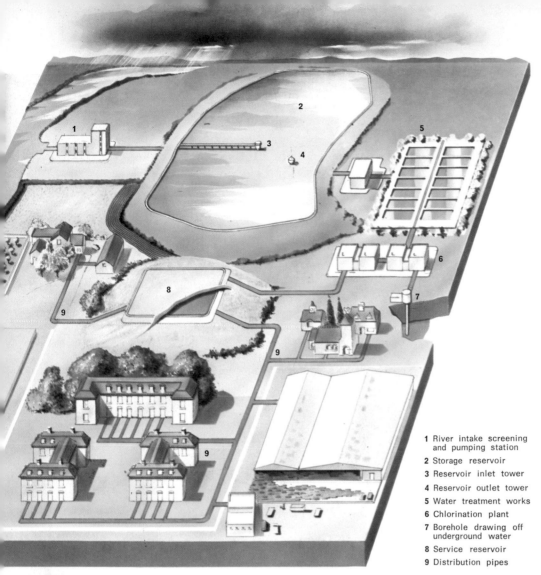

1 River intake screening and pumping station

2 Storage reservoir

3 Reservoir inlet tower

4 Reservoir outlet tower

5 Water treatment works

6 Chlorination plant

7 Borehole drawing off underground water

8 Service reservoir

9 Distribution pipes

Above: A typical water supply system. Here, water taken from a river is screened to remove debris and pumped into a storage reservoir. It is then filtered, purified and chlorinated before distribution to the consumers. Water pumped up through boreholes drilled into underground water sources needs only chlorination before it is distributed.

Left: Part of Israel's National Water Carrier, which carries water to the Negev desert.

Weir Pumps Ltd

Above: Three *pumpsets*, each consisting of a pump and an electric drive motor, at the Ross Priory pumping station in Scotland. These pumpsets, which have a total capacity of 227 million litres (50 million gallons) of water per day, pump water from Loch Lomond for distribution to reservoirs and treatment works supplying central Scotland.

Left: A reservoir in North Wales. Reservoirs play an important part in the purification of water. While the water is standing in the reservoir, the larger solid impurities settle to the bottom, the large surface area allows the oxygen in the air to attack other impurities, and the various physical, chemical and biological conditions set up within the water during storage have a destructive effect on any harmful bacteria.

Picturepoint

tion of possible contamination. Combined with hydrogen (forming ammonia, $NH_3$), it indicates pollution by organic matter. In the form of nitrites and nitrates, it points to inorganic pollutants such as fertilizers and chemical wastes.

## Water treatment

Before it can be distributed to consumers, water must undergo a series of physical and chemical treatments to remove the impurities. The number and nature of the cleaning processes varies from one works to another, because some sources of raw water are much cleaner than others. The following is an exhaustive series of treatments, not all of which will be necessary in every case.

The first treatment is quite simple—the water is stored in large reservoirs or settling basins for several weeks. This allows the larger particles to sink to the bottom of the basin. During this period chemical reactions, which take place naturally and slowly in the water, tend to neutralize any acidity or alkalinity. The most important advantage of storage, however, is that the number of toxic bacteria in the water is strikingly reduced. Shortage of suitable food, a low temperature in the depths of the storage basin, the effects of sunlight, and the competition from harmless micro-organisms all contribute to the decline in the bacterial population.

The next stage in the treatment is to pass the water through a fairly coarse screen which removes leaves and other debris. At this stage chlorine is usually added to kill off the remaining bacteria. Chlorine is not the only possible disinfectant. Some European countries use ozone ($O_3$), which is rather more expensive, and in some small plants the water may be sterilized by irradiating it with ultra-violet light. A second screening usually follows, which removes algae and small particles. This is done by a *microstrainer*, a rotating filter drum covered with a very fine stainless steel mesh. The holes in the mesh are less than one micron (one millionth of a metre) in diameter, and the water passes through them from the inside of the drum outwards.

Even after passing through the extremely fine mesh of the microstrainer, water still contains many small suspended particles. Some of these are insoluble minerals, others are dead bacteria, and all make the water look cloudy and sometimes discoloured. They can be trapped by a process known as *coagulation and flocculation*.

In cloudy water the suspended particles are in continuous rapid motion and are never in close contact with each other for long enough to stick together. If a chemical coagulant such as aluminium sulphate ($Al_2 (SO_4)_3. 14H_2O$) or ferric sulphate ($Fe_2 (SO_4)_3. H_2O$) is added, the particles can be trapped by it so that they slowly aggregate together and eventually form a single, amorphous mass, leaving the water clear. This coagulated mass has a woolly appearance and settles in a sort of blanket about halfway down the tank; it is called a *flocculent precipitate* or *floc* for short. A small residue of the coagulant remains dissolved in the water and may make it harder and more corrosive.

By this stage the water is considerably purer than it was at its source, but it

27

## MULTI-STAGE FLASH DESALINATION PLANT

sea water for cooling and feed

condenser

condenser

uncondensed gases

vapour condensing

product water

brine flows from left to right

chemical dosage tank

steam to heat brine

cooling sea water for discharge

heat exchanger

recirculating brine

condensed steam from heat exchanger

**Top:** A *multi-stage flash desalination* plant in Abu Dhabi, capable of producing over 9 million litres (2 million gallons) of fresh water per day.

**Above:** The multi-stage flash desalination plant distils fresh water from salt water by heating it and then reducing the air pressure around it. Sea water is heated by steam, and then passed through a series of chambers in which its pressure is progressively reduced. This causes fresh water to 'flash' (evaporate because of the low pressure) out of it and condense onto the condenser tubes.

**Left:** The *reverse osmosis* process is a potentially important desalination method. In this process, salt water is forced against a *semi-permeable membrane*, one which allows the solvent of a solution to pass through it but not the dissolved substances, in this case pure water and salt respectively. The membranes are made from suitable polymer materials such as cellulose acetate.

must still undergo further cleaning in filter beds. Filtering is one of the most important processes of all. There are two main methods of filtration. *Slow sand filtration* may be used for water which comes from a relatively pure source and has not undergone any previous treatment. The water flows into beds of fine sand, and seeps through the sand and an underlying bed of gravel into an underground drainage system.

*Rapid sand filters* are filled with coarser sand, often with a layer of crushed anthracite below and sometimes with a layer of fine sand above. Rapid sand filters are the most commonly used because they allow faster rates of flow, but they are generally suitable only for water that has been previously cleaned to some extent by coagulation and flocculation. Rapid filters are cleaned daily by *backwashing*, passing water through them in the opposite direction to the normal flow. Slow filters are cleaned about once every two months by removing the top layer of sand and replacing it with clean sand.

After filtration, water is usually *aerated* to increase the amount of dissolved oxygen it contains. This improves the colour and freshness of taste as well as reducing acidity by eliminating dissolved carbon dioxide. There are several different types of aerator. One, the *spray aerator*, forces the water through fine nozzles into the air. Another, the *cascade aerator*, has a series of steps over which the water falls.

No amount of filtration, sedimentation or coagulation, however, will rid water of substances that are completely dissolved in it, and a large group of such substances—the salts of calcium and to a lesser extent magnesium—are responsible for the 'hardness' of water. Hard water makes washing with soap more difficult, hinders the extraction of meat and vegetable juices in cooking, and deposits scale in kettles, boilers and pipes, and chemical treatment is often necessary to reduce hardness to an acceptable level. In areas where the water is exceptionally hard, a softening process may be carried out at the treatment works if costs permit, but it is usually left to individual consumers to install their own softening units if they require soft water. There are two kinds of hardness, *permanent* and *temporary*.

Temporary hardness is due to calcium bicarbonate ($Ca(HCO_3)_2$) and magnesium bicarbonate ($Mg(HCO_3)_2$), and causes scale when the water is heated because the bicarbonates break down into insoluble carbonates which settle out of the water and stick to the surface of the container. This kind of hardness can be removed by treating the water with lime (calcium hydroxide, $Ca(OH)_2$), which reduces the bicarbonates to carbonates, so that they precipitate out without the need for heating.

Permanent hardness cannot be removed by boiling. It is caused by sulphates and chlorides of calcium and can be reduced by treatment with sodium bicarbonate ($NaHCO_3$). This leads to an *exchange reaction*, in which the carbonate group of atoms is transferred from the sodium to the calcium atoms to make an insoluble compound which settles out of the water. The sodium atoms receive in exchange the chloride and sulphate groups, making salts which do not contribute to hardness.

The Lower Laithe
Reservoir at
Stanbury, Yorkshire
— a stunning example
of modern techni-
logical achievement.

# Building Technology

The Ouse Bridge over the M62 motorway,
near Goole in Yorkshire. A mile (1.5km)
long, its 29 spans are of composite plate
girder construction.

# Road Building

The invention of the wheel and the establishment of stable civilizations led to the development of the first paved road systems, the forerunners of our modern road networks. Although the great caravan routes between Europe and Asia and the system of roads that helped hold China together were older than the Roman Empire, it is the Roman roads that are best known. The Romans were first-class engineers and pioneered most of the elements of modern road construction: efficient drainage, a good foundation, an even surface, a planned network with well-sited 'service areas', and regular maintenance. When this regular maintenance ceased in the turbulent decline of the Roman Empire, the roads fell into decay and disuse. It is even claimed by some that the neglect of this vital road system contributed to the decline of that empire. Much of Europe, though, including England (but not Scotland) owes the outline of its road system to the Romans.

The Middle Ages were a time of great neglect of the roads, but in the wake of the Renaissance and the voyages of discovery, however, came a new need for travel and for better roads. Towards the end of the eighteenth century the science of road building flourished in Britain as a result of the work of two Scottish engineers, Thomas Telford (1757-1834) and John Loudon McAdam (1756-1836), the latter giving his name to a system of road building ('tarmacadam', 'tarmac' or 'coated macadam') still the basis of most modern road construction. In Scotland earlier in the eighteenth century, General Wade had laid the foundations of today's Scottish road network in order to open up and pacify the Highlands.

This development in Great Britain was interrupted by the (historically speaking) brief interlude of the railway age, but the invention of the internal combustion engine late in the nineteenth century, and the advent of the motor car, created a great demand for good roads. Today an extensive and well-maintained road network is a basic necessity of life for every civilized community.

As we have seen, in European countries such as Britain the road networks acquired their present shapes over the centuries. However, the British *motorway* network, now over 2,500 km (1,550 miles) long, was not begun until the 1950s. The construction of a motorway is, therefore, a good example of all stages of modern road building.

## Planning

Once the need for a particular motorway has been established, the precise route has to be mapped out. First a general survey is taken to avoid wherever possible centres of population, good agricultural land and areas of outstanding beauty, as well as areas of vital industry such as coal mining. Often the engineers will plot a number of alternative routes and examine each for the various advantages and disadvantages they present. Once the route has been chosen, a more detailed survey is made and the provisional line of the road is determined. This becomes the basis for the publication of a *draft scheme*, and it is at this stage that

Right: A road under construction near Nairobi, Kenya. The construction principles being used for this road are similar to those developed by the French engineer Pierre Trésaguet (1716-1796) and by Thomas Telford. A foundation of heavy stones is laid on to the levelled topsoil, and this is covered by a layer of smaller stones and a wearing surface of gravel.

Below: The principal Roman roads of England and Wales, compared with the modern network of motorways. The motorway network serves the same purpose as did its Roman predecessor: to facilitate rapid travel between important locations.

Bottom: An early stage in the construction of the first section of the M1 (London to Leeds) motorway, the first road of its type to be built in Britain. This section, 88 km (55 miles) long, included 134 bridges and was completed in 1959. The construction time for this section was 19 months. Britain now has well over 2,500 km of motorway.

Picturepoint

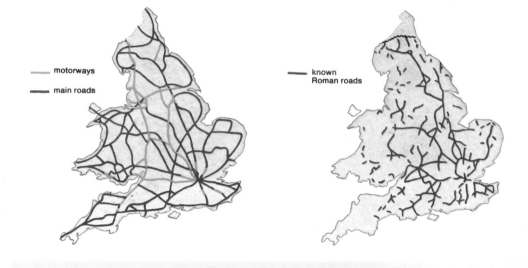

— motorways

— main roads

— known Roman roads

John Laing & Son Ltd.

objections may be lodged by parties affected. In some cases a public inquiry may be held, which can—and often does—bring about changes in the draft scheme.

Many hundreds of detailed working plans are now prepared, and the engineer in charge will have to co-ordinate these for the construction of the road itself, for the junctions and slip roads, and the bridges, underpasses, culverts and other structures needed. Indeed, the organization of this work is now so complex that special computer programs have been developed to handle it.

### Earthworks and drainage

Depending on the type of terrain, site clearance may involve the removal of many obstacles or simply consist of the cutting of the original construction 'scar'

across the countryside. This is followed by what is perhaps one of the biggest and least appreciated tasks of the road builder: the physical movement of enormous quantities of earth. Over 16 million tonnes of earth and rock were shifted, for example, in the construction of the first 88 km (55 miles) of the M1 motorway.

Valuable topsoil is always removed and saved for covering verges, slopes and central reservations. These areas, on modern motorways, have provided a new type of nature reserve for plants and wild life. In order to provide as even a profile as possible for the road, much 'muck shifting' consists of excavating earth from some parts of the line and shifting it to other parts to form embankments. This kind of working is called *cut and fill*.

Very early in the design of the road, consideration is given to the important subject of drainage. *Primary drainage* takes care of the run-off water from the entire pavement structure, and an extensive system of drains is laid well before the *formation level*—the platform of subsoil on which the road pavement is laid—is built up. Surface water from the pavement, once the road is built, is conducted to the sides of the road and thence into the drainage system by means of the *camber* of the road—its curved profile. The Romans ensured good drainage (and provided against flooding) by always raising their roads high above the ground on either side—possibly the origin of the word 'highway'.

### The pavement

The road pavement is the actual structure of the road, built up on the subsoil which is usually called the *subgrade*. It consists of three principal parts—the *sub-base*, the *roadbase* and the *surfacing*. The primary purpose of the pavement is to distribute the traffic loads in such a way that the subgrade is not *deformed* (damaged). Permanent deformations would lead to unevenness in the road and therefore detract from its usefulness for fast and heavy traffic. A great deal of attention is, therefore, given to pavement design so that the right structure can be selected for each class of traffic and the anticipated traffic density. An additional function of

**Top left:** A heavy *bulldozer*, one of several types of earthmoving machinery used in road construction. These machines are driven by large diesel engines, and the blade position is controlled by hydraulic rams.

**Left:** A large *motor scraper*, which scrapes up earth and carries it away in the large scraper box mounted between the axles. As the vehicle is driven forward, the leading edge of the open-fronted box is pushed a little way into the ground so that earth is scooped up into the box. The original type of scraper, the *scraper trailer*, consists of a scraper box mounted on wheels and pulled along by a tractor.

**Below left:** Laying concrete pavement by means of *slip form machines*. The first machine in the 'train' (not shown here) spreads the concrete on the roadbase, and the second machine, the one in this picture, compacts it into a firm slab.

**Below:** Laying the wearing course of coated chippings on top of the base course of a flexible pavement. The wearing course is the road's surface.

Richard Costain Ltd.

John Laing & Son Ltd.

Asphalt & Coated Macadam Association

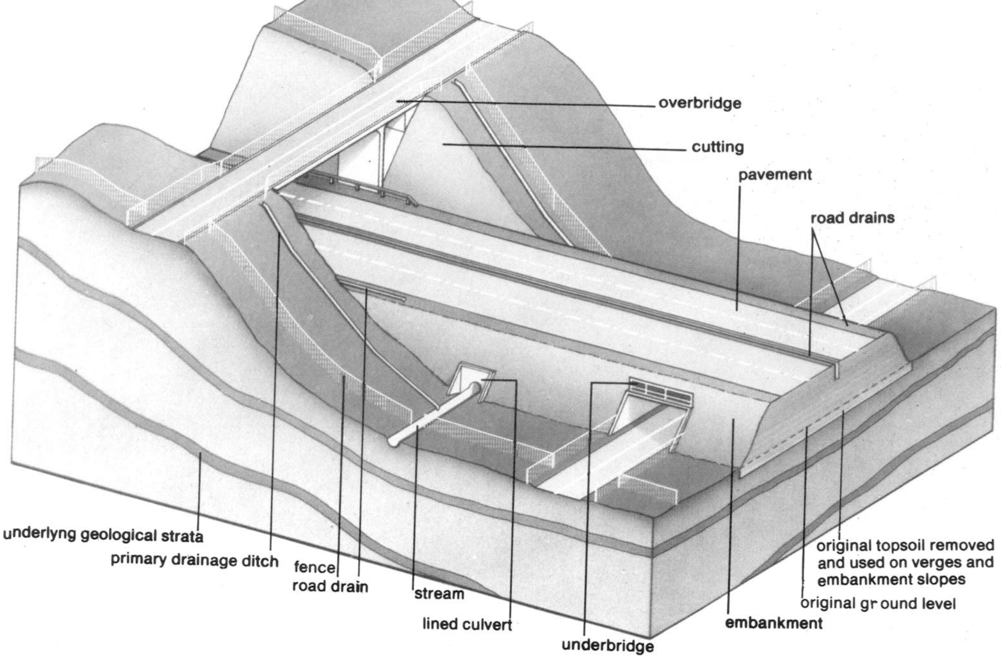
overbridge
cutting
pavement
road drains
underlyng geological strata
primary drainage ditch
fence
road drain
stream
lined culvert
underbridge
embankment
original topsoil removed and used on verges and embankment slopes
original gr ound level

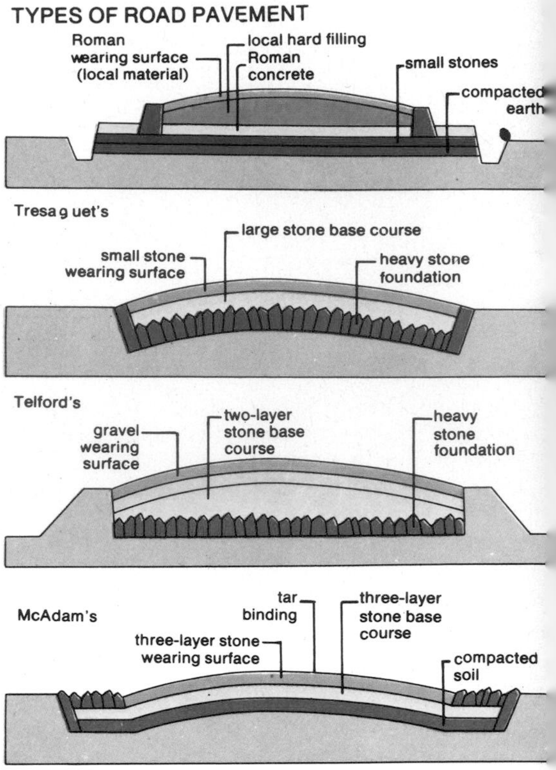
TYPES OF ROAD PAVEMENT
Roman
wearing surface (local material)
local hard filling
Roman concrete
small stones
compacted earth
Tresa g uet's
large stone base course
small stone wearing surface
heavy stone foundation
Telford's
gravel wearing surface
two-layer stone base course
heavy stone foundation
McAdam's
tar binding
three-layer stone base course
three-layer stone wearing surface
compacted soil

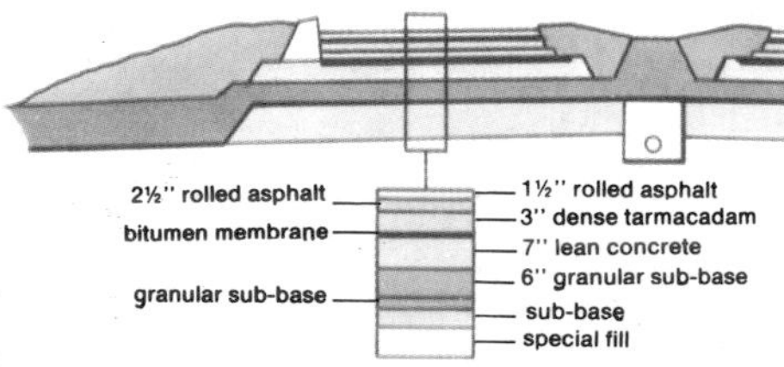
2½" rolled asphalt
bitumen membrane
granular sub-base
1½" rolled asphalt
3" dense tarmacadam
7" lean concrete
6" granular sub-base
sub-base
special fill

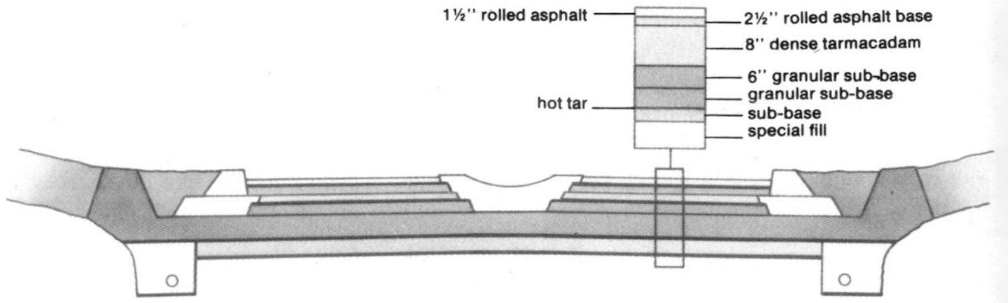
1½" rolled asphalt
hot tar
2½" rolled asphalt base
8" dense tarmacadam
6" granular sub-base
granular sub-base
sub-base
special fill

Courtesy of Michael Overman, *Roads, Bridges and Tunnels*. / Aldus Books

the surfacing is to prevent the entry of water to the road structure, allowing traffic to run smoothly in all weathers.

There are two types of pavement: *rigid*, consisting of concrete, and *flexible*, consisting of layers of various types of *coated materials*. These are composed of aggregates such as stone and sand, mixed with varying percentages of *tar* (extracted from coal) or *bitumen* (derived from oil), and are delivered hot to the site. They are variously known as *tarmacadam*, *bitumen macadam*, *hot rolled asphalt*, and *dense tar surfacing*; all are often referred to as *black top*.

For both types of pavement the sub-base is much the same: a layer of granular material such as stones or gravel laid upon the compacted formation and then itself compacted to form a firm base for the next stage. This, in the case of rigid construction, is a roadbase of *lean cement concrete*, a concrete containing a relatively small percentage of cement. The same material is sometimes used to provide the base for flexible surfacing, but fully flexible construction calls for a roadbase of coated materials, laid (often in several layers or *courses*) by a mechanical finisher and compacted by rollers. In some instances a roadbase of coated materials is also used for rigid pavements: this is known as *composite construction* and has been used on many motorways and airfield runways in Europe. The base is a vital part of the pavement, and it is rightly said that 'a road is only as good as its base'.

For rigid construction the final slabs of concrete are now laid. The roadbase is covered with plastic sheeting, steel mesh reinforcement is laid on top (this may be omitted if the concrete road is not carrying heavy traffic), and the concrete is poured to a thickness of at least 250 mm (10 in). Although the concrete, to allow for expansion and contraction, is poured in sections called *bays*, and the joints are then filled with a flexible and waterproof bituminous compound, the whole operation is highly mechanized, using a complex *concrete train* proceeding slowly along the road.

Flexible pavements can use the principle of *stage construction*. Relatively thin layers of coated materials are laid down as and when traffic conditions demand, the whole becoming one strong and homogenous pavement. Normally, the surfacing laid on the roadbase will consist of a *base course* averaging from 45 to 60 mm (1.8 to 2.4 in) thickness, followed by a final *wearing course* which may be between 25 and 40 mm (1 and 1.6 in) thick. Both are prepared to stringent specifications, and laid with a mechanical finisher to closely controlled levels. The stone for the wearing course is carefully selected to ensure a skid-resistant surfacing and, especially on motorways, coated chippings (hard stones with a coating of bitumen) are applied for extra resistance to skidding. Various types of road rollers (smooth-wheeled, pneumatic-tyred or vibrating) are used to compact each layer while it is hot.

## The finishing touches

Before the motorway can be opened to traffic the lane markings, signs, barriers, emergency telephones and other equipment have to be installed. White lane

**Top: A sectional drawing of a short length of completed road, showing some common construction features, and cross-sections of some important types of pavement structure from Roman times to the present day. The composite pavement shown here is similar to a flexible pavement but incorporates a lean concrete roadbase like that of a rigid pavement. Other composite types use a roadbase of coated materials with a concrete surface.**

**Right: The bridge over the River Avon near Bristol, England, carrying the M5 motorway which runs from Birmingham to Exeter.**

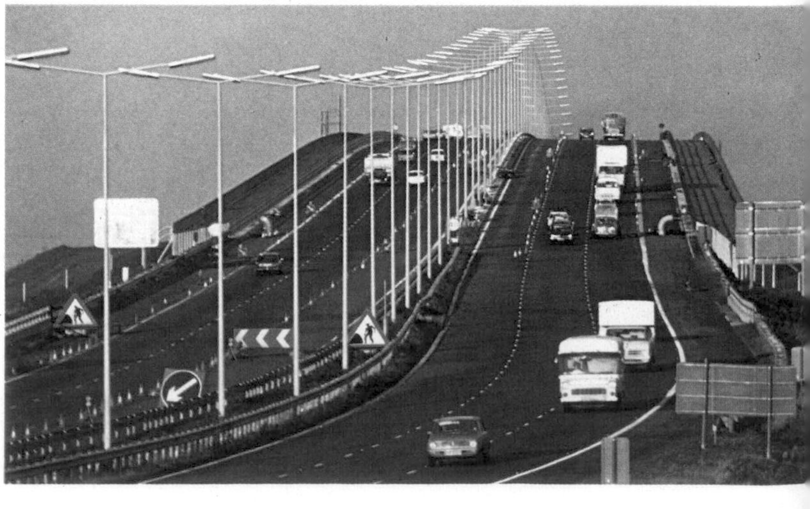

Picturepoint

Left: The M62 motorway in northern England divides into two to bypass a farm in the Pennine hills. The 53 km (33 mile) long M62 connects the busy industrial regions of Lancashire and Yorkshire.

Above: Applying an anti-skid road surface. The road is first coated with a binder consisting of bitumen and epoxy resin, and when the binder has cooled to road temperature an aggregate of calcined bauxite is spread over it. The coating takes between two and five hours to set hard enough to be driven on. It has a very high skid resistance even when wet, and is often used at junctions and other hazardous sites.

markings on British motorways are generally provided with reflecting road studs known as 'cat's eyes' and these may be coloured red, yellow or green for special purposes. A variety of directional and warning signs must be provided, and many of the latter are now centrally controlled and can display electronically a range of appropriate warnings and instructions.

Metal crash barriers are erected along the central reservations and at other critical points. On urban stretches motorway lighting is installed. Emergency telephones are spaced at reasonable intervals, and all the appropriate wiring has to be accommodated in waterproof conduits along or under the sides of the road. At the same time, the slip roads have to be similarly fitted out and advance directional signs pointing to the motorway have to be erected over a wide area of the feeder road network.

## Maintenance

The opening of the motorway is by no means the end of the story; in some ways the highway engineer's work has only just begun. Planned regular maintenance of both the fabric of the road and the many ancillary installations is essential to protect the original investment and to give a long and useful life to the road.

Maintenance includes such items as grass, tree and bush cutting to keep the line of the road clear and visible, the cleaning and repair of signs and lamps, and the general cleaning of the road. Winter maintenance includes snow clearing, gritting and salting. The maintenance of the actual road structure may consist of simple patching, or of *surface dressing* whole stretches to restore skid resistance. This is done by spraying tar or bitumen on to the road, spreading stone chippings, and then rolling it. For more lasting maintenance, the road is provided with a relatively thin overlay of coated materials (sometimes the existing surface is heated or burned off), which renews the surface and adds strength to the whole of the road structure.

Above: The M56/M63 motorway interchange near Manchester, England. The design of interchanges such as this one is nowadays aided by the use of specially-developed computer programs.

Left: A *road planer*, a machine which strips off the worn surface layer of a road when a new wearing course is to be laid. The road surface is heated to about 1,000°C (1,830°F) by a propane-fired heater unit, and broken up by rotary cutters. The loose material is scraped up and conveyed to the truck backed up behind the planer. The machine is self-propelled, and is powered by a 56 kW (75 bhp) four cylinder diesel engine.

# Tunnels

Some of the earliest tunnels constructed were those connected with supplies of water. Long before the birth of Christ *qanaats* were used in many Middle Eastern countries to supply water for irrigation and domestic purposes. The qanaat system of winning water (still in use today) employs a tunnel driven more or less horizontally into a wadi bed or similar formation until it encounters water-bearing strata. The first such tunnels were, however, relatively short, and it was not until Roman times that tunnels of any appreciable length were engineered. These formed part of the aqueduct systems that carried water from distant springs to Rome and other cities of the Empire.

**The development of tunnelling**
Modern tunnelling owes its conception and birth to the canal era that began with the commissioning of the Duke of Bridgewater's canal in northwest England in 1761. The great problem that all canal engineers, from James Brindley (1716-72)

Howard Humphreys & Sons

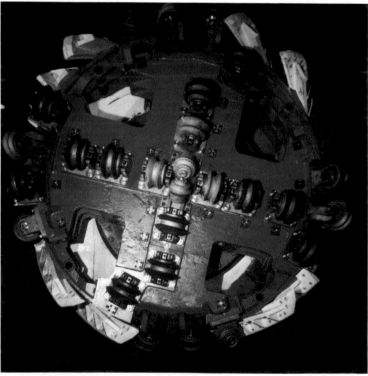

Thyssen

Left: The cutting head of a Thyssen FLP 35 full face hard rock tunnelling machine. The 4.2 m (13.8 ft) diameter head rotates at 4.5 rpm, and the machine has a forward thrust of 400 tonnes. The machine is guided with the aid of a laser unit positioned 150 to 300 m (492 to 984 ft) from the cut face.

Above: The tunnelling shield used in driving one of the twin tunnels on the Newport to Monmouth trunk road in Wales. The tunnel face was blasted out 1.2 m (4 ft) at a time; after each blasting the shield was moved forward to support the roof, then the concrete lining was put into place behind it.

Below: The rotating cutting head, mounted on a hydraulically-controlled, movable boom, of a Thyssen Titan roadheader tunnelling machine. The machine moves forward on crawler tracks, and the boom moves the cutting head across the entire area of the tunnel face. The water jets suppress the dust.

Thyssen

onwards, had to face was the lack of water at the summit where a canal passed from one catchment to another. Seldom was the amount available sufficient for the operation of the long chain of locks that would have been needed to carry it over the top. At the start of the era, experience in the construction of tunnels was very limited and consequently the early canals tended to follow the contours of the countryside.

This meant that routes were long and circuitous, and as competition between canal companies increased so did the need to provide shorter and more economical routes. This required the increasing use of tunnels, and as experience was gained so construction methods and techniques improved. The old Harecastle tunnel built by Brindley on the Trent and Mersey

Canal in England, for example, took 11 years to construct, but when the second Harecastle tunnel was built some 60 years later only three years were needed.

But even before that tunnel was completed, in 1827, there was evidence that the days of the canal were numbered. In 1825 the opening of the Stockton and Darlington Railway heralded the dawn of the railway age, and in the following 25 years, in a great explosion of activity, the old canal system was reduced to obsolescence by this new and exciting form of transport. The 'navigators' who had built the canals were transformed into the railway 'navvies' of the nineteenth century, bringing with them the skill and experience in the construction of tunnels which was as essential to the railways as it had been to canals.

In the construction of these early tunnels there was little in the way of machinery available and most of the excavation was done by hand, the spoil being loaded into skips and hauled from the tunnel by ponies. If the tunnel was long, a number of shafts would be sunk so that extra faces could be opened up and the rate of progress increased. Spoil was hauled to the surface by horse *gins* (hoists) and removed by horse and cart. At Box tunnel, on the Paddington to Bristol railway line, I. K. Brunel used a force of over 4,000 men and 300 horses working night and day. The cost was high even by modern standards, amounting to some £6.5 million.

Another railway tunnel constructed at about the same time was the Woodhead tunnel through the Pennines, which is

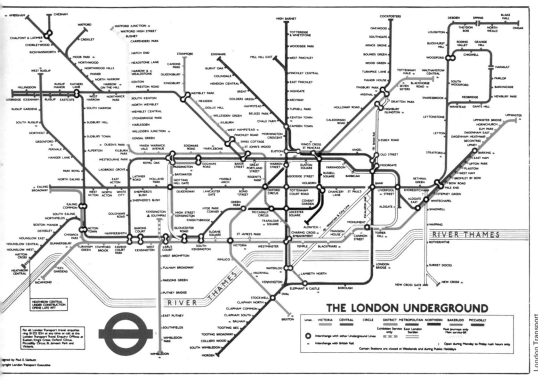

**THE LONDON UNDERGROUND**

Lines: VICTORIA CENTRAL CIRCLE DISTRICT METROPOLITAN NORTHERN BAKERLOO PICCADILLY

Left and below left: In 1977 London Transport was operating over 400 km (250 miles) of railway, of which some 122 km (76 miles) were in bored tunnels. 35 km (22 miles) were in sub-surface tunnels built by 'cut-and-cover' tunnelling, which involves digging a large trench and then roofing it over.

Above: A Markham soft-ground tunnelling machine.

Below: The charges used in blasting a tunnel face are sealed in place with gel-filled ampoules. These retain the blast within the rock, and the explosion atomizes the gel into a fine mist which absorbs the dust and fumes.

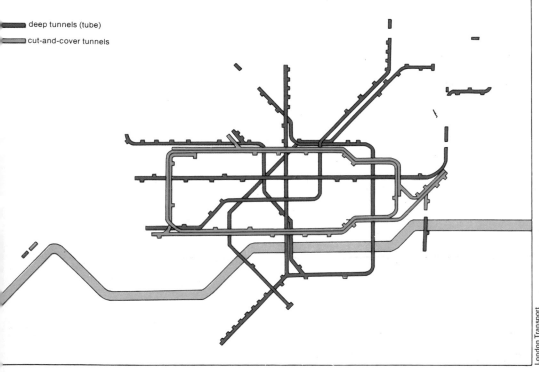

deep tunnels (tube)
cut-and-cover tunnels

more than twice the length of the Box tunnel. At one time nearly 1,500 labourers were employed on the project, driving the tunnel through the treacherous millstone grits, shales, soft red sandstones, slate and clay that were encountered. In these circumstances injuries and deaths were frequent occurrences.

One of the first tunnels to be built under a river was constructed between Rotherhithe and Wapping in London. In 1805, the Thames Archway Company first proposed the tunnel, but the venture did not develop and was abandoned in 1808. However, it was revived in 1823 following the invention by Marc Isambard Brunel, the father of Isambard Kingdom Brunel, of the first ever *tunnelling shield* in 1818. The tunnelling shield supports the surrounding earth during excavation, and

is moved forward as work progresses.

For a while good progress was made, but in 1827 a great inflow of mud and water occurred, bringing construction to a halt. By the end of 1827, as the result of great determination and unremitting labour, the problems were overcome and work restarted. To celebrate this triumph over disaster, in the true spirit of the age, a banquet was staged under the river at which a company of 50 dined and listened to music provided by the Coldstream Guards. Unfortunately, mounting costs and further trouble led to more delay and the tunnel was not completed until 1843.

The idea of a tunnel beneath the English Channel to link England and France was first proposed in 1802 by a French engineer called Albert Mathieu, but little happened until 1865 when Sir John Hawk-

shaw carried out borings and took samples in St Margaret's Bay and at sea. Further sampling from the seabed was carried out in 1875-76, and in the late 1870s pilot headings, each a mile long, were driven out to sea on both sides of the channel using Colonel Beaumont's newly-invented mechanical tunnelling machine. In 1882, however, British fears that the French would use the tunnel to mount an invasion brought work to a halt, and although various studies were made subsequently at different times no further work was undertaken until 1973. Further exploratory drives were then again made from each shore but rapidly escalating cost estimates led in 1975 to a further cessation of work. A new proposal, put forward in 1977, suggested that the tunnel should be funded by the European

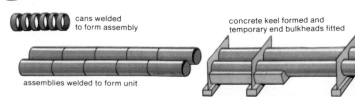

plates welded
to form can

cans welded
to form assembly

concrete keel formed and
temporary end bulkheads fitted

assemblies welded to form unit

Richard Costain Ltd

Courtesy of Richard Costain Ltd

Thyssen

Economic Community.

By the end of the nineteenth century construction techniques had improved immeasurably, helped greatly by new machinery then becoming available. Sweden in particular pioneered the use of compressed air tools and excavators which could be used underground where ventilation was poor.

## Modern tunnelling

Most of the hazards encountered in tunnelling arise because the ground conditions encountered have not been predicted. Before a tunnel is built, detailed geological surveys are carried out by means of boreholes and trial excavations, but as the samples obtained by such methods are minute compared with the volume of material which can affect the tunnel, difficult ground conditions are not always revealed. Typical problems include areas of broken and shattered rock in an otherwise unbroken rock formation due to folding or faulting. The presence of water in such faults is a further hazard which may lead to sudden and uncontrollable inflows, especially if the tunnel is deep or subaqueous.

Sometimes small-size pilot tunnels are driven so that the strata can be examined at first hand, but the driving of such a tunnel can itself be a hazardous undertaking. Nowadays the use of pilot tunnels is less frequent but some indication or warning of dangerous conditions can be obtained by probing ahead of the face.

For construction purposes tunnels can be divided into two types, those in rock and those in soft ground. Tunnels in rock are generally excavated by drilling and blasting. At one time, in the case of tunnels with a large cross-sectional area, a top heading was often driven both to provide a working platform and to permit the placing of roof support with the minimum lapse of time after excavation. Even in badly-jointed rock the roof will stand unsupported for a while, but if support is not provided quickly rock falls are bound to occur. This is because the excavation of a tunnel leads to some readjustment of the

**Above: The Hong Kong Cross-Harbour Tunnel,** which was built by the *immersed tube* method. The twin-tube tunnel sections, which were up to 114 m (374 ft) long and made of steel lined with reinforced concrete, were fabricated on shore, floated out into the harbour, and then sunk into place on the harbour bed. The ends of the tubes were sealed with steel plates, which were cut away when the sections were joined together.

**Above right: A tunnel** driven under the North Sea during exploration of the coal deposits off the coast of northeast England.

**Right: The entrance to** one of the two tunnels of the 28 km (17 mile) Chesapeake Bay bridge-tunnel scheme linking Virginia with Maryland. The scheme consists of a raised causeway incorporating two bridges and two tunnels that provide navigation channels for shipping.

**Below: Two of the fan** units which provide ventilation for the tunnels of the Naples ring road system.

Photri

Woods of Colchester

stresses in the rock that are caused by the weight of the material above it.

Support is generally provided by means of steel arches and timber lagging, but reinforced concrete arches are also used. A recent development is the use of *shotcrete*. This is a carefully-graded concrete sprayed, at high pressures, onto the exposed faces of the formation as soon as possible after excavation. Many tunnels in sound rock, however, require no support at all for much of their length, even in some cases for all of it, and in such cases *full face* work is now adopted.

This method of tunnelling has been made possible by improvements to the lighting and ventilation of tunnels so that heavy excavators and dump trucks can be used. Drilling is carried out from hydraulically-controlled rigs and blasting is

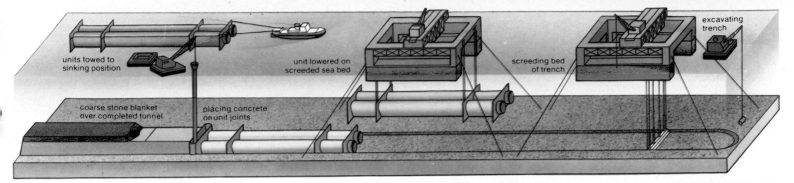

**Above:** The construction of the Hong Kong Cross-Harbour Tunnel. The prefabricated steel tube sections of the tunnels were sunk on to a bed consisting of a screed of crushed granite laid in a trench dredged across the harbour bed. The construction began in 1969, and the tunnel was opened in 1972.

**Below:** An artist's impression of the construction of the proposed rail tunnel under the English Channel, and (bottom) the likely route and section of such a tunnel. The proposal envisages three parallel tunnels; two single-track railway tunnels with a smaller service tunnel linked

to them every 250 m (820 ft). The tunnels would be some 98 km (32 miles) long, about 70 km (23 miles) being below the sea.

**Right:** The British end of the Channel Tunnel workings. Work was halted in 1975 because of escalating costs, and is unlikely to restart in this form.

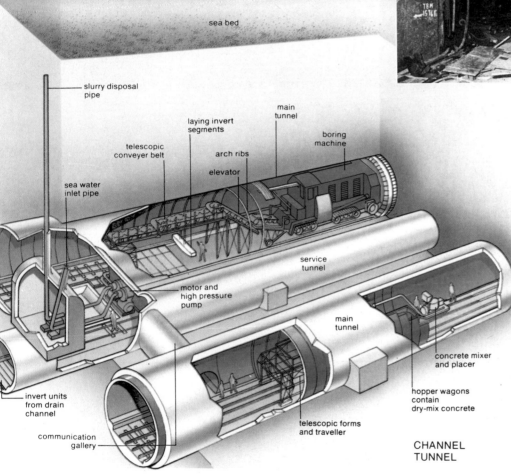

CHANNEL TUNNEL

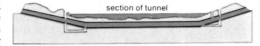

PROPOSED ROUTE OF CHANNEL TUNNEL

now a well-developed and very accurate operation. A thin cover of shotcrete is frequently applied to prevent surface deterioration due to weathering and to reduce the risk of accidents.

Tunnels in soft ground require a different technique. In the past, excavation has been carried out by using hand-held pneumatic tools, and the spoil loaded mechanically on to railway skips. The tunnel must be supported as close to the face as possible, and segmental cast iron or precast concrete rings are used for this. The face is advanced by, for instance, about 60 cm (2 ft), and a ring erected before further excavation is undertaken. These methods are now however being replaced by the use of tunnelling machines. In the case of smaller tunnels such machines frequently have a single, large, rotating

head equipped with cutters, but for larger tunnels a *roadheader*, a machine with a rotating cutting head mounted on a movable, hydraulically-controlled boom, is used.

In situ concrete provides a frequently-adopted alternative to the use of precast segmental rings. Specially-made steel formwork is used in such cases, but temporary support may still have to be provided by means of steel rings. After erection or placing, both precast and in situ linings are 'tightened' by injecting cement grout between them and the formation so that all voids are filled. This is done to prevent deterioration and loosening of the strata which might impose a high loading and lead to failure of the lining.

In very bad ground such as silty gravels, and especially if the tunnel is below water, compressed air may have to be used to prevent inflows and to support the face. Alternatively, the formation may be sealed with cement or chemical grouts.

Another method of construction, especially for subaqueous tunnels in soft material at comparatively shallow depths, is the *immersed tube* method. It was first suggested at the end of the eighteenth century by Trevithick, but has only recently become practical. It involves the construction on dry land of sections of tunnel, which are then floated into position and sunk into a dredged trench which is subsequently backfilled with sand. When all the sections are in position and the ends are above water level, the joints between the sections are sealed and the tunnel is pumped dry ready for internal finishing.

So the science of tunnelling has advanced from the early qanaats, using lining rings of baked clay, to the elaborate structures of today. The Seikan railway tunnel in Japan, linking two of Japan's larger islands, is probably the most notable currently under construction. On completion, scheduled now for 1982, it will be nearly 54 km (33.6m) long and 9.6 m (31.5 ft) in diameter, and will be up to 100 m (328 ft) beneath the seabed with a depth of water of up to 140 m (460 ft).

# Bridges

Modern industrial and developing economies depend upon increasingly sophisticated overland transport systems, in which bridges play a vital part. Bridge builders have always been faced with the same set of basic questions. Will the span be great enough? Will the structure be economical and durable enough? Will it bear the loads of the prevailing transport system? The answers to these questions can only be reached after computing many complex equations in which the main variables are the bridge types, the differing materials available and their relative abilities to withstand the differing types of stress that they encounter during use.

The *beam bridge*, basically a flat beam supported at each end, is the simplest type of bridge. Each end of the beam exerts a force directly downwards, and in the beam itself the *bending moment* (weight x distance from support) increases towards the middle of the span. The upper surface of the beam will be *compressed*; the lower surface will be in *tension*, or stretched. The strength of a beam will depend on its ability to withstand these opposing forces created by its own weight plus any applied load. Within certain limits, the deeper the beam is, the greater its strength will be.

*Cantilever* bridges work like a pair of springboards facing each other. The shore ends are anchored down and the main weight is carried by supports placed a certain distance from each anchored end. The bending moments in the projecting parts increase towards each tip. The forces in the cantilevered part are thus in *tension* on the upper surface and in *compression* in the lower zone of the material. If the tips cannot be made to meet because the distance to be spanned is too great, they may be linked by a short *suspended span*.

The *arch* works by converting the *downward* force of gravity acting on the material into an *outward* thrust at each end. The forces within the arch 'ring' are thus exclusively those of compression, and the *abutments* must be strong enough to maintain this force by holding the end of the arch in. In multi-span arches, some of the outward thrust of each arch may be taken up by the opposing thrusts from the arches on either side.

The converse of the arch is the *suspension* principle, where the road is hung from cables which are exclusively in *tension*. The weight of the bridge is taken by the towers which hold the cables aloft. The extreme ends of the cable have to be anchored to maintain a downward and outward force. Much attention has been paid to the problem of stiffening the roadway itself to counteract the effect of wind-induced oscillations and of *torsional* (twisting) forces caused by uneven loading of the deck.

Few modern bridges are built using only one of these basic forms. New combinations are always being sought—the great Swiss designer Robert Maillart, for example, integrated the concrete beam and arch in original and complex ways. *Cable-stayed* bridges combine the cantilever and the girder principles. The *box girder* principle used in this type of bridge has also found wide application in

**Above:** The Postbridge, an ancient bridge over the East Dart River on Dartmoor in southwest England. This bridge, which possibly dates back to the thirteenth century, is a *clapper bridge*, consisting of several slabs of granite resting on heavy stone piers. The basic design is of prehistoric origin.

**Below:** A primitive form of suspension bridge, made from cane and liana, spanning the Tsau River in the Central Highlands of New Guinea. Suspension bridges made from these and similar materials are to be found in many parts of the world, including South America, Africa and South-East Asia.

**Right:** Many of the bridges built by the Romans are still standing today. This is the Ponte Sant' Angelo over the Tiber in Rome, built in AD 136 during the reign of the Emperor Hadrian. It is one of the eight masonry bridges (of which six remain) built in Rome between 179 BC and AD 370.

G. F. Allen/Bruce Coleman Ltd

Brian Coles/Bruce Coleman Ltd

Michael Holford

Michael Holford

*continuous beam* bridges (where each span of a multi-span beam bridge acts with a cantilever effect on its neighbours), and also in providing the roadway deck for suspension bridges.

**Bridge development**

From Roman times to 1779 (the date of the world's first iron bridge at Coalbrookdale in Shropshire, England), the development of bridges had been the story of the masonry arch. The main improvements over that period included the use of ribbed arches, a progression from semicircular shape to shallower, segmental and elliptical profiles, and the lightening of the *spandrels* (the areas above each 'shoulder' of an arch) by pierced channels. Iron worked well enough in compression for several notable arches of 60 m (200 ft) and more to be built, such as Rennie's Southwark Bridge (1819) over the Thames. Telford even proposed a single 183 m (600 ft) span of cast iron to replace the ancient London Bridge.

The advent of steel, however, offered much greater possibilities, both for the creation of much larger spans and for the use of the cantilevering method of construction. The first great steel arch bridge was the celebrated Illinois and St Louis bridge of 1874, which was designed by Captain James Eads. The *fixed end* principle used by Eads, however, was superseded by the *two-hinged* arch pioneered by Gustave Eiffel in his wrought iron Barabit Viaduct of 1884. The hinges at abutments allow the slight temperature-induced movements in the bridge to take place without causing extra stresses. The greatest such arch is

Above: The Pont Valentré which spans the River Lot at Cahors in southwest France. This bridge, a good example of a medieval fortified bridge, was completed in 1355 after almost 50 years of building. A large number of fortified bridges were built in Europe during the Middle Ages.

Below left: The Iron Bridge over the River Severn at Caolbrookdale in Shropshire, England, the first large iron bridge in the world. The original design for the bridge was prepared by Thomas Farnolls Pritchard, but this was modified by Abraham Darby, who built it in 1779.

Below: London Bridge since 1500. The first three drawings show the bridge in the sixteenth, seventeenth and eighteenth centuries; the fourth shows John Rennie's London Bridge, built in 1831 about 55 m (180 ft) upstream from the old bridge, and the fifth shows the present bridge, which was opened in 1973.

c. 1500

1651-1666

1762-1831

1831

1973

the 503 m (1,650 ft) span Syndey Harbour
Bridge, opened in 1932, itself modelled on
the 1916 prototype *through arch*, the Hell
Gate in New York.

Concrete, with its enormous strength
in compression, also offered possibilities
for the construction of arches, though
their construction usually required more
*falsework* or *centering* (temporary sup-
porting framework) than did steel arches.
Maillart pioneered the delicate and
economical *stiffened slab arch*, using very
thin reinforced concrete for the arch-ring.
Freyssinet in France applied pre-stressing
techniques to through arches, for
example over the Seine at St Pierre de
Vouvray and in a design for a 1,000 m
(3,281 ft) structure over the Hudson river.
Interestingly, one of the most recent
concrete arches, the 305 m (1,000 ft)
Gladesville Bridge in Sydney, Australia,
was built by the ancient construction
technique of centering, though with
sophisticated precast hollow box *voussoirs*
(wedge-shaped sections put together to
form an arch) post-tensioned together.

In the development of beam bridges the
designers' main concern was to evolve
beams and girders of sufficient depth with
the least possible weight. The *truss*, an
open framework of short struts, was first
developed in timber, though early designs
often incorporated an arch rib. Development was particularly rapid in eighteenth
and nineteenth century America where
designs were rapidly modified in iron, then
steel, to provide the many short-span
bridges required by the burgeoning railway systems.

Two British beam bridges by Robert
Stephenson are of particular interest. The
High Level Bridge across the Tyne at
Newcastle, opened in 1849 and still in use,
is a fine example of the *bowstring girder*
principle. Though the main structural
element in each of the six spans is a
wrought iron arch, the outward thrust at
each end is taken up by members tensioned betweem them like the string of a
bow. The complete unit thus rests directly
downwards on its piers, a principle later
employed in many steel and concrete
bridges.

The Britannia Bridge, opened in 1850,
was the prototype box girder bridge.
Though Stephenson only had rivets and
46 x 13 cm (18 x 0.5 in) wrought iron strips
as basic materials, he planned four spans,
each composed of twin rectangular boxes,
through which the London to Holyhead
railway would run over the Menai Straits.
The complete spans were constructed on
shore then floated out and hoisted into
place. The spans, once in position were
further locked together so that the bridge
became a continuous structure.

The continuous box girder has come
into prominence as the most important
structural principle of recent years.
Modern box girders, however, differ from
Stephenson's in that they are made of
steel plate, are welded together, use the
top of the box as the running surface and
are often aerodynamically shaped. Since
the strength of the box girder derives
principally from its shape, any buckling
of the thin steel plate used would be
dangerous, and stiffening *stringers* are
welded inside the sections to prevent
distortion. The box girder concept allows
the engineer to work economically by
designing much closer to the maximum
possible stresses of steel, though the
collapse of the West Gate Bridge in Mel-

Left: Isambard Kingdom
Brunel's wrought iron
railway bridge across
the River Tamar at
Saltash in Cornwall,
completed in 1859. This
picture, taken in 1858,
shows the second of the
two 142 m (465 ft) main
spans being raised into
position. The outward
thrust of the arched
top tube of each span
is contained by the
curved suspension
chains below it.

Below: The Forth
Railway Bridge, a steel
cantilever bridge
designed by Benjamin
Baker and Sir John
Fowler. The bridge,
which was opened in
1890, has three main
towers carrying the
cantilevers, with a
short section called a
*suspended span* between
each of them.

Left: The Nosslach
Bridge in Austria, a
reinforced concrete
arch road bridge. The
first concrete bridge
was built in 1840 over
the Garonne Canal in
France, and other early
concrete bridges were
built in Germany,
Switzerland and the US
during the second half
of the nineteenth
century. Concrete is
strong in compression
but weak in tension, so
until the advent of
steel-reinforced
concrete at the end of
the century the arch
was the only feasible
form of construction
for concrete bridges.
The first large
reinforced concrete
bridge was built by
Francois Hennebique
over the River Ourthe
in Belgium in 1905.

Right: The Europe
Bridge near Innsbruck,
Austria, is a steel box
girder bridge carried
on reinforced concrete
piers. There are six
continuous spans, of
81 m (266 ft), 108 m
(354 ft), 198 m
(650 ft), 108 m, 81 m
and 81 m, and the
tallest pier is 160 m
(525 ft) high. Europe's
highest bridge, the Lao
Bridge in Italy, is
260 m (853 ft) high.

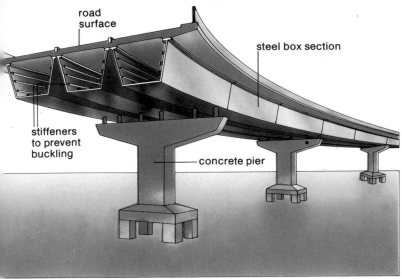

road surface

steel box section

stiffeners to prevent buckling

concrete pier

**Above left:** The structure of a steel box girder bridge with three trapezoid sectioned box girders. Box girder bridges generally have one, two or, more rarely, three girders, which may be of either rectangular or trapezoidal cross-section.

**Above:** The Ponte Presidente Costa e Silva bridge over the Rio Niteroi, Brazil, during construction in 1973. The centre section of the bridge (shown here) over the navigation channels of the river, is a cantilevered steel twin box girder structure; the approaches to the centre section are of reinforced concrete box girder construction. The bridge, opened in 1974, is over 8 km (5 miles) long.

**Left:** The Severins Bridge over the Rhine at Cologne is a *cable-stayed* bridge, the bridge deck being supported by cables attached to a tower. The bridge is assymetric, having one span of 151 m (495 ft) and one of 302 m (991 ft), and it was opened in 1959.

bourne and the Milford Haven Bridge in Wales highlighted the dangers of too narrow margins.

Cantilever bridges have been built on traditional patterns from wood and stone since time immemorial, particularly in Asian regions such as China and Kashmir. However, modern cantilevers date from the advent of steel, and the Forth Railway Bridge (1890) remains one of the greatest and earliest examples.

A reaction against the 'unnecessarily' high safety margins of the Forth Bridge caused the principle to be more economically tried in the Quebec Bridge. During construction in 1907, however, a lower main compression chord buckled and the bridge collapsed. The modified design called for the central suspended span to be completed and then hoisted into position. Quebec's second disaster occurred when the 5,000 tonne section dropped into the river during lifting operations.

Other notable steel cantilevers include the Viaur Viaduct (on the Toulouse to Lyons railway line in France) where the deck runs flush with the level (tensioned) upper chords of the structures; and the New Howrah Bridge over the Hooghly River in Calcutta, where the roadway runs flush with the level (compression) lower chords.

Concrete has also been used in several cantilever structures, notably in Riccardo Morani's Maracaibo Lake Bridge in Venezuela. The principle used in the five central spans is very similar to that of the Forth Bridge, though each lower, compression member is formed by the horizontal roadway slab. Each cantilever tower is independent from its neighbour (though linked by a suspended span) to minimize damage caused by the regular earth tremors experienced in the area.

Though many so-called 'primitive' suspension bridges were (and still are) built with considerable sophistication, the use of the suspension principle in European bridges required the development of materials strong and reliable in tension. The first notable spans in Europe were constructed with wrought iron chains. Telford's Menai Bridge (1826) was one such, in which each of the 15 chains for the central span were hoisted, complete, into position.

In the US, John Roebling developed an alternative method of constructing weight-bearing suspension cables. Working first with iron wire he devised a system of travelling *sheaves* (pulleys) which could cross and recross the opening between the two towers of the bridge, on each passage

Bay Bridge, completed in 1936, is over 8 miles long, spanning San Francisco Bay. A double-deck road bridge, it has 2 suspension spans, 20 arches and a tunnel.

**Above: The Nanking
Bridge over the Yangtze
River, China, opened in
1968, is a continuous
truss double-deck
bridge. The upper deck
carries two lanes for
vehicles, two for
cycles, and two
footpaths, and the
lower carries a double
track railway.**

**Left: Completed in
1956, the Richmond-San
Raphael Bridge across
San Pablo Bay,
California, is a two-
deck road bridge over
6 km (4 miles) long.**

**Below: The Severn
Bridge, England, is a
suspension bridge with
a steel box girder
deck. The main span is
988 m (3,240 ft) long,
and the side spans are
each 305 m (1,000 ft)
in length.**

laying down a single strand. When
sufficient strands had been strung, they
would be gathered then clamped together
into a thick cable. Using steel wire, this
method of *cable spinning* has since become
standard for virtually all suspension
spans. Among early bridges thus constructed was Roebling's Niagara Railway
Bridge of 1855.

Roebling used deep trusses and radial
cables to add stiffness to the roadway,
though later US refinements progressively
lightened the trusswork and heightened
the towers to create longer and longer
spans. Successes include the George
Washington Bridge, 1931 (1,067 m, 3,500
ft) and the Golden Gate Bridge, 1937
(1,280 m, 4,200 ft). The light plate girder
stiffening and narrow roadway of the
Tacoma Narrows Bridge, 1940 (853 m,
2,800 ft), however, led to its collapse from
progressive harmonic oscillations brought
on by a moderate wind.

Subsequent intensive research into the
effects of wind on suspended decks highlighted the need to reduce *vortex shedding*
(the creation of severe air turbulence) by
the decks, and later suspended spans (for
instance the Verrazano Narrows and the
Forth Road Bridges) featured more open
trusswork and longitudinal vents in the
roadway to prevent the build-up of air
pressure above and below.

A more original solution, however, was
used for the Severn Road Bridge in England, 1966 (988 m, 3,240 ft), which incorporates aerodynamically-shaped trapezoidal box sections for the road deck.
This relatively light structure has also
been adopted for the construction of the
world's longest span (1,410 m, 4,626 ft),
the bridge over the River Humber in
northeast England.

Fixed bridges are often not feasible
over busy shipping channels flanked by
low-lying banks, and so movable bridges
are often necessary. *Bascule* spans hinge
at the landward end on *trunnion bearings*
or rock upwards on *Scherzer rolling
bearings*. Tower Bridge in London is the
best known example of a *double-bat
bascule*. *Vertical lift* Bridges usually
consist of a trussed deck with each end
supported at the base of a tower. The
bridge is opened by hydraulically raising
the ends up the towers. Other types of
moving bridge include the *swing bridge*,
pivoted for horizontal rotation, and the
*transporter bridge*. In this rare type a
short section of roadway is suspended
from a wheeled trolley running along a
high truss, and pulled to and fro from
bank to bank.

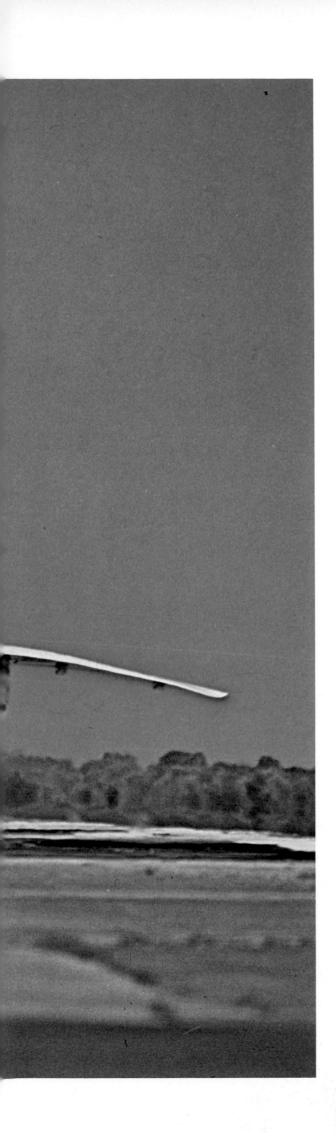

# Transport Technology

Concorde is capable of speeds of Mach 2 (1,354m.p,h.). It is powered by 4 Rolls-Royce engines, situated in ducts under the wings, giving 38,050lbs (17,260kg) of thrust.

# Aircraft

To defy the force of gravity and take to the air was for many centuries one of man's greatest ambitions. From the end of the eighteenth century, there were a number of successful attempts at flight —in balloons, gliders and a variety of strange flying machines—but in 1903 the dream finally seemed to have come true. In that year the Wright brothers made the first-ever 'sustained' flight in a powered airplane. The freedom of long distance flight, and ultimately space-travel, was then only decades away.

The essential principle involved in flight is the need to create enough force to overcome gravity and lift a craft into the air. Then this force must somehow be maintained, otherwise the aircraft will sooner or later be pulled back to earth.

An airplane which is unpowered, like a glider, is given the initial force required to launch it by the pull of a towing truck or light aircraft. This gives it sufficient *lift,* the force which keeps it in the air, until it picks up a rising air current or 'thermal' upon which it can soar. Without this fresh impetus from air currents, the glider will slow down and sink because of the combined effects of air resistance, or *drag,* and gravity.

Powered aircraft, however, can overcome drag and gravity through the force of their engines. It is these that provide the necessary forward motion to generate lift on the wings.

## Newton's laws of motion

The laws of motion, first formulated by Sir Isaac Newton in the seventeenth century, explain why a lifting force is necessary for flight. The first law of motion states that a force must be applied to any object before it will change its position, its speed or its direction of travel; thus an object will remain quite still or continue moving in a straight

Hit a ball into the air with a racket and it climbs for a while before gradually falling back to earth. In so doing it is obeying Newton's first law of motion, which states that an object stays still or continues to move in a straight line at a constant speed unless it is interfered with in some way by an external force. In other words, the ball would not have climbed into the air spontaneously. It required an initial external force from the movement of the racket by the arm to launch it. Once in the

air, in the absence of any external forces, the ball would continue on and up along its original course. Instead it follows a smooth curve because the invisible force of the earth's gravity pulls it down all the time while the air friction slows it. The action of these external forces constantly and subtly modifies the direction and speed of the ball, eventually bringing it back to earth. When the ball is given a light tap with the racket it does not travel as high or as far as when it is

line at a constant speed unless some external force acts upon it. This tendency to oppose any change in its state of rest or motion is called the object's *inertia.*

The second law of motion states that, providing the *mass* of a body remains constant, a force acting on it will produce an *acceleration* which is proportional to that applied force. The mass of a body is a measure of the amount of matter it contains. This is not necessarily the same as a body's weight, which is a measure of the pull exerted on it by the force of gravity. The difference is easily demonstrated in space flight, where a body becomes increasingly weightless the further it travels into space, as the force of the earth's gravity gets weaker; the body's mass, however, remains constant.

The third law of motion states that action and reaction are equal and op-

posite. According to this law, when an aircraft is standing on the ground the ground is providing an equal and opposite reaction to its weight—otherwise it would either sink into the ground or rise into the air. In flight, however, the air itself must be made to provide the necessary reaction to the action of the aircraft's weight. This reaction or upward force is provided by the lift, a force created largely by the wings as the aircraft is pushed or pulled through the air by its engines.

Any structure, such as an aircraft wing or tailplane, which is shaped to produce aerodynamic lift is known as an *aerofoil* (airfoil). Looking at an aircraft wing in cross-section, the upper surface is curved slightly upwards, while the lower surface is almost flat. As it moves through the air, the wing's rounded front or leading

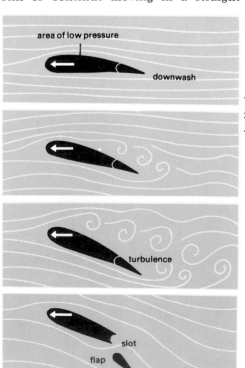

area of low pressure

downwash

turbulence

slot

flap

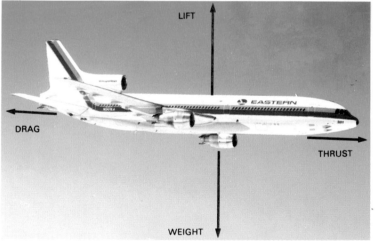

LIFT

DRAG

THRUST

WEIGHT

Lockheed

Left: The way an aircraft moves in the air depends upon the action of four basic forces. When an aeroplane is flying at a constant speed along a perfectly straight course these forces are in equilibrium. The lift from the wings exactly matches the weight; the forwards thrust balances the air resistance or drag.

Below: A model of an aeroplane in a wind tunnel shows the formation of turbulence. A swirling mass of air is created when the smooth airflow breaks away from the wings. Wind tunnels are used to test the airflow over new aircraft designs. Smoke is introduced into the tunnel to make the airflow visible.

Left: The airflow over a level wing or aerofoil is smoothly curved downwards, giving good lift. Tilting the wing up slightly boosts its lift. At larger angles the airflow starts to break away from the wing. As it is tilted further the turbulence moves forwards so that less of the wing gives lift. Eventually a critical angle of attack is reached when the airflow separates from the wing completely. Then so little of the aerofoil is creating lift that the aircraft 'stalls' and drops sharply.

Bottom left: Lowering the flaps on the wing exaggerates the profile of the whole aerofoil, increasing its lift and the critical stalling angle.

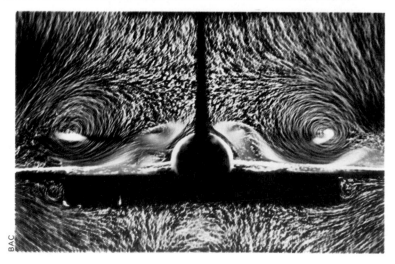

BAC

given a much stronger hit. According to the second law of motion, provided the mass of an object is kept constant, the force applied to it is proportional to its acceleration. While the mass of the ball is the same, the force applied by the racket in each case is different. The greater the force, the further the ball flies because of its greater acceleration.

When the ball lands, it bounces up again in accordance with the third law of motion. This states that to every action there is an equal and opposite reaction. As it hits the ground, the ball depresses the earth fractionally, but because the earth is so much larger than the ball, this dent is invisible to the naked eye. The earth reacts, however, by pushing back with exactly the same force as the force of impact, trying to return to its original shape. If the ground is soft, a slight depression might be visible where the ball landed because the soil was not strong enough to resist the sudden rapid acceleration of impact.

edge deflects the air into two streams, one of which passes over the wing and the other under it. Early attempts at heavier-than-air flight used wings with a flat cross-section, but designers soon realized that much more lift could be obtained if suitably curved aerofoil surfaces were used.

The shape is specifically designed to create lift, and is effective for two reasons. Firstly, as the aircraft moves forward, air has to rush in behind it to prevent a vacuum forming. Secondly, because the curved upper surface of the aerofoil is longer from front to back than the relatively straight lower surface, the upper airstream must travel faster than the lower airstream, in order to reach the trailing edge of the wing at the same time. That these actions create lift is explained by a principle discovered by the eighteenth-century Swiss scientist Daniel Bernoulli.

According to Bernoulli's principle, if the speed at which a *fluid*—that means a gas or a liquid—flows across a surface is increased, the pressure which it exerts on that surface will decrease. The faster airstream over the top of the aerofoil therefore exerts a much lower pressure than the slower one under it. This situation of reduced pressure above a wing creates a very powerful upward force, or lift.

The flow of air over the curved wing surface is known as *laminar flow;* it is made up of successive layers of air flowing smoothly over each other. The layers next to the surface of the wing, known collectively as the *boundary layer,* travel more slowly than the rest of the laminar flow, because of the friction between them

and the wing. This boundary layer is very thin, less than a fraction of a millimetre thick.

The *angle of attack,* that is the angle at which the wing meets the airstream, has an important bearing on the amount of lift the wings generate. The wing meeting the air at a slightly up-turned angle gives a slightly increased pressure on the underside, which backs up the effects of the low pressure above the wing in creating lift. Increasing the angle of attack increases lift—up to a certain critical angle of about 15°. After that point, lift falls off sharply and the result can be a *stall*.

## Turbulent air

The fall-off in lift is caused by *turbulent* air. At small angles of attack the boundary layer leaves the upper surface of the wing at or near the trailing edge; this is the *separation point*. Behind the separation point, the air flowing over the wing is no longer streamlined—in line with the direction of the wing—but *turbulent,* breaking up into swirling vortices. Turbulent air creates a lot of drag but very little lift. As the angle of attack increases, the separation point moves further and further forward on the wing, so that an increasingly small area of the wing is producing lift. Finally when the critical angle is reached, so little of the wing is contributing lift that the aircraft stalls and drops sharply. Similarly, when a plane runs into weather conditions that are causing turbulent air, this disruption of the smooth airflow can produce the same stalling effect. To correct a stall in mid-air the pilot needs to level-off the angle of attack and increase lift; the usual manoeuvre is a shallow dive, which will help the aircraft pick up speed and generate more lift.

Alternatively the lift of a wing can be increased at low speeds by extending different types of slats and flaps that effectively change the whole profile of the aerofoil. A small, adjustable aerofoil, or *slat,* positioned in front of the main wing with a small gap, or *slot,* between the two

CONTROL SURFACES

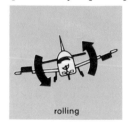

rolling

pitching

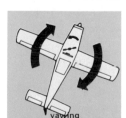

yawing

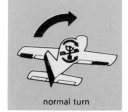

normal turn

**Above and left:** A normal aircraft is manoeuvred about three axes by three sets of control surfaces.

**Rolling:** Turning the control column in the cockpit moves the ailerons, causing the aircraft to roll. When an aileron is lowered the wing creates more lift and rises. Raising the aileron on the other wing reduces its lift.

**Pitching:** Pushing the control column moves the elevators, tipping the aircraft up or down.

**Yawing:** Turning the rudder makes the aeroplane yaw, or turn. A normal banking turn combines yawing the aircraft and rolling it into the turn.

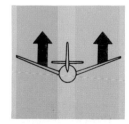

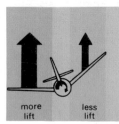

more lift    less lift

**Left:** The upwards tilting, or dihedral, of the wings stabilizes the aircraft. When equally inclined to the horizontal, both wings create equal lift. As the aircraft rolls, a sideways airflow hits the lower wing at a larger angle than the upper wing, so that it generates more lift, righting the aeroplane.

**Right:** A delta winged aircraft has no separate tailplane. The wings are swept back so far that the control surfaces, or elevons, on the trailing edges can serve as both elevators and ailerons. To roll the aeroplane, one elevon is raised and the other is lowered. For a climbing turn, one elevon is raised while the other remains level.

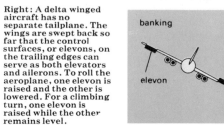

banking    elevon    banking and climbing

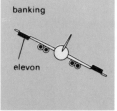
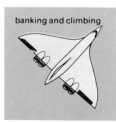

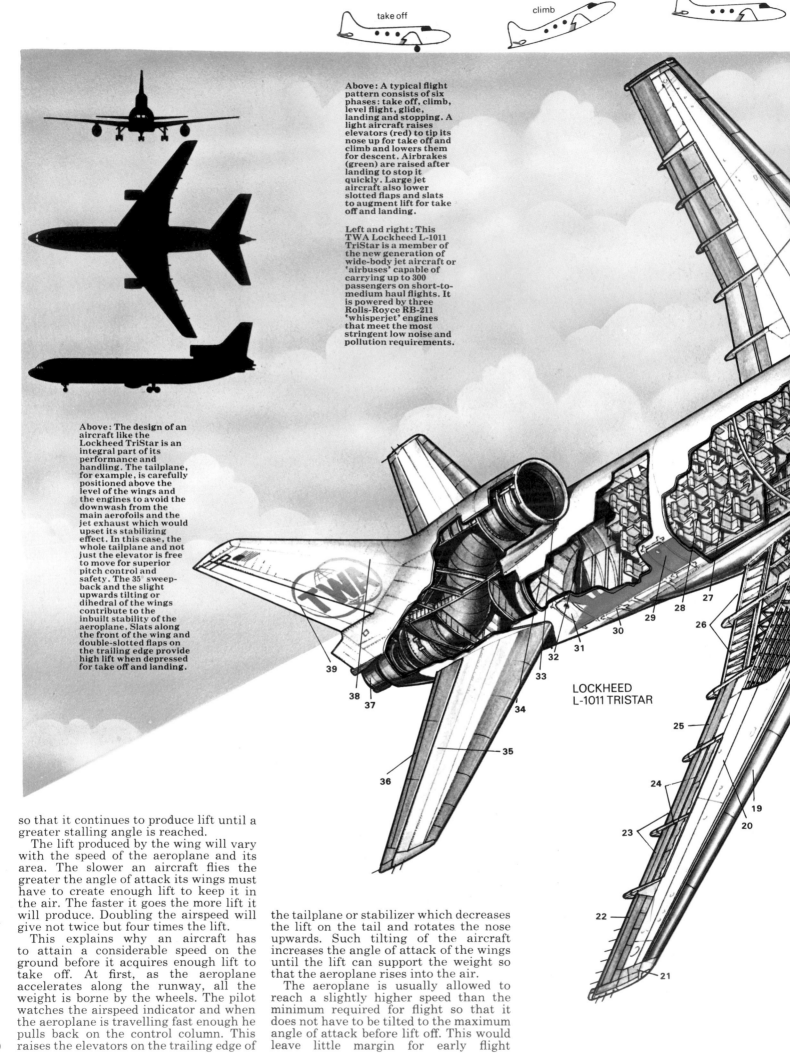

**Above:** A typical flight pattern consists of six phases: take off, climb, level flight, glide, landing and stopping. A light aircraft raises elevators (red) to tip its nose up for take off and climb and lowers them for descent. Airbrakes (green) are raised after landing to stop it quickly. Large jet aircraft also lower slotted flaps and slats to augment lift for take off and landing.

**Left and right:** This TWA Lockheed L-1011 TriStar is a member of the new generation of wide-body jet aircraft or 'airbuses' capable of carrying up to 300 passengers on short-to-medium haul flights. It is powered by three Rolls-Royce RB-211 'whisperjet' engines that meet the most stringent low noise and pollution requirements.

**Above:** The design of an aircraft like the Lockheed TriStar is an integral part of its performance and handling. The tailplane, for example, is carefully positioned above the level of the wings and the engines to avoid the downwash from the main aerofoils and the jet exhaust which would upset its stabilizing effect. In this case, the whole tailplane and not just the elevator is free to move for superior pitch control and safety. The 35° sweep-back and the slight upwards tilting or dihedral of the wings contribute to the inbuilt stability of the aeroplane. Slats along the front of the wing and double-slotted flaps on the trailing edge provide high lift when depressed for take off and landing.

LOCKHEED
L-1011 TRISTAR

so that it continues to produce lift until a greater stalling angle is reached.

The lift produced by the wing will vary with the speed of the aeroplane and its area. The slower an aircraft flies the greater the angle of attack its wings must have to create enough lift to keep it in the air. The faster it goes the more lift it will produce. Doubling the airspeed will give not twice but four times the lift.

This explains why an aircraft has to attain a considerable speed on the ground before it acquires enough lift to take off. At first, as the aeroplane accelerates along the runway, all the weight is borne by the wheels. The pilot watches the airspeed indicator and when the aeroplane is travelling fast enough he pulls back on the control column. This raises the elevators on the trailing edge of the tailplane or stabilizer which decreases the lift on the tail and rotates the nose upwards. Such tilting of the aircraft increases the angle of attack of the wings until the lift can support the weight so that the aeroplane rises into the air.

The aeroplane is usually allowed to reach a slightly higher speed than the minimum required for flight so that it does not have to be tilted to the maximum angle of attack before lift off. This would leave little margin for early flight

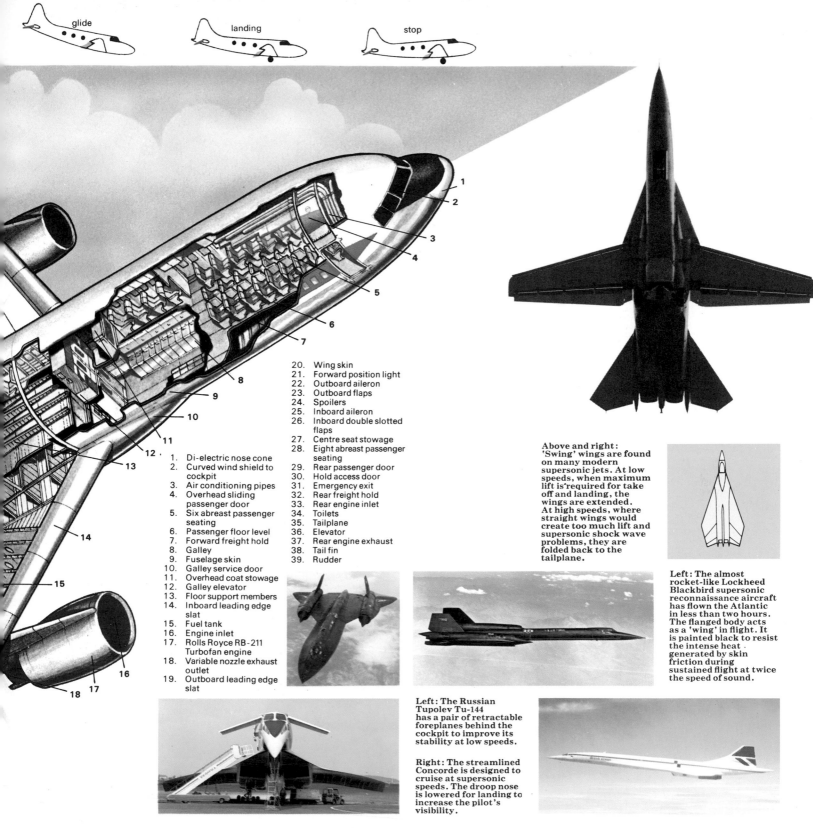

glide

landing

stop

1. Di-electric nose cone
2. Curved wind shield to cockpit
3. Air conditioning pipes
4. Overhead sliding passenger door
5. Six abreast passenger seating
6. Passenger floor level
7. Forward freight hold
8. Galley
9. Fuselage skin
10. Galley service door
11. Overhead coat stowage
12. Galley elevator
13. Floor support members
14. Inboard leading edge slat
15. Fuel tank
16. Engine inlet
17. Rolls Royce RB-211 Turbofan engine
18. Variable nozzle exhaust outlet
19. Outboard leading edge slat
20. Wing skin
21. Forward position light
22. Outboard aileron
23. Outboard flaps
24. Spoilers
25. Inboard aileron
26. Inboard double slotted flaps
27. Centre seat stowage
28. Eight abreast passenger seating
29. Rear passenger door
30. Hold access door
31. Emergency exit
32. Rear freight hold
33. Rear engine inlet
34. Toilets
35. Tailplane
36. Elevator
37. Rear engine exhaust
38. Tail fin
39. Rudder

Above and right: 'Swing' wings are found on many modern supersonic jets. At low speeds, when maximum lift is required for take off and landing, the wings are extended. At high speeds, where straight wings would create too much lift and supersonic shock wave problems, they are folded back to the tailplane.

Left: The almost rocket-like Lockheed Blackbird supersonic reconnaissance aircraft has flown the Atlantic in less than two hours. The flanged body acts as a 'wing' in flight. It is painted black to resist the intense heat generated by skin friction during sustained flight at twice the speed of sound.

Left: The Russian Tupolev Tu-144 has a pair of retractable foreplanes behind the cockpit to improve its stability at low speeds.

Right: The streamlined Concorde is designed to cruise at supersonic speeds. The droop nose is lowered for landing to increase the pilot's visibility.

manoeuvres. Sometimes in large jet aircraft flaps are lowered for take off to increase the lift of the wings and enlarge the angle of attack the aeroplane can reach safely before stalling.

Raising these flaps prematurely after take-off can have tragic consequences. For if the aeroplane is still climbing steeply when the flaps are raised, the wings may be inclined at an angle of attack greater than the critical stalling angle. In which case the aircraft stalls and, because it may not have gained sufficient height to give the pilot time to correct the situation by tilting the nose down into a glide until it has picked up enough airspeed to restore lift, it plummets to the ground out of control. Fortunately the chances of this error occurring are extremely slight because of the numerous warning systems built into the control panel in the cockpit.

Since lift also depends on the mass or density of the air, airports at high altitudes and in tropical countries where the air pressure is lower than at sea level or in temperate regions have longer runways. This allows the aeroplane more room to build up the slightly higher speed it needs before it can generate an equivalent amount of lift. Similarly, after take off, as the aeroplane climbs into thinner air at high altitudes, it must either go faster or fly at a greater angle of attack to maintain lift.

For landing, the elevators are lowered to tip the nose down into a gradual descent to the runway. On the final approach, the aeroplane adopts an increasingly nose-up posture, giving the wings a high angle of attack to sustain lift at the reduced speed. Flaps are also lowered during landing to boost lift. One potential danger in landing is that the nose will tip back so far that the aeroplane will stall and drop on to the runway. Depressed flaps help to minimize this risk of stalling by increasing the operative angle of attack of the wings.

Landing transfers the lift from the wings to the ground again. The pilot aims to bring the aeroplane into contact with the runway at the slowest possible vertical velocity and a low ground speed. Aircraft usually land into the wind in order to cut their ground speed. After landing, the aeroplane is slowed rapidly by raising air brakes or *spoilers* to increase drag and cut lift and by reversing the engine thrust to stop it as quickly as possible.

51

# Helicopters and Autogyros

A conventional fixed wing aircraft is able to fly because of the lift generated on its wings as they move forward through the air. On a helicopter or autogyro, however, the fixed wings are replaced by a set of thin wings called *blades* attached to a shaft. The rotation of this set of blades, or the *rotor,* through the air creates the lift necessary for flight.

An autogyro or a helicopter will climb when the total lift of the rotor exceeds the weight of the machine. The helicopter will hover when the sum of all the lift forces on the rotor blades is equal to the weight of the machine.

A helicopter has a rotor which is driven by an engine, but an autogyro has a rotor which gets its power from the motion of the airstream blowing through it, rather like a windmill. Thus the autogyro needs some other device, usually an engine-driven propeller, to pull or push it through the air horizontally.

## Hovering and climbing

As the rotor turns, it traces out a circle in the air which is known as the *rotor disc*. The total lift generated by the rotor acts through the centre of this disc and at right angles to it. This means that when a helicopter is hovering the lift forces are acting vertically upwards through the centre of the rotor. To make the machine climb, the lift generated by each blade must be increased. This is done by increasing the *angle of attack*—the angle at which the leading edge meets the airstream—of each blade equally, thus increasing the total lift without changing the direction in which it acts. The pilot controls this by means of a lever known as the *collective pitch control*.

In order to make the helicopter fly forwards the rotor disc must be tilted forwards slightly, so that part of the rotor acts to pull the machine in that direction. The rotor disc is tilted forwards by increasing the angle of attack of each blade as it travels around the rear of the disc, and decreasing the angle as each blade travels around the front of the disc. As a change in the angle of attack means a change in lift, the lift is increased at the rear of the rotor disc and decreased at the front, causing the disc to tilt forwards.

These changes in the angle of attack of the blades can be made to occur at any point around the rotor disc, tilting the disc accordingly. This enables the helicopter to fly in any direction. The pilot controls the tilt of the rotor disc by means of the *cyclic pitch control lever*.

## The importance of blade speed

When a helicopter is hovering, the speed of the blades through the air is due to their speed of rotation and is constant at all points around the rotor disc. When the helicopter is moving forwards, however, the speed of a blade through the air changes as it travels around the disc. When a blade is travelling towards the front of the disc, its air speed is its speed due to its rotation plus the speed of the aircraft (just as a bullet fired forwards

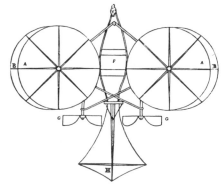

Right: Designed by Sir George Cayley in 1843, this early idea for a vertical take-off and landing aircraft used two sets of rotors to provide lift, and two propellers to provide forward thrust. It was intended that the fan-like rotors would fold flat to form circular wings to create lift during forward flight.

Below: This helicopter was built in France by Paul Cornu in 1907 and during several short flights in November of that year it reached a height of almost 2 m (6 ft). It was powered by a 24 hp Antoinette engine driving a pair of rotors mounted in a tandem configuration, and the pilot sat next to the engine.

Radio Times Hulton Picture Library (above also)

Russ Kinne, Photo Researchers

Above: The helicopter produces the vertical force needed to lift it from the ground by forcing air downwards, creating the down draught which is making the circular ripple patterns on the surface of the water. When a helicopter is hovering, about 70 per cent of its power is used in creating this force.

Left: The down draught is strongest beneath the points on the rotor at which the most lift is generated, shown here by the arrows above the rotor blades. The sea directly below the helicopter fuselage is relatively calm, as it is shielded from the down draught by the body of the helicopter and by the tail.

Gazelle helicopters escorting army scout cars during Queen Elizabeth II's Jubilee Review in Germany in 1977. Seventy years earlier (1907) Paul Cornu had built the first helicopter capable of carrying a man.

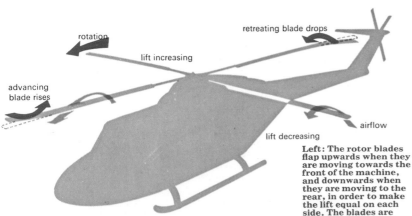

**Left:** The rotor blades flap upwards when they are moving towards the front of the machine, and downwards when they are moving to the rear, in order to make the lift equal on each side. The blades are at their highest flap position when pointing forward and at their lowest when they point to the tail.

**Right:** The Westland/ Aérospatiale Lynx has hingeless rotor blades and is powered by two Rolls-Royce BS-360 Gem turboshafts which give it a top speed of 160 knots at sea level. Main rotor diameter is 12.8 m (42 ft), and the overall length of the aircraft is 15.2 m (49.75 ft). The army version is shown here.

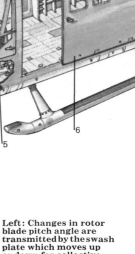

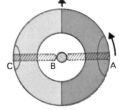

from a gun on a moving train will travel at the speed at which it left the gun plus the speed of the train on which the gun was travelling).

When a blade is travelling towards the rear of the disc, however, its air speed is reduced by the speed of the aircraft, which at that point is effectively travelling in the opposite direction to it. As the lift on a blade varies according to its speed through the air, the forward-moving blade has more lift than the rearward-moving one.

If the rotor was a completely rigid structure, these differences in lift would cause it to tilt towards the rearward-moving side, and the helicopter would tend to fly sideways instead of straight ahead. To overcome this problem, the rotor blades are hinged at the roots to allow them to flap up and down a certain amount. This allows the forward-moving blade to rise slightly, in effect reducing its lift. The blades thus rise when moving forwards and drop again when moving backwards in order to keep the actual lift on them constant.

Certain helicopter designs, such as the Westland/Aérospatiale Lynx, have replaced the flapping hinge with a controlled stiffness, or flexible, section near the root of the blade. The blade moves in a way which is broadly similar to that of the fully articulated blade described above but the control power at the pilot's command is greatly increased, allowing a number of flexible manoeuvres.

**Changing direction**

Newton's third law of motion states that every action produces an equal but opposite reaction. In other words, if a body exerts a force on another in one direction, it will itself be subject to an equal force acting in the opposite direction. Thus a main rotor which is rotated by an engine in the fuselage will set up a reaction which will result in the fuselage rotating in the opposite direction. To prevent this, a torque, or twisting force, compensating system is installed, such as the small anti-torque rotor at the tail of single main rotor helicopters.

Directional control can be achieved by varying the amount of torque compensation applied. Over-compensating turns the fuselage in the same direction as the main rotor, and under-compensating allows it to turn in the opposite direction. Where compensation is by means of an anti-torque rotor, the amount of compensation is controlled by varying the *pitch,* or angle of attack, of the blades.

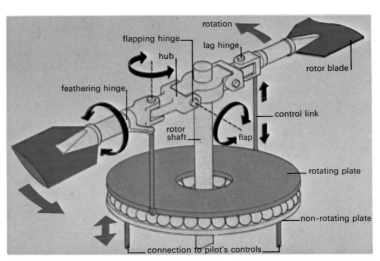

**Left:** Changes in rotor blade pitch angle are transmitted by the swash plate which moves up or down for collective pitch changes, and tilts to give cyclic pitch changes. Blade pitch angle depends on the swash plate height. If it is tilted the pitch of a blade is increased as it passes the high side.

**Above:** A plan view of a rotor shows the points at which problems can occur when travelling at speed. At point 'A' the blade speed nears the speed of sound and drag is high; at 'B' the airspeed is too low for useful lift; and at 'C' the blade tip stalls as the pilot increases blade pitch to maintain lift.

**Right:** A tandem rotor helicopter can move sideways by tilting both rotors towards the appropriate side. In order to turn the helicopter, the rear rotor is tilted to one side and the forward rotor to the other, so that the nose and tail of the craft are moved in opposite directions, causing it to turn.

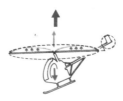

**Left:** Forward flight is achieved by tilting the rotor forwards. Then the lift from the rotor acts at an angle which provides forward thrust as well as the vertical lift. If the load of a helicopter is towards the front, the fuselage will tilt to keep the centre of gravity beneath the centre of the rotor.

**Right:** With helicopters like the Lynx, which have a semi-rigid rotor construction without blade hinges, greater control is available. This makes it possible to fly upside down and to perform many other manoeuvres that were impossible with other less flexible craft using the conventional hinged rotors.

Westland

54

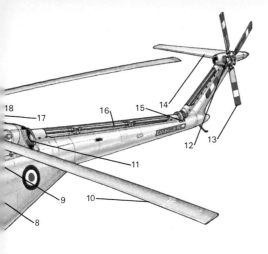

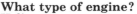

## WESTLAND/ AEROSPATIALE LYNX

1. pilot's seat
2. cyclic pitch stick
3. tail rotor control pedals
4. co-pilot's collective-pitch lever
5. co-pilot's seat
6. main door
7. wheel attachments
8. forged frame
9. Rolls-Royce BS.360 gas turbine engines
10. rotor blade
11. exhaust outlet
12. tail rotor power unit
13. tail rotor
14. tailplane
15. intermediate gearbox
16. tail rotor drive
17. rotor hub
18. drag hinge damper
19. pitch control rod
20. main gearbox
21. collective pitch linkages

**Below and right:** These four illustrations show how helicopters overcome the effects of torque - without a second rotor, the spin of the main rotor would set the whole craft turning in the opposite direction.

A small tail rotor is the most common anti-torque device (above). The reaction torque can also be cancelled out with two main rotors turning in opposite directions (top and bottom right). The co-axial layout has two rotors, one turning above the other (centre right).

## What type of engine?

Helicopter rotors are usually driven through a shaft fitted to the rotor hub (shaft drive), but some have been built with small jet thrust units fitted at the rotor blade tips (tip drive).

Shaft drive rotors can be driven by any form of aero engine. Originally all helicopters were powered by piston engines, but the *turboshaft*, or gas turbine, engine is now used on all but the smallest machines. Rotary engines, like the Wankel engine invented in Germany, are being considered for these small machines.

## Dealing with engine failure

In the event of engine failure, the rotor rapidly slows down and loses lift, but it is possible for the pilot to land safely by use of *autorotation*. By rapidly lowering the collective pitch lever the pilot can set the blades so that their leading edges are pointing slightly downwards from the horizontal. As the aircraft is descending, the new position of the blades means that a positive, or upwards, angle of attack is maintained against the upward flow of the airstream. This generates forces on the blades to keep them spinning, and as the helicopter nears the ground the pilot raises the collective pitch lever slightly, so that the spinning rotor provides enough lift to slow down the machine before it lands.

## Helicopter speed limits

The conventional helicopter cannot fly at more than about 400 km/h (250 mph) because at high speeds the air speed of the forward-moving blade approaches the speed of sound and that of the rearward-moving blade is very low. The result of this is that the drag on the forward-moving blade is greatly increased and it begins to lose lift because of the break-up of the airflow over it. The rearward-moving blade loses lift because of its low air speed. At a critical speed, when pointing directly to the tail of the aircraft, the blade stalls, because air is flowing from the rotor hub to the blade tip—not across the blade to give lift.

A partial solution to this problem has been put forward by the Sikorsky Company. This is the Advancing Blade Concept (ABC) which uses two identical rotors, positioned one above the other and turning in opposite directions. The system balances the forces on the advancing side of each rotor, thus balancing the helicopter by cancelling out the loss of lift on the rearward-moving side of each rotor.

*Textron's Bell Aerospace Division, N.Y.*

**Left:** The Sikorsky Skycrane can carry a heavy load of up to 9,072 kg (20,000 lb). The anchor points for the load are directly below the rotor hub, so that the centre of gravity of the load is below the centre of the rotor. This prevents the helicopter from becoming unstable when fully laden.

**Above left:** Helicopters are often used as air taxis, linking a city's airports with each other and with the city centre, or ferrying passengers to and from remote areas. They can take off and land in such confined or rough places as the roof of a skyscraper, or an off-shore oil rig or in a field.

**Above:** The Bell X-22A experimental vertical take-off aircraft. For take-off and landing the ducted propellers were tilted into the horizontal position, as shown in the upper picture; for forward flight they could be tilted forwards as in the lower picture. Its highest speed was 518 km/h (325 mph).

**Left:** The rotor of an autogyro is turned by air blowing through it. Lift is only created when the rotor is spinning, and so an autogyro must be moving forwards before it can take off.

*Russ Kinne, Photo Researchers*

**Right:** Autogyro rotor blades, like those on a helicopter, flap up and down to maintain equal lift across the rotor. Autogyros use propellers for forward thrust and are steered by rudders.

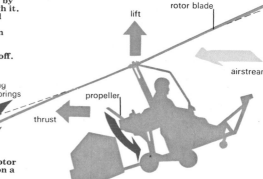

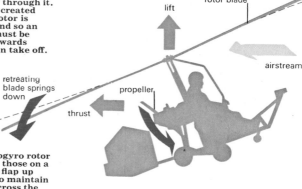

lift

rotor blade

advancing blade bends upwards

airstream

retreating blade springs down

propeller

thrust

# Hovercraft and Hydrofoils

In 1953 the British inventor Christopher Cockerell began investigating methods of making boats go faster. It was one of his successful experiments that gave the first real impetus to the development of vehicles supported by a layer of air. A number of names are used to describe air cushion supported craft, including *hovercraft*, *air cushion vehicles* (ACV), *ground effect machine* (GEM) and *surface effect ships* (SES).

Cockerell's idea was to trap air beneath the hull of a boat, thereby eliminating the friction between the hull and the water which slows down conventional craft. Originally this was achieved by blowing air into a shallow upside-down hull at a pressure slightly higher than atmospheric and trapping it by means of a curtain of very high pressure air around the edge of the hull. This *air cushion* trapped within an *air curtain* provided two to three times more lifting force than if the same air was simply directed downwards as an even jet of air. Cockerell produced a free-flight model using this system, followed by the construction of a full-scale manned hovercraft.

## Flexible skirts

One of the disadvantages of the early system was that it required an excessive amount of power to generate the air curtain. The next important step in the development of an economic hovercraft was the introduction of a *flexible skirt system* in 1961. This is a rubberized material fringe that hangs down around the edge of the vessel. The skirt serves the same function as the air curtain in containing the air cushion.

In marine vehicles the air cushion permits speeds three times faster than a ship, with relatively low water resis-

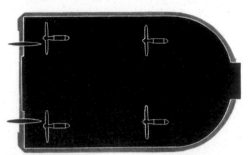

Above and right: The SR.N4 hovercraft travels on a 2.5 m (8 ft) deep cushion of air and is powered by four Rolls-Royce Marine Proteus gas turbine engines. The SR.N4 is 39 m (130 ft) long with a beam (width) of 24 m (78 ft). Overall height on its landing pads is 11.5 m (38 ft), and it weighs 160 tons.

Below and right: Air blown into the space between two cans creates a curtain of air around the lower rims. This traps a cushion of air below the inner can which gives the needed lift. On measuring the pressure on a scale Cockerell proved that the force of lift was greater than that achieved by one can.

National Research Development Council

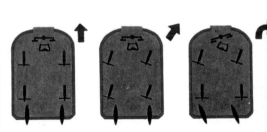

Below: Directional control of the SR.N4 is determined by the angle of the fins at the rear of the craft and of the pylons, the propeller mounts, on the roof of the craft. These are controlled by the rudder bar, shown at the top of the diagram, and the handwheel just below it.

NRDC HOVERCRAFT

HOVERLLOYD    GH-2005

British Hovercraft Corporation

Right: Hovercraft are used to provide ferry services in many parts of the world. SR.N4s, the world's largest amphibious hovercraft, operate a regular service across the English Channel, each carrying 254 passengers and 30 vehicles. Larger passenger-carrying hovercraft are being developed.

Left: The world's first hovercraft, the SR.N1, was built by aircraft makers Saunders-Roe and financed by Britain's National Research Development Corporation. SR.N1 made the first hovercraft crossing of an open body of water when it crossed the English Channel from Calais to Dover in 1959.

Popperfoto

## TYPES OF HOVERCRAFT

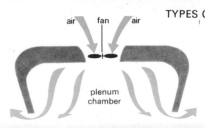

air    fan    air

plenum chamber

OPEN PLENUM

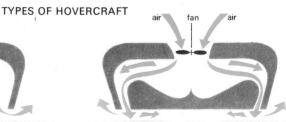

air    fan    air

PERIPHERAL JET

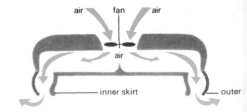

air    fan    air

air

inner skirt    outer

FLEXIBLE SKIRT

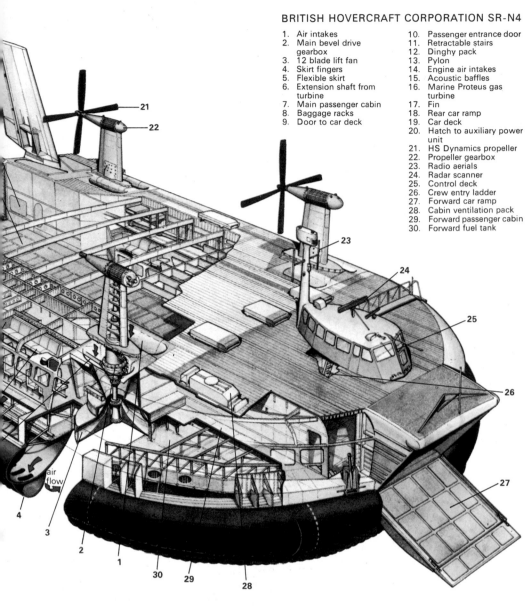

## BRITISH HOVERCRAFT CORPORATION SR-N4

1. Air intakes
2. Main bevel drive gearbox
3. 12 blade lift fan
4. Skirt fingers
5. Flexible skirt
6. Extension shaft from turbine
7. Main passenger cabin
8. Baggage racks
9. Door to car deck
10. Passenger entrance door
11. Retractable stairs
12. Dinghy pack
13. Pylon
14. Engine air intakes
15. Acoustic baffles
16. Marine Proteus gas turbine
17. Fin
18. Rear car ramp
19. Car deck
20. Hatch to auxiliary power unit
21. HS Dynamics propeller
22. Propeller gearbox
23. Radio aerials
24. Radar scanner
25. Control deck
26. Crew entry ladder
27. Forward car ramp
28. Cabin ventilation pack
29. Forward passenger cabin
30. Forward fuel tank

tance. Craft using a full peripheral skirt can travel from one kind of surface to another with little perceptible change in the craft's motion. This means that amphibious movements — travelling from land to sea — and over-ice operations are possible. Non-amphibious marine hovercraft have been developed with side walls or keels immersed in the water, sealing the sides of the cushion, with the ends sealed by flexible curtains. These craft offer greater economy of power as far as the cushion is concerned but require relatively higher driving power because of the sidewall resistance in the water.

### Moving forwards

Hovercraft can be propelled by a variety of means, including ducted or unducted propellers, with low tip speeds for quietness, and centrifugal fans. Propulsive devices which operate by contact with the ground are being considered for use in Arctic regions where the sloping terrain demands substantial side forces to control the craft effectively.

Redirection of the propulsive thrust is one common steering method. Many craft employ rudders operating in the fan or propeller slipstream to swing the craft into a turn. Sideways facing air nozzles are also used on some designs to help turn the craft at low speeds. For purely marine hovercraft, control can be very effectively obtained by the use of conventional rudders, and craft with immersed sidewalls can be steered by turning the sidewalls.

Braking of amphibious hovercraft is not as effective as for wheeled land vehicles unless a surface contacting device is used. Cutting off the lift-creating air to stop the craft by letting it settle on the surface is only advisable over water or smooth surfaces. Drawing to a halt is thus a very gradual process for amphibious craft — reverse thrust of the propellers is used, which provides only about one third of forward thrust.

Hovercraft are now used quite extensively as passenger and cargo ferries, and many are also in military use as patrol craft and troop carriers. *Hovertrains*, running along concrete tracks have been developed — but the future here seems to be with levitation by magnets (maglev) rather than air cushions. Another proposal, by the French company Bertin, is the use of air cushion landing gear for heavy freight aircraft, and SEDAM are presently building 225-ton air cushion ferry craft.

Rapid progress has been made in the development of air cushion platforms and strap-on skirt systems for the movement of large, heavy items such as oil storage tanks and electrical transformers. Air cushion platforms range in size from small ACV pallets a few feet square to large ACV platforms capable of handling loads weighing hundreds of tons. Basically these consist of flat boxes, sealed except for an inlet at one edge which is connected to an air pump and vents in the bottom through which the air escapes to form the air cushion. The use of these ACV pallets hovering a few inches above the ground means that heavy items like aero-engines or large castings can be easily be moved around by hand.

Ice-breaking is another dramatic role for ACV platforms. The reasons why ice-breaking occurs beneath an air cushion are not yet fully understood, but in

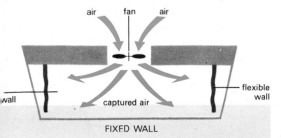

**Left: Fixed sidewall hovercraft ride on 'captured air bubbles' and are nicknamed CABs. Thin but solid sidewalls extend into the water to block air leakage from the chamber beneath the hovercraft deck. Increasing the air pressure lifts the craft, thus reducing water drag.**

**Below: ACV pallets are used to move heavy loads. Air is pumped into the pallet and, as pressure builds up, escapes through thin lubricating seals. This creates an air cushion between the pallet and the ground, making the pallet and its load airborne. It can then be moved with little effort.**

Beken of Cowes

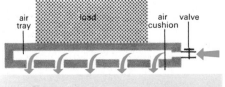

air ... fan ... air

captured air

flexible wall

wall

**FIXED WALL**

air tray ... load ... air cushion ... valve

**ACV PALLET**

Canada 69 cm (27 in) thick ice has been broken by the passage of a 220–ton ACV.

## Hydrofoils

A hydrofoil boat works on the same principle as an aircraft. It has a boat-shaped hull to which 'wings', or *hydrofoils,* are attached at the front and back by means of vertical, leg-like struts. As they travel through the water these hydrofoils produce lift in the same way the aerofoil shape of an aircraft wing provides lift in the air.

A stationary hydrofoil boat floats on the surface of the water like a conventional boat. As it gathers speed it begins to rise in the water until, when it is travelling fast, the lift created by the flow of water over the hydrofoil is sufficient to raise the hull clear of the water. A hydrofoil boat in full flight looks rather like an ordinary boat on water skis. Once out of the water the hull no longer suffers resistance from friction between the hull and the water or from waves in rough water and therefore gives a faster, smoother ride.

## Water wings

The thicker the medium through which a foil is travelling, the more lift it can produce. As water is several hundred times denser than air, hydrofoils can be much smaller than an aircraft's wings and yet still create considerable lift. An aircraft's wings, however, operate in air whose density changes little over the range of altitudes at which they fly. The hydrofoil boat's 'wings' are working very close to the surface of the water where there is a massive and abrupt change in density between air and water. If the foils break through the surface a large drop in lift occurs because the pressure difference between its upper and lower surfaces is destroyed when the water no longer flows over the top.

The upper and lower limits of the depth within which the foils must operate are too fine to be controlled by hand. To ensure a nearly constant flying height, the foils need some form of automatic control. This in-built stability is achieved differently by the two principle types of hydrofoil design.

## Surface piercing hydrofoils

In the *surface piercing* hydrofoils, the foils actually break the surface of the water as the craft moves forward. When lift is lost due to the hydrofoil breaking through waves, the craft sinks deeper into the water, thereby immersing a greater foil area which in turn creates more lift. This very simple design is used in almost all the commercial hydrofoil ferries in the western world.

## Fully submerged hydrofoils

In the *fully submerged* hydrofoils, the foils are completely immersed in water all the time. The amount of lift produced is controlled by altering the angle of attack of the foils with hydraulic rams. These are rods moved by liquid under pressure which press down on or pull back from the hydrofoil to change its angle of inclination.

The movement of the hydraulic rams themselves is directed by signals from a sonic device in the bow which sends out pulses of high-frequency sound waves and listens for echoes from on-coming waves in order to assess the wave's height. It then automatically instructs the hy-

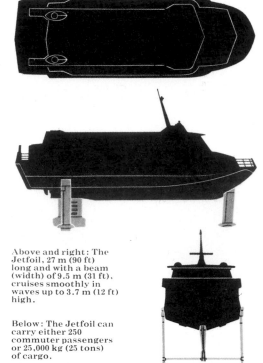

Above and right: The Jetfoil, 27 m (90 ft) long and with a beam (width) of 9.5 m (31 ft), cruises smoothly in waves up to 3.7 m (12 ft) high.

Below: The Jetfoil can carry either 250 commuter passengers or 25,000 kg (25 tons) of cargo.

Right: The waterjet propulsion system draws water in through a duct in the aft strut to two pumps. It is then discharged at high pressure to drive the craft forward.

Below: The Jetfoil's retractable struts and foils allow operation in shallow water.

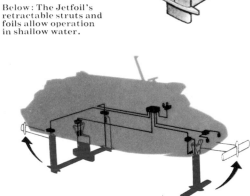

Below: The torpedo-shaped HD4 hydrofoil boat was designed by Alexander Graham Bell and Casey Baldwin. Nicknamed the 'Water Monster' and weighing over 5,100 kg (5 tons), it achieved lift even at low speeds. In 1918 it reached a world speed boat record of 114.4 km per hour (70.86 mph).

Right: The Tucumcari, a Patrol Gunboat Hydrofoil, was designed to United States Navy specifications under a programme initiated in 1965. Its maximum foilborne speed of 50 knots made it ideally suited to Vietnam war service. The craft was scrapped in 1972 after running aground in the Caribbean.

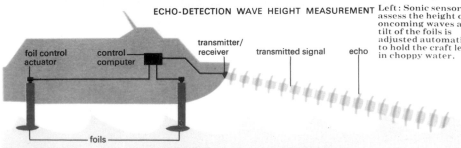

**ECHO-DETECTION WAVE HEIGHT MEASUREMENT**

foil control actuator — control computer — transmitter/receiver — transmitted signal — echo — foils

Left: Sonic sensors assess the height of oncoming waves and the tilt of the foils is adjusted automatically to hold the craft level in choppy water.

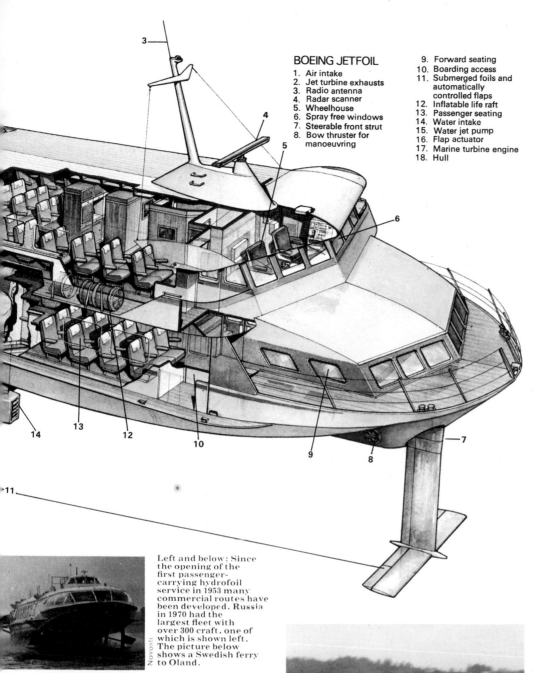

## BOEING JETFOIL

1. Air intake
2. Jet turbine exhausts
3. Radio antenna
4. Radar scanner
5. Wheelhouse
6. Spray free windows
7. Steerable front strut
8. Bow thruster for manoeuvring
9. Forward seating
10. Boarding access
11. Submerged foils and automatically controlled flaps
12. Inflatable life raft
13. Passenger seating
14. Water intake
15. Water jet pump
16. Flap actuator
17. Marine turbine engine
18. Hull

draulic system to make the appropriate adjustments to the angles of the hydrofoils so that the hull is held steady. Gyroscopes in the hull which sense the craft's pitch, roll and heave motions also feed information into this control circuit and help to keep the hydrofoil boat level. These systems are very expensive; the principal user of fully submerged hydrofoils is the US Navy.

### Propulsion systems

An early type of hydrofoil arrangement was the 'ladder' type, in which the amount of lift generated depends on the number of rungs immersed — the greater the number of rungs covered, the greater the lift.

Some designs of either type of hydrofoil have most of the weight carried by a large foil or foils at the front while on others the main foils are placed towards the rear. The smaller foil which carries the remaining weight is usually pivoted for steering the craft.

Commercial hydrofoil boats are usually powered by marine diesel engines, but high speed military craft often use gas turbine engines. There may be two separate propulsion systems, one for use when the craft is being carried by the foils and another for when it is moving very slowly and floating on its hull.

### Problems at high speed

At speeds above 50 knots, hydrofoils can suffer from the effects of *cavity flow*. As a result of increasingly turbulent water flow across the top of the foil, cavities are formed along the foil surface which cut its lifting force. These cavities subsequently fill with air or water vapour.

When the craft is travelling very fast, the water pressure on the upper foil surface may drop below atmospheric pressure. Under such circumstances, air from above the surface of the water may be sucked down the strut and along the foil to fill the cavities. This effect is called *ventilation* and again causes a variation in lift.

If the pressure across the top of the foil falls low enough, the water will vaporize, forming bubbles of water vapour which break up the smooth flow of water over the upper surface, thereby reducing lift. This phenomenon, known as *cavitation*, not only upsets efficient lift production but can also seriously erode the foil over a period of time. As the bubbles burst they smash minute jets of water against the foil surface with sufficient force to damage the metal.

Left and below: Since the opening of the first passenger-carrying hydrofoil service in 1953 many commercial routes have been developed. Russia in 1970 had the largest fleet with over 300 craft, one of which is shown left. The picture below shows a Swedish ferry to Oland.

Novosti

Picturepoint

Above: FRESH 1 (foil research experimenting super cavitating hydrofoil) holds the hydrofoil speed record of 84 knots. When foilborne the craft is powered by a fan jet producing 8,200 kg (18,000 lb) of thrust. The craft has a catamaran hull linked with a bridge to which test foils are fitted.

Right: The Little Squirt in full flight can do 50 knots. Built in 1962 as a research vessel it was the first craft to be fitted with a waterjet system of propulsion. Trailing edge flaps were fitted to the foils and foil controls introduced—both features used in later hydrofoil designs like the Jetfoil.

The Boeing Company

## TYPES OF HYDROFOIL

SURFACE PIERCING          SHALLOW-DRAFT          SUBMERGED          LADDER

# Bicycles and Motorcycles

The bicycle is a very efficient form of personal transport. Its history dates back over 200 years to the early designs of the second half of the eighteenth century. The most famous of the early machines was the 'Célerifère', later named the 'Vélocifère', built by the Comte de Sivrac in France in 1791. This was a two-wheeled wooden horse, propelled by the rider pushing his feet against the ground, and it must have been difficult to steer as the front wheel was not pivoted.

The first machine with a steerable front wheel was demonstrated by the German Baron von Drais de Sauerbrun in 1818. Known as the Draisienne or 'hobby-horse', it had a simple wooden frame and two large, spoked wooden wheels fitted with iron tyres. The hobby-horse was enormously popular during the following 20 years, but interest declined and production ceased about 1830.

The next development was the pedal operated bicycle invented in 1839 by Kirkpatrick Macmillan, a Scottish blacksmith. The pedals were fitted to the ends of two levers pivoted at the front of the frame above the front wheel, and the forward and back motion of the levers was transmitted by connecting rods to cranks driving the rear axle. Little progress was made in the development of drive mechanisms until the 1860s, when Pierre and Ernest Michaux of Paris fitted pedals and cranks to the front wheel of a hobby-horse type machine, which they called a 'vélocipède'.

During the 1860s, wire-spoked wheels and rubber tyres were introduced, and this led to the evolution of the 'Ordinary' or 'Penny-farthing' bicycles of the 1870s. This type of bicycle had a large front wheel, driven by pedals and cranks fitted to its axle, and a small rear wheel about half the diameter of the front one. The frame was a single metal tube and the saddle was mounted on it above the front wheel, close to the handlebars.

The forerunner of the modern design was the 'Safety' bicycle developed between 1870 and 1890. This type of cycle had two wheels of approximately equal diameter, with wire spokes and rubber tyres and a chain drive to the rear wheel. By 1895 the diamond-shaped frame was standard, as were pneumatic (air filled) bicycle tyres which had been patented in 1888 by J. B. Dunlop. Pneumatic tyres had, in fact, been invented in 1845 by R. W. Thompson, but were not adopted at that time and were forgotten.

The basic design of bicycles changed little during the first quarter of the twentieth century, but in the late 1920s improvements in materials and construction methods permitted the development of lightweight sports and touring machines.

One of the most radical changes in bicycle design came in 1962, with the introduction of the small-wheeled Moulton cycle and its many successors. These small-wheeled machines soon became popular, and contributed to the general revival of interest in cycling during the 1960s and 1970s.

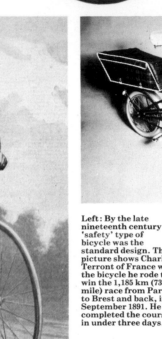

Above: An 'ordinary' or 'penny-farthing' bicycle, built in 1878 by Bayliss Thomson.

Left: The first pedal-driven bicycle, built in 1839 by Kirkpatrick Macmillan. He was also the first person to be fined for a cycling offence, after knocking over a child in Glasgow in 1842.

Left: By the late nineteenth century the 'safety' type of bicycle was the standard design. This picture shows Charles Terront of France with the bicycle he rode to win the 1,185 km (736 mile) race from Paris to Brest and back, in September 1891. He completed the course in under three days.

Above: One of the many makes of small-wheeled bicycle built since 1962 when Alex Moulton designed the first of this type. Unlike most of its successors, the Moulton cycle had a suspension system, using a coil spring on the front and a rubber shock absorber at the rear.

Below: A derailleur gear mechanism. Operating the hand lever moves the change mechanism towards or away from the wheel. As it moves, it transfers the chains from one sprocket to another. The system shown has a double chainwheel, which doubles the number of gear ratios available.

Right: A modern lightweight sports bike. Competition cycles can be very expensive, due to the high standards of workmanship employed, the small numbers produced and the use of expensive materials such as titanium. The frames are usually made of manganese-molybdenum steel.

low gear   high gear

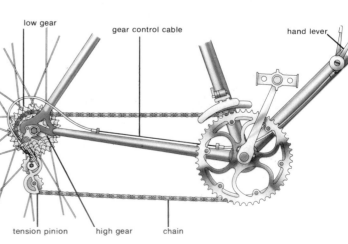

low gear        gear control cable        hand lever

tension pinion    high gear    chain

With their chunky tyres and robust construction, BMX machines are designed for the roughest of cross- country track racing. These bicycles are now made by many manufacturers worldwide.

Left: The motorcycle built by Gottlieb Daimler in Germany in 1885. The drive from the single cylinder petrol engine was transmitted to the rear by a belt and pulley arrangement. A small gear fixed to the driven pulley turned the ring gear attached to the spokes of the rear wheel.

Right: Early machines were basically strengthened pedal cycles fitted with engines. This 1903 Triumph has an ordinary pedal drive on one side for starting and to assist the engine on uphill runs, and the belt drive from the engine on the other side.

Above: One of the most powerful road bikes built, the 903 cc (55 in³) four cylinder Kawasaki 900 Z1. The engine produces over 60 kW (80 hp) at 8,500 rpm, giving it a top speed of 200 kph (125 mph). Its basic weight is 232 kg (511 lb). Braking is by a front disc brake and a rear drum brake.

Right: This unusual motorcycle and sidecar combination was photographed in Berlin in 1928. The bike is an NSU, and the sidecar carries a duplicate set of controls and handlebars so that the combination can be driven from the sidecar or from the bike itself.

Above: Speedway bikes are single cylinder, single gear machines. They have no brakes or gearchange, the only controls being the clutch and throttle.

Below: Cross-country racing is a popular sport in many countries, using tough, purpose-built bikes. This one is a Spanish Bultaco.

Modern mass-produced bicycle frames are made from high-quality lightweight steel alloy tubing, with steel or light alloy handlebars. The wheels have steel or alloy rims and hubs, with steel wire spokes.

The pedals and cranks are fitted to a short axle running through the bottom bracket of the frame; this axle also carries the chainwheel. The chain is made of steel and connects the chainwheel with the rear drive sprocket mounted on the hub of the rear wheel. Except for track racing bikes, this rear sprocket incorporates a freewheel mechanism which allows the rear wheel to turn freely, enabling the rider to coast downhill without having to keep pedalling.

Many bicycles are fitted with gears, either the fully-enclosed type built into the rear wheel hub or the derailleur type comprising a set of rear sprockets of different sizes. The enclosed type is a miniature form of the epicyclic gearbox, the type of gearing used on many vehicle transmission systems, and gearchanges are accomplished by engaging different combinations of gear wheels within the hub.

Gear changing on a derailleur system is achieved by shifting the chain from one sprocket to another, the smallest sprocket giving the highest gear ratio.

### Motorcycles

The first motorcycle was built in Germany in 1885 by Gottlieb Daimler, but the motorcycle industry did not really begin until the end of the nineteenth century. Early motorcycles were modified bicycles fitted with engines, but manufacturers were soon designing and building frames especially for motorcycles.

Most modern bike frames are made of steel tubing, with the engine mounted on twin tubes which form the bottom section of the frame. Suspension is provided for both wheels to give greater comfort to the rider and to improve the roadholding of the machine. The front suspension is by coil springs and telescopic hydraulic damper units incorporated in the front fork legs. The rear suspension uses a pair of spring and damper units. With one on each side, the upper ends are fixed to the frame below the saddle and the lower ends to the rear fork. The rear fork extends back almost horizontally from the frame, and it is pivoted to allow it and the wheel to move up and down under the control of the spring units.

The hydraulic damper units, or shock absorbers, regulate the up and down motion of the suspension. For example, when the wheel hits a bump in the road it is pushed upwards, compressing the spring. The spring pushes it back down on to the road again and it then tends to rebound back up, starting the whole process over again. If no dampers were fitted, this wheel bounce would make the machine uncomfortable to ride and difficult to control, especially at high speeds. The dampers smooth out these unwanted oscillations of the suspension by resisting the up or down movement of the spring.

The upper part of the damper is in effect a cylinder of oil, fixed to the frame in the case of rear dampers or to the upper part of the forks in the case of front dampers. The lower part, which moves up and down with the wheel, is connected to

Above: 250 cc (15.25 in³) racing bikes at the Daytona racetrack in Florida, USA. The technical experience gained from racing is of great benefit to the designers of ordinary machines.

Below: Competitors in a sidecar race at Brands Hatch racetrack in England.

a piston within the oil cylinder. This piston has small holes drilled through it and as it moves the oil has to pass through these narrow holes. This means that the speed at which the piston can move is limited by the speed at which the oil can pass through the holes.

The speed at which the suspension unit can be compressed or expand again is thus limited to that of the piston, and this prevents the oscillations of the spring that could cause wheel bounce.

The wheels themselves have steel rims and spokes, except for motor scooter wheels which are usually made of pressed steel. Aluminium alloy rims and cast magnesium alloy wheels are also now frequently used.

## Engines and transmissions

Modern motorcycle engines range in capacity from just under 50 cc (3 in³) to over 1200 cc (73 in³). They may be two or four-stroke petrol engines or rotary Wankel-type engines, either air cooled or water cooled. Some small electrically-driven machines have been produced for town use.

The crankshaft motion is transmitted to the gearbox via the primary drive, which is either a chain drive or a set of gears, and the clutch. The final drive from the gearbox to the rear wheel is usually by chain, but some of the more expensive machines use a drive shaft.

Most two-stroke bikes have magneto ignition systems, self-contained units driven directly from the engine that generate the power to run the ignition, lighting and horn circuits. The ignition coil and the contact breaker are built in to the unit.

Four-stroke machines use battery and coil ignition systems, with either a dc dynamo or an ac alternator, driven by the engine, to keep the battery charged and provide electrical power when the engine is running. Many bikes now use electronic ignition systems in place of the conventional mechanical contact breaker sets.

## Brakes and controls

Motorcycles may be fitted with either drum or disc brakes, or have a disc brake on the front wheel and a drum brake on the rear. The drum brake consists of a brake drum built into the wheel hub and a pair of brake shoes lined with an asbestos-based material, which press against the inside of the drum when the brake is applied.

The disc brake is a steel disc mounted on the wheel hub, with a pair of brake pads which are pushed against the disc from either side to grip it as the brake is applied.

The front brake is operated by a lever mounted on the right of the handlebars, the rear brake by a foot pedal, on the right hand side on modern machines. Drum brakes are usually operated mechanically, by cable on the front and by a rod on the rear, but disc brakes use hydraulic systems.

Engine speed is controlled by a twist-grip control on the right hand side of the handlebars, connected to the carburettor or carburettors by a cable. The clutch is operated by a lever on the left of the handlebars and smaller machines and motor scooters often use a twistgrip control, also on the left, to operate the gearchange.

Below right: the BMW R90 S, a large, luxurious touring bike. The 898 cc (55 in³) horizontally-opposed twin cylinder engine develops 50 kW (67 hp) at 7,000 rpm, and the transmission is by fully enclosed drive shaft. Top speed is 200 kph (125 mph), and it weighs 215 kg (474 lb).

BMW R90S

1  fuel tanks
2  cockpit fairing
3  turn indicator
4  telescopic front fork
5  twin disc brakes
6  horizontally-opposed twin cylinder engine
7  carburettor
8  footbrake
9  gearbox and final drive shaft
10 rear suspension
11 drum brake
12 rear lights
13 saddle

# Cars, Trucks and Buses

1875 Marcus

1886 Benz

1902 Wolsely

The idea of using an engine to drive a wheeled road vehicle first became a practical reality in Paris in 1769, when Nicolas Cugnot built a steam powered carriage that ran at about 4 kph (2½ mph). Many steam cars and trucks were built during the following 150 years, and in 1906 a steam car designed by the Stanley brothers in the USA reached a speed of 204 kph (127 mph).

By this time, however, the more efficient internal combustion engine was rapidly taking over as the source of power for road vehicles. Steam vehicle building had virtually ceased by the middle of the 1920s. Despite the overwhelming dominance of the internal combustion engine, however, a few people are still designing steam cars and indeed steam-powered vehicles may yet come back into use.

Battery powered vehicles have been somewhat more successful than steam vehicles, but the main limitation is the size and weight of the batteries. In practice a great deal of the vehicle's power is used up simply carrying the batteries around, and this means that its range and speed are restricted. Until sufficiently light and powerful batteries have been developed, electric cars are unlikely to become a viable alternative to conventional vehicles.

Yet there are some applications of battery power which are possible even now. Large numbers of battery vehicles are in use, for example, performing duties such as milk or mail delivery which do not involve high speeds or long distances. They are quiet and pollution-free, and ideal for work involving a lot of stopping and starting which would soon wear out a diesel or petrol engine.

Mains-type electric vehicles, such as trolley buses and tramcars, do not have the problem of carrying their energy around with them since they pick it up as they go. Many cities are now building tramway systems again, in some cases less than 30 years after abandoning trams in favour of ordinary buses.

## Cars

Although the credit for the building of the first automobiles powered by internal combustion engines is usually given to Karl Benz and Gottlieb Daimler, several such machines were built during the previous 60 years. Benz and Daimler produced their first cars in 1885 and 1886 respectively, but a car running on hydrogen gas had been built by Samuel Brown in London in the early 1820s. The Belgian engineer J. J. E. Lenoir built a car in 1862, and this was followed by the two built by Siegfried Marcus in Austria in 1864 and 1875.

The achievement of Daimler and Benz, however, is important because they envisaged the use of the car as a popular means of transport, and their efforts led directly to the creation of the motor industry. The earlier pioneers appear to have had little real interest in the future possibilities of their inventions, and did not persist in their development.

The drawings above and at the bottom of the page show how the shape of car bodies has evolved since the nineteenth century. Top row: Early cars were open vehicles with no weather protection, but body design progressed rapidly during the 1900s. The mass-produced Model T Ford was introduced in 1908 and over 15 million were built in its 19-year production run. The move towards fully enclosed designs continued during the 1920s, and in the 1930s body lines became more graceful and flowing.
Bottom row: Designs changed little during the 1940s, but the introduction of unitary construction in the 1950s allowed designers to produce longer, lower and more adventurous shapes. Small cars like the Mini became very popular in the 1960s, and during the 1970s the clean, efficient 'wedge' shape evolved.

Right: A drawing of a 1903 Mercedes.

Below: A 1909 Buick, with a front-mounted engine driving the rear wheels through a chain and sprocket final drive.

Above right: The 1955 Lincoln is a good example of American car design of that period. The body is long and low, and the large windows and windshield give the driver excellent visibility.

Right: During the 1920s mass production techniques enabled manufacturers to build large numbers of cheap and reliable cars. The relative affluence of the period provided them with large sales, particularly in the US and western Europe, until the economic collapse of the early 1930s.

1948 Vauxhall

1954 Oldsmobile

1908 Ford

1922 Austin

1937 Rolls-Royce

Michael Holford

Right: The operation of a four-speed manual gearbox. The gear lever moves the yokes to lock the required gears to the drive shaft. Here only one of the two yokes is shown at a time, and the line of power transmission is shown in red. The drive from the engine enters the box through the clutch shaft which drives the layshaft. First, second and third gears are selected by locking the required gear to the transmission shaft, taking up the drive from the layshaft. Top gear is selected by locking the clutch shaft directly to the transmission shaft. Reverse gear, not shown, is selected by connecting the transmission shaft to the layshaft via a separate idler gear.

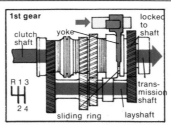
1st gear: clutch shaft, yoke, locked to shaft, R 1 3 / 2 4, sliding ring, transmission shaft, layshaft

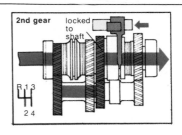
2nd gear: locked to shaft, R 1 3 / 2 4

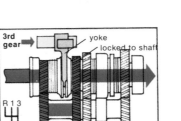
3rd gear: yoke, locked to shaft, R 1 3 / 2 4

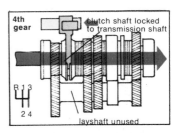
4th gear: clutch shaft locked to transmission shaft, R 1 3 / 2 4, layshaft unused

Michael Holford

Daymark

Left: Racing cars have evolved into highly specialized designs. On this one the engine is sited between the driver and the rear wheels. The cowling above and behind the driver's head is the air intake for the carburettors. Aerofoils at the front and back keep the wheels firmly on the ground at high speeds.

Top: Most car suspensions use coil springs, as in this example, but hydraulic or pneumatic systems are also used. The horizontal rod with the rubber dust seal is one of a pair linking the front wheels to the steering mechanism. When the steering wheel is turned the rods move sideways to pivot the front wheels.

Above: The rear suspension and drive shafts of a Lotus car.

Right: A cutaway of a Chevrolet Stingray, a powerful American sports car which has a lightweight body built on to a steel girder chassis. The use of chassis-type construction has continued for a number of sports cars despite the use of unitary construction for most modern cars.

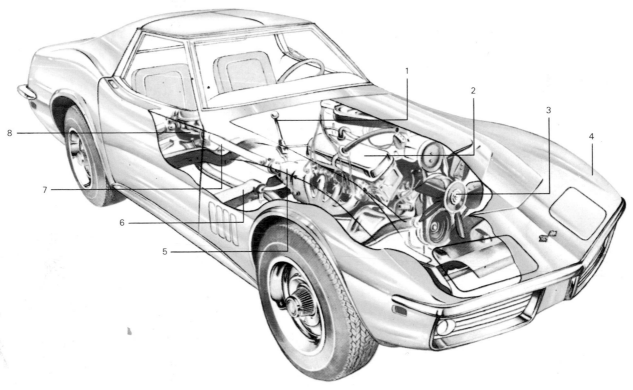

CHEVROLET STINGRAY
1 gearshift
2 engine
3 cooling fan
4 lightweight body
5 gearbox
6 chassis
7 drive shaft
8 differential

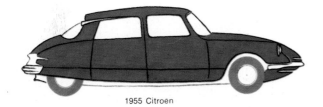
1955 Citroën

1959 Mini

1975 Vauxhall

The early Benz and Daimler cars used single cylinder engines. But engine design progressed rapidly and by 1900 multi-cylinder engines were well established. During the first decade of the twentieth century, the design practice of putting the engine at the front of the car and taking the drive from there to the rear wheels was adopted by most manufacturers. This is still the most widespread layout, but the trend towards smaller cars has made other layouts, such as front engine, front wheel drive and rear engine, rear wheel drive, common.

The drive from the engine is taken via the clutch to the gearbox, and from there by drive shafts to the driving wheels. The clutch used with manual gearboxes has three main components: the clutch plate, the pressure plate and the flywheel on the end of the engine crankshaft. When the clutch is engaged, the pressure plate presses the clutch plate against the face of the flywheel. As the flywheel turns, the clutch plate turns with it, and so the drive is transmitted into the gearbox.

When the clutch pedal is depressed, the pressure plate is forced away from the clutch plate by hydraulic pressure. The clutch plate is then no longer being pressed against the flywheel and turned by it, and so the drive from engine to gearbox is disconnected.

Automatic transmission systems use hydraulic couplings in place of the friction type clutch. The flywheel drives a saucer-shaped impeller which is enclosed within a casing full of oil. As the impeller turns, oil is flung outwards by radial vanes on its inside face. The oil is deflected against similar vanes on the inside of another saucer-shaped unit, the turbine, which faces it. The force of the oil turns the turbine, which is connected to the gearbox by a shaft.

The various combinations of gears within an automatic gearbox are selected by clutch mechanisms within it. The clutches are activated hydraulically or electrically by devices which sense the engine and car speeds, and the position of the accelerator pedal, to determine the correct ratio required. These devices can be over-ridden by the driver, using the gear selector lever, so that the car can be held in any particular gear or put into reverse or neutral.

Cars use disc or drum brakes, or a combination of both with discs on the front and drums at the rear. The brake pedal operates all four brakes via a hydraulic system, but the handbrake operates only the brakes on the two non-driving wheels. The handbrake lever is linked to the brakes by steel cables or rods, and as it is independent of the hydraulic system it can provide some braking if the main brake system fails.

Until the 1950s, almost all cars had a steel girder chassis on to which the pressed-steel body was built, but during this period mass-produced cars were beginning to be built without a chassis. This method is called *unitary construction*.

The body and chassis parts are built together as a single unit from welded steel pressings. The method is lighter and cheaper than chassis type construction, and better suited to mass production techniques. Apart from this and styling considerations, body designers also have to take into account such factors as passenger safety and the aerodynamics of the body shape.

Above: The petrol-engined Albion of 1914. The development of trucks was stimulated by their use during the First World War. After the war the large numbers of surplus military trucks which were sold did much to encourage the spread of motor transport in Europe and the US.

Right: This ancestor of the modern double-decker bus is a 1910 type 'B' which belonged to the London General Omnibus Company. There is no roof to the upper deck and the wooden seating accommodates thirty passengers. The tyres are solid rubber, and its speed was 20 kph (12 mph).

Top: A large articulated truck with a twin-axled semi-trailer.

Above: A heavy duty articulated low-loader carrying a motor grader, a large earthmoving machine. Special low-loaders have been built which can carry loads of over 400 tonnes.

Right: A cutaway drawing of a three-axle rigid truck, showing the strong ladder-type steel chassis, the engine, the transmission and suspension. The drive is transmitted to both rear axles, and the use of double wheels on these axles allows heavier loads to be carried.

**FODEN TRUCK**
1 driver's cab
2 engine and gearbox
3 fuel tanks
4 drive shaft
5 final drive gearboxes
6 frame chassis
7 brake drum
8 rear suspension
9 front suspension
10 steering box

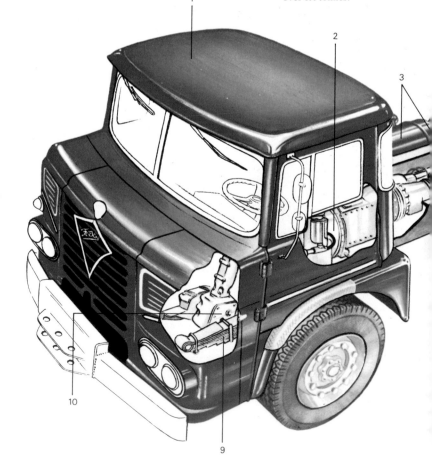

Above: A rear-engined tour bus. Bus safety is improved by using multiple braking circuits. Many buses are also fitted with electro-magnetic retarders which exert a strong magnetic force on the vehicle's drive shaft to slow it down, thus supplementing the action of the brakes.

Below: A one-man-operated London bus. The driver collects the passengers' fares as they enter, and it has seats for 68 passengers with room for 21 standing. The six-cylinder 114 kW (153 hp) diesel engine and the four-speed gearbox are mounted across the rear chassis.

Right: A pair of four-axled rigid tipper trucks used for carrying quarried stone. The tipper body is mounted on pivots at the rear, and the front end can be raised by hydraulic jacks to tip the load off at the back. The hydraulic system is driven by the truck's engine.

Below: The triple-circuit braking system of an articulated tractor unit. The tractor and semi-trailer brakes are independently operated by compressed air from a compressor driven by the engine.

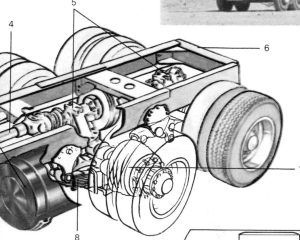

- air from compressor
- tractor pressure line
- tractor brake line
- trailer pressure line
- trailer brake line
- park brake pressure line
- park brake line
- emergency line
- anti-compounding line

During the development of a new model, extensive testing of mock-ups and prototypes is carried out. The design has to comply with international safety regulations, which cover many aspects including the size and position of the lights and the height and strength of the bumpers.

Prototypes are crashed into walls and other vehicles in order to evaluate the strength of the passenger compartment, and the ability of the front and rear body sections to absorb the impact created by a collision.

Wind tunnel testing is also used to improve the aerodynamic qualities of the body shape. This leads to better road-holding and acceleration, higher top speeds and greater fuel economy.

## Commercial vehicles

Commercial vehicles are an important part of the transport systems of most of the countries of the world, particularly since the comparative decline of the railways. Early commercial vehicles were powered by steam, electricity or petrol engines, but most are now diesel powered.

The diesel engine was invented by Rudolf Diesel in Germany in 1897. Despite its success in marine propulsion, however, satisfactory road vehicle versions did not appear until 1922. On most commercial vehicles today the engine is mounted at the front, ahead of or beneath the driver's cab. Some manufacturers fit the engine beneath the chassis, and many buses and coaches use this layout or have the engine at the rear.

There is a wide range of commercial vehicle diesel engine, both two-stroke and four-stroke. Most are water-cooled, the main exceptions being the air-cooled engines produced by Magirus Deutz in Germany.

Light vans and some buses are often of unitary construction, without a chassis, but larger vehicles usually have a ladder-type frame chassis on to which an enormous variety of bodies can be built. Trucks may be either rigid or articulated. The rigid type has a single chassis carrying the cab, engine and body or load platform, and can have from two to four axles.

The articulated truck consists of a short tractor unit comprising the cab, engine and transmission. There is a 'fifth wheel' or turntable on top of the chassis, above the rear axle or pair of axles, to which the trailer is attached. The articulated trailer unit, called a semi-trailer, has no wheels at the front, being supported by the tractor, but one or more axles at the rear. Rigid units are often used for drawbar operation, towing trailers which are linked to them by a steel towing bar.

Most truck gearboxes are manually operated, and the number of gears available from the main gearbox can be doubled by means of an extra set of gears called a 'range splitter', or by using a two-speed driving axle. Automatic or semi-automatic transmissions are used on some heavy trucks and many buses.

Until recently, truck cabs were designed to be purely functional, unlike cars where driver comfort and convenience have always been carefully considered. Modern truck cabs, however, incorporate similar standards of seating, sound insulation and easily operated controls to those used in cars. This type of ergonomic design helps to reduce the driver fatigue which is a potential cause of accidents.

# Railways

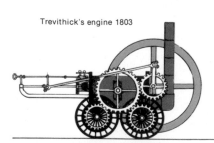

Trevithick's engine 1803

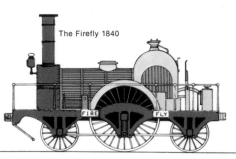

The Firefly 1840

On August 31, 1975, a grand cavalcade of locomotives was held to mark 150 years of rail travel in Britain. Since the opening of the Stockton and Darlington Railway in 1825, railways have become one of the most widespread forms of transport, serving almost every country in the world.

At the beginning of the nineteenth century Britain was still in the throes of the Industrial Revolution. Manufacturing industry, with its demand for power and raw materials, and its output of mass-produced goods, was altering the pattern of life. Not only merchandise but people also needed to be transported all over the country to help weave the web of commerce. The rutted and muddy roads were totally unable to meet this demand, while the canals were handicapped by the need for locks to overcome changes in water level. But by 1800 the public was already familiar with the two elements that were to combine to make the steam railway the transport of the future.

Railways had already existed in Britain for over 200 years, the first examples being wooden trackways along which horses could haul wagons of coal from the mines to the nearest water transport—canal, sea or navigable river. In time the wooden rails changed to iron, and the flat 'plateways' changed to edged rails along which flanged wheels were guided.

The other vital element was steam power, the moving force. This too had been developed as an adjunct of the mining industry, where low pressure steam engines were used to pump water from the underground workings. The Cornish mining engineer, Richard Trevithick, was the first to conceive the idea of building a high pressure engine and mounting it on wheels.

Trevithick's first two steam locomotives were in fact road vehicles: the idea of a steam engine running on rails only came about as the result of a wager. Much impressed by the potential of this new invention, Samuel Homphray, a South Wales iron master, bet a friend that a railway engine could be built to haul a ten ton load along the newly opened Penydarren Tramway at Merthyr Tydfil, a feat which Trevithick's specially built locomotive duly performed on Tuesday February 21, 1804.

In the years that followed, experimental railway engines were tried on various mineral railways. George Stephenson, the giant among the early railway builders, was, like Trevithick, a mining engineer. His particular achievement was to synthesize the best available knowledge and thus develop not only a serviceable and reliable locomotive but also the concept of the steam-worked railway.

1825 was the year of his first great triumph, the opening of the Stockton and Darlington Railway, the first public railway to be worked by steam traction. The opening train was hauled by Stephenson's *Locomotion*, preceded by a mandatory horse rider bearing a red flag.

Such exploits were at first regarded as highly dangerous by the general public, but in spite of widespread suspicion the construction of new railways proceeded apace and by 1841 the skeleton of Britain's railway network was already in existence.

Adam Woolfitt/Susan Griggs

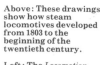

Above: These drawings show how steam locomotives developed from 1803 to the beginning of the twentieth century.

Left: The *Locomotion* was built in 1825 by George Stephenson, and in that year became the first steam engine to haul a train on a public railway, between Stockton and Darlington.

Right: The Furness Railway's locomotive number 9, built in 1855 by Fairbairn and Company. Steam engines can be classified by their wheel layouts; this one is an 0-4-0, having no wheels in front or behind its four driving wheels. These classifications do not include the wheels of the tender.

Ronan

American History Library

Below: Steam engines at a depot in West Germany. Steam engines are sturdy and reliable, but of the total heat energy supplied to them from the burning fuel only about six per cent is converted into useful mechanical energy. The unused energy escapes as heat in the exhaust steam and smoke.

Below right: A cutaway drawing of a steam engine. The steam from the boiler passes into the steam chest, and when the valve is opened it enters the cylinder. In the cylinder it expands, forcing the piston along. The piston's motion is transmitted to the driving wheels by the connecting rod.

ZEFA

## STEAM LOCOMOTIVE
1. Cylinder
2. Smoke deflectors
3. Steam chest
4. Piston
5. Chimney
6. Valve gear
7. Connecting rod
8. Coupling rods
9. Sanding pipes
10. Water injector
11. Safety valve
12. Boiler tubes
13. Fire box
14. Regulator
15. Steam brake lever
16. Whistle
17. Vacuum brake lever
18. Reversing gear
19. Sand lever

Right: The *Dolbadarn*, a small, narrow-gauge locomotive on the Llanberis Lakeside Railway, Wales. Steam engines need to take on water frequently, either from trackside tanks, as in this case, or by scooping it up from troughs—between the rails at intervals along the track—as they travel.

Below: Southern Pacific locomotive number 2372 was the first of the twelve Class T-32 4-6-0 engines which were built at Sacramento, California, during the First World War. This particular locomotive was completed in 1918 and remained in use until it was scrapped in 1956.

Picturepoint

The Mallard 1935

Stanier Coronation class 4-6-2 1938

Above: Three twentieth-century steam engines. The streamlined *Mallard* set the world steam engine speed record of 202.8 kph (126 mph) in 1938. *Evening Star* was the last steam locomotive to be built by British Railways.

Left: The A-3 class *Flying Scotsman*, built in the 1920s and now restored. The extra tender was added to carry water, as watering facilities no longer exist on the British Rail network.

Right: A powerful diesel locomotive used for hauling trains along the line from Whitehorse in the Yukon Territory, Canada, to the port of Skagway in Alaska.

Railway construction had by this time spread to Europe and North America. The first lines on the continent were built by British engineers and used British-built locomotives. In France the first public steam railway was the 61 km (38 mile) long Lyons and St. Etienne line, opened in 1828. Germany followed a few years later with a short line from Nuremberg to Furth. Its first locomotive, Der Adler, was delivered complete with a British driver, William Wilson, who had been one of Stephenson's pupils.

British engineers later pioneered lines in many other European countries. Thus the 1.435 m (4 ft 8½ in) gauge adopted by Stephenson eventually became standard in most of the world.

### Railways in the Wild West

In the United States and Canada, railways were built largely across virgin territory, where few restrictions of private ownership applied. North American railways were thus built to one of the most generous loading gauges in the world, even though the track was the standard 1.435 m (4 ft 8½ in). In the West, lines were built to open up the country, the towns arriving after the railway rather than vice versa. Many such lines converged on Chicago, which became the greatest railway town in the world. On May 9, 1869, a golden spike was driven to mark the completion of the first transcontinental railroad.

By 1850 some 10,460 km (6,500 miles) of line were in operation in Great Britain. Subsequent lines were generally of lesser importance, being either branch lines or competing routes. The working life of many of these has been relatively short, the rule of 'last opened, first closed' seeming to apply.

On the continent the railways were generally state owned rather than under private ownership. Lines were built for strategic or economic reasons, and on the whole a less dense but more efficient network has resulted.

The First World War left the European railways battered, and it was some time before pre-war standards were regained. However, the war had also encouraged the mass production of motor vehicles, and for the first time the dominance of the railway was challenged. During the depression of the 1930s there was little money available to carry out much-needed modernization plans and in only a few countries such as Switzerland and France was progress made with electrification. Experiments were made with diesel traction, including the high-speed *Flying Hamburger* from Hamburg to Berlin, but steam remained the dominant form of power.

The Second World War once again put enormous strains on Europe's railways, which suffered severely from bomb damage. In the post war era, car ownership came within the reach of most families, while an increasing proportion of freight traffic was carried by road. British Railways were nationalized and subsequently modernized. Many branch lines were closed and steam was replaced by diesel and electric traction.

The handling of individual wagon loads of freight began to be phased out in favour of bulk train loads, with automatic loading and unloading at terminals. Freightliner container trains now travel at speeds of 113 kph (70 mph) between most parts of the country. On the passenger side the emphasis is on fast and frequent services linking major cities, while suburban and minor cross-country trains are given lower priority.

### Rolling stock

Steam power was the force that made the railways great, even though it has now been almost entirely replaced by diesel and electric traction. Steam locomotives can still be found at work in South Africa, India and China and eastern Europe, while in Britain various branch lines such as the Severn Valley Railway have been reopened by railway enthusiasts in order to run steam trains.

The steam locomotive is a robust and simple machine. Steam is admitted under pressure from the boiler to the cylinders.

Above: *Venus*, a British Railways 'Britannia' class steam engine, number 70023. The 4-6-2 Britannia class locomotives, which were introduced in 1951, were the first express passenger steam engines to be built by British Railways after they were nationalized on 1 January 1948.

Below: A French electric locomotive. The power is picked up from the overhead cable by the pantograph on the top of the locomotive. The voltages used by electric trains vary from one railway system to another, from 600 V (direct current) to 25,000 V (alternating current).

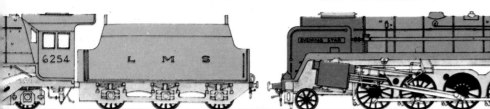

Evening Star — Last British Steam Locomotive 1960

Picturepoint

ZEFA

Above: Mountain railway cars may be self propelled, the driving wheel being a large cog that engages with a toothed rack between the rails, or they may be pulled along by a cable from a fixed winch.

Left: Monorail trains, running on single overhead rails, are used in some cities as an alternative to underground railways.

Below: British Rail's Advanced Passenger Train, designed to run at 240 kph (150 mph) on existing tracks. Its unique suspension system enables it to travel at 200 kph (125 mph) around bends which would limit ordinary trains to 130 kph (80 mph).

British Transport

In the cylinder, steam expands and pushes a piston to the other end. On the return stroke a port opens to clear the exhaust steam. By means of mechanical coupling rods, the travel of the piston turns the driving wheels of the locomotive.

Diesel locomotives are of three main types: diesel-electric, diesel-hydraulic and diesel-mechanical. In the diesel-electric locomotive, the diesel engine drives a dynamo, and the electrical output from the dynamo powers electric motors which drive the wheels. In the diesel-hydraulic, the engine drives a hydraulic transmission, which turns the wheels by a form of miniature turbine, while in the diesel-mechanical locomotive the transmission is by a gearbox, just as in a diesel road vehicle. Diesel-electrics are by far the most common type, although diesel-mechanical locomotives are often used for shunting.

The third main form of motive power is electric traction. The first electric locomotives were powered by batteries, but modern locomotives take current from overhead wires or from a third rail. On the third rail system the current is supplied via the third rail and returned via the running rails. Four-rail systems are also used, on underground railways for example, which have two conductor rails for the supply and return of the current. Modern transmissions and traction motors are small enough to be housed in the bogie of the locomotive, rather than above footplate level as in older designs. Electric locomotives have a very high power-to-weight ratio as they do not have to generate their own power or carry fuel.

The design of railway rolling stock has undergone a development parallel to that of the locomotive. The latest passenger carriages are air-conditioned and are designed to travel at speeds in excess of 161 kph (100 mph). Freight vehicles show a tremendous variety in shape and size, depending on the type of load they have to carry. Modern freight trains are fitted with continuous brakes and can travel at much higher speeds than the old loose-coupled freights.

The track and signalling of modern railways has undergone a similar improvement to cope with faster and more frequent train services. Lengths of continuously welded rail (CWR) a quarter of a mile long considerably reduce the number of rail joints in comparison with standard 18.28 m (60 ft) rail lengths, and most main lines are now laid with CWR. Coloured lights have now largely replaced the old crank-operated semaphore signals and a single control box can now operate a section of line that was formerly controlled by numerous signal boxes.

Before modernization the railways were extremely labour-intensive, but rationalization is now the rule. It is even possible to do away with train drivers altogether, and one-man, semi-automatic trains have been in use on London Transport's Victoria Line since its opening in 1968.

# Military and Space Technology

The space shuttle, a re-usable manned
aircraft, is launched like a rocket from
the parent 'plane, and returns
unpowered to a runway landing. The
liquid-fuel tank is discarded after use.

# Guns

Although the Chinese were using *gunpowder* in rockets and fireworks almost a thousand years ago, there is no hard evidence to show that it was used as a propellant in firearms until the formula reached Europe some time in the thirteenth century. The reason for this lay in the level of technology necessary to construct a suitable barrel, which only existed in the Western world. By the end of the fourteenth century the knowledge of guns was widespread.

Early guns were shaped like flower vases and shot arrows. Arrows were quickly replaced by bullets of metal or stone, although some muskets were still being loaded with arrows at the time of the Spanish Armada. From the very beginning, guns were made in two sizes, the larger for bombardment and the smaller for carrying and firing by hand.

Early hand guns were about 30cm (12in) long, made of iron or bronze and mounted on a long stick so that they could be held in one hand and pointed at the target with the stick tucked under the arm for steadiness. The other hand wielded a glowing match and the charge was ignited through a touch-hole. The cannon were larger and were given pivots or trunnions. They were mounted on wooden carriages derived from farmcarts and dragged by horses. Although they were heavy and cumbersome, needing a large crew to service each gun, they were effective and heralded the end of the mediaeval castle. For over 300 years the design of such guns hardly changed and improvements were only made to ancillary items, not to the overall weapon.

## Firing mechanisms

Things went differently for the handguns, which developed rapidly. The first improvement was the firing mechanism. Carrying the match in one hand was impractical for general use, and the match was soon put into an S-shaped metal lever pivoted on the side of the stock. Pulling the lower end of the lever pushed the match into the touchhole.

The next improvement was to make the match holder in two parts with a finger-lever, or 'tricker' to operate it. The whole mechanism was known as the *matchlock*, and it was used, with very few exceptions, on shoulder arms, muskets and Hackbuts or Arquebus as they came to be known. Pistols were not made with matchlocks, although oddly enough they appeared later on in China and Japan.

Early in the sixteenth century the *wheel-lock* was invented. This used the principle of flint and tinder to produce a spark to ignite the powder. The wheel-lock was far more practical for ordinary use and many were produced, particularly in Germany where the clockmaking industry was ideally suited to making the mechanism required. The successor to the wheel-lock was not long in appearing, and before the end of the sixteenth century the first *flintlocks* were in use.

The flintlock proved to be the most durable and widespread of all the early forms of ignition for it remained in general use for almost 350 years. The flintlock used the same principle of flint and steel as the wheel-lock, but it employed it in a

Photoresources

Above: The 'Tsar's Great Cannon'. This is the largest cannon in the world. It is 5.7 m (17.5 ft) long with a bore of 91.7 cm (36.1 inches) and weighs 40 tonnes. Made from cast iron, it was cast by Andrey Chokhov in 1586 in Moscow.

Right: Bombards on portable gun carriages— from an engraving published in 1575. The mobility of artillery pieces had become an important feature by the end of the fifteenth century; previously the emphasis had been placed on size.

Below: (Top) A brass-mounted flintlock pistol manufactured by Twigg and Bass of London in the late eighteenth century. (Centre) Tap action, boxlock, flintlock pistol. (Bottom) Metal powder flask of the size usually associated with pistols.

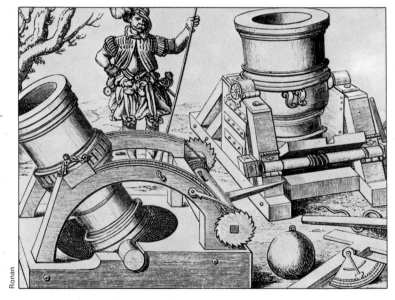

Ronan

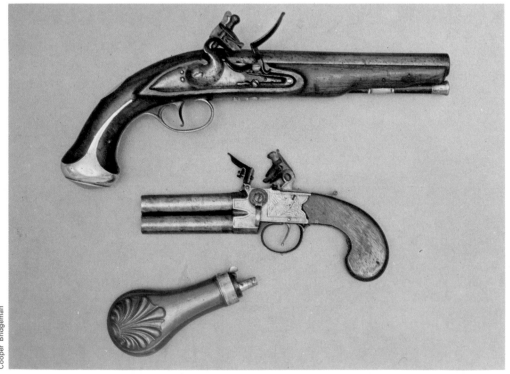

Cooper Bridgeman

Until the 15th century the barrels of portable firearms were fixed to long, straight wooden hafts. Later these were shortened, broadened and curved, so that the recoil was directed upwards instead of straight back against the user.

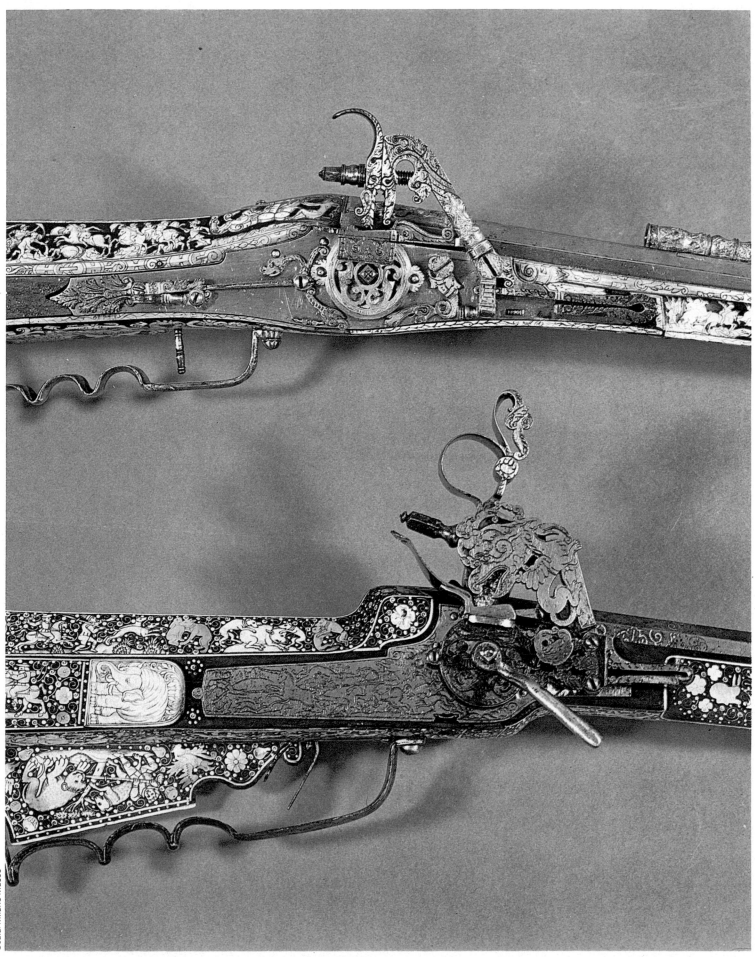

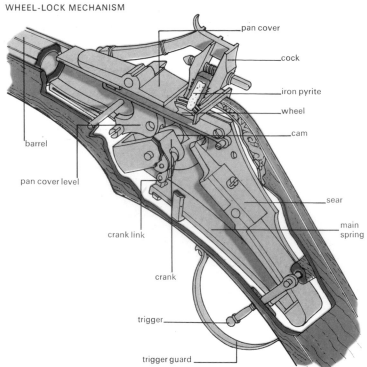

WHEEL-LOCK MECHANISM

- pan cover
- cock
- iron pyrite
- wheel
- cam
- barrel
- pan cover level
- sear
- main spring
- crank link
- crank
- trigger
- trigger guard

FLINTLOCK MECHANISM

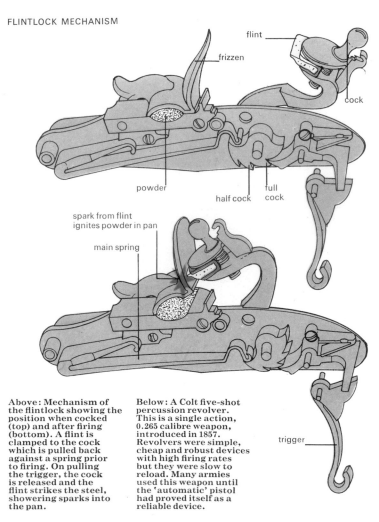

- flint
- frizzen
- cock
- powder
- half cock
- full cock

- spark from flint ignites powder in pan
- main spring
- trigger

COLT REVOLVER MECHANISM

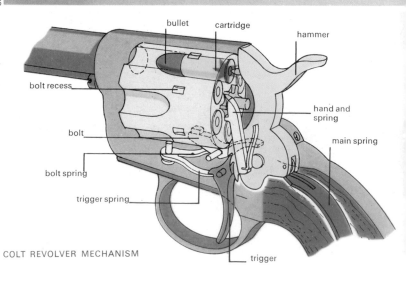

- bullet
- cartridge
- hammer
- bolt recess
- hand and spring
- bolt
- main spring
- bolt spring
- trigger spring
- trigger

**Above: The wheel-lock mechanism.** This involves a steel wheel which is wound up using a winding spanner. A piece of iron pyrite is clamped in the cock which is held under spring tension. A small pan surrounding the wheel contains the primer. Sparks shower onto this when the cock hits the moving wheel.

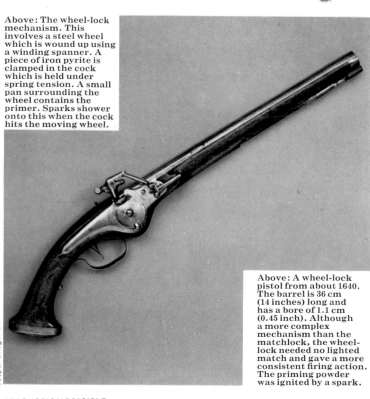

Cooper Bridgeman

**Above: A wheel-lock pistol from about 1640.** The barrel is 36 cm (14 inches) long and has a bore of 1.1 cm (0.45 inch). Although a more complex mechanism than the matchlock, the wheel-lock needed no lighted match and gave a more consistent firing action. The priming powder was ignited by a spark.

**Above: Mechanism of the flintlock showing the position when cocked (top) and after firing (bottom).** A flint is clamped to the cock which is pulled back against a spring prior to firing. On pulling the trigger, the cock is released and the flint strikes the steel, showering sparks into the pan.

**Below: A Colt five-shot percussion revolver.** This is a single action, 0.265 calibre weapon, introduced in 1857. Revolvers were simple, cheap and robust devices with high firing rates but they were slow to reload. Many armies used this weapon until the 'automatic' pistol had proved itself as a reliable device.

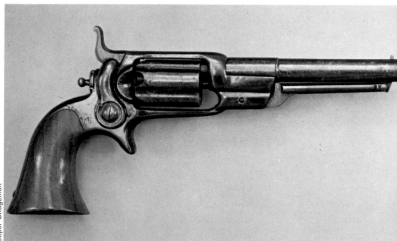

Cooper Bridgeman

PERCUSSION PRICIPLE

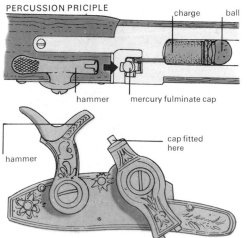

- charge
- ball
- hammer
- mercury fulminate cap
- hammer
- cap fitted here

**Left: The percussion-cap mechanism.** Mercury fulminate was used as the detonating compound and contained in a small inverted cup. This was placed over a narrow steel tube connected to the main chamber containing the charge. On release, the hammer struck the cap and the flash passed down to the main charge.

**Right: The Colt revolver mechanism.** This is the single-action type which means that the chambers are advanced by the action of cocking the hammer; pulling the trigger only releases the hammer. To ensure exact alignment of chamber and barrel, a catch engages with a recess in the cylinder.

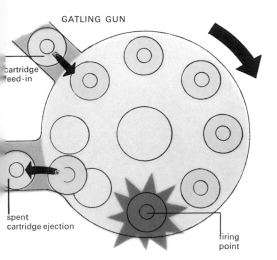

## GATLING GUN

cartridge feed-in

spent cartridge ejection

firing point

**Above: Operation of a multi-barrel Gatling gun. The cartridges were gravity-fed from a hopper above the gun and fired when the barrel reached its lowest position. The cartridge was then ejected. The Gatling gun could fire up to six rounds a second, but modern aircraft types can exceed this.**

**Right: The 1921-model Thompson sub-machine gun with a 20-round box magazine of .45 inch cartridges. The firing rate of this weapon was so great that it could discharge its magazine in less than two seconds. Sub-machine guns are lighter than machine guns with a limited supply of ammunition stored in the magazine.**

Ronan

**Above: A Gatling gun fitted to a camel saddle, from an engraving published in 1872. As the first practical machine gun, the Gatling gun was used in the American Civil War and some were issued to the British Army. Its size and weight, however, limited its potential and it was soon replaced by other designs.**

**Below: The new British 105 mm light field gun. After a prolonged period of development and lengthy acceptance trials, this gun has replaced the Italian designed 105 mm pack howitzer. The great advantage of light field guns is that they can be dismantled for transportation over rough terrain.**

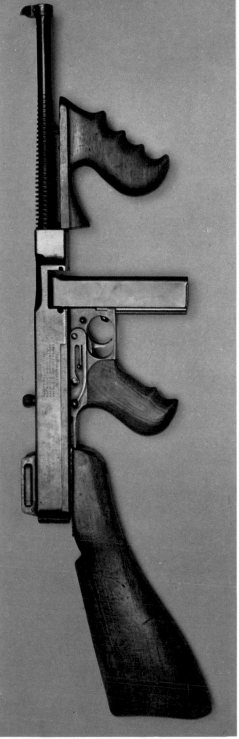

Cooper Bridgeman

Peter Russell/Spectrum

simpler, neater and more reliable way. It was sufficiently cheap to be employed in military arms whereas no army had been able to afford the expensive and delicate wheel-lock guns.

The end of the flintlock era came through the activities of a clergyman. It had been known from the seventeenth century that certain metallic salts such as mercury fulminate would explode if struck sharply and around 1800 the Reverend Alexander Forsyth used these compounds to ignite the main charge. Thus was introduced the last form of the muzzle-loaders, the *percussion cap* gun. They did not last for long.

### Breech-loading guns

About 12 years after the first percussion cap gun was made, a Paris gunmaker, Pauly, made a gun which was loaded at the breech end using a paper cartridge with a metal base. Few were made and an improvement soon appeared. This was the needle gun, using a long needle which travelled through the length of the paper cartridge and struck a percussion cap on the base of the bullet. It was an instant success and led directly to the German victories in the Danish and Austrian wars of the 1860s. But another feature of the needle gun was even more successful: this was the breech mechanism. The breech was closed by a rotating bolt, not unlike a door-bolt. It was strong, simple and highly reliable, and rapidly became the most widely used rifle mechanism of all time. Within a hundred years many millions of bolt action rifles had been made.

Rifles, as opposed to smooth bore guns, were made from the earliest times. Some matchlock guns from about 1500, for example, had *rifling* grooves cut into the barrel, to give the bullet a spin and thus greater accuracy. Others soon followed this example. The difficulty with muzzle-loaded rifles was that they soon became blocked, preventing the bullet from being loaded. Breech loaders had no such trouble, and progress in rifling forms and bullet shape was rapid with the cartridge-loaded weapons. By the middle of the nineteenth century all-metal cartridges had replaced the earlier paper and metal ones, and design was rapidly becoming standardized.

The cartridges were detonated by one of two methods: *rim-fire* or *centre-fire*. In rim-fire cartridges the detonator compound was contained in a thin ring around the inside of the cartridge rim. The striker crushed a small portion of the rim against the breech and so ignited the charge. The advantage of this method lay in the fact that the case could be in one piece and the cost was therefore reasonably low. The centre-fire cartridge, on the other hand, had a percussion cap let into a hole in the centre of the base of the case, which was struck by a pin or hammer to fire the charge. The centre-fire cartridge was more expensive to make, but it withstood greater pressures and gave a more even ignition. Today only very small cartridges, such as the 0.22 inch target and sporting ammunition, use rim-fire detonation. Centre-fire is used in all others.

Many of the first breech loaders used a hinged block to close the breech but these were only suitable for firing single shots. With the introduction of the metal cartridge case, however, designers devised

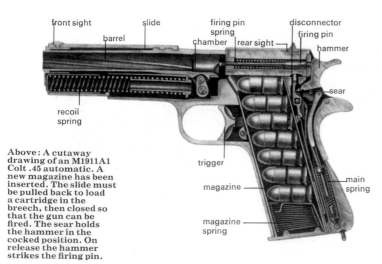

Above: A cutaway drawing of an M1911A1 Colt .45 automatic. A new magazine has been inserted. The slide must be pulled back to load a cartridge in the breech, then closed so that the gun can be fired. The sear holds the hammer in the cocked position. On release the hammer strikes the firing pin.

Labels: front sight, slide, firing pin spring, chamber, rear sight, disconnector, firing pin, hammer, barrel, sear, recoil spring, trigger, magazine, main spring, magazine spring

Right: The Oerlikon MkII anti-aircraft machine gun. A MkII shell with high explosive, incendiary and tracer components is shown below. The gun had a length of 2.4 m and weighed 67 kg (gun only). Its rate of fire was 465 to 480 rounds per minute. Maximum range at 45° elevation was about 1.8 km.

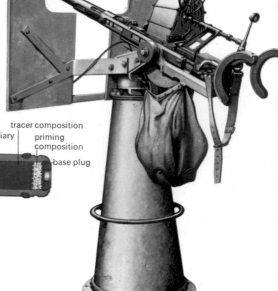

Labels: compression ignition fuse, rear disc, waxed cloth disc, detonator, high explosive filling, incendiary filling, tracer composition, priming composition, base plug

repeating action mechanisms where the cartridges are loaded and fired successively using some hand-operated lever to work the system. One of the earliest of these was the Winchester under-lever repeater so well known from cowboy books and films.

The Winchester rifle carried its ammunition in a tube under the barrel, from where it was fed backwards by spring pressure to a point under the breech. Working the under-lever downwards opened the breech, ejected the empty cartridge case and placed the loading platform opposite a fresh round. The spring pushed the round onto the platform and the action of closing the lever brought the platform up to the breech and pushed the round in, all in one movement. The breech then closed. The mechanism was somewhat complicated, but it was enormously successful and remained in manufacture for over 50 years.

The popular bolt action was made into a hand-operated repeater by placing a magazine beneath the bolt and allowing the bolt to strip a fresh round off the magazine platform as it went forward, pushed by the firer's hand. This was far simpler than the Winchester system and better suited to long, powerful cartridges.

### Revolvers

Wheel and flint-lock mechanisms enabled practical pistols to be made and with the arrival of percussion ignition multibarrel pistols became fashionable. From these the *revolver* was quickly developed. In this, the rounds are stored in the chambers of a cylinder which line up in turn with a single barrel.

The automatic pistol was not invented until the end of the nineteenth century, and the first practical one was made in Germany by Borchardt. This pistol used the force of recoil in the firing of a 9 mm round to push the barrel backwards and operate a mechanism which ejected the spent case, cocked the hammer and fed another round into the breech. The Borchardt was followed by the Mauser and Luger which were derivatives of it, and at the same time a flood of other designs poured out from factories all over the world.

In 1900 in Belgium, the firm of Fabrique Nationale made a compact automatic pistol to the design of the American gunsmith John Browning. This pistol operated by a combination of recoil and blowback, in which the force on the cartridge case actually pushed the bolt backwards.

Peter Russell/Spectrum

Left: An M109 155 mm SP gun at maximum elevation. Note the narrow track and large rear entry doors. These SP (self propelled) guns come into the medium-sized artillery range, with a firing range of between 16 and 24 km (10-15 miles) depending on the size of the shell—usually between 25 and 50 kg.

Below: 35 mm twin anti-aircraft field gun. This is one of the most modern all-weather, medium-range anti-aircraft guns with fully automatic control equipment. It has an effective range up to 4000 m and a firing rate for each gun of 550 rounds per minute. The ammunition is fed automatically.

Below: A German MG 42 machine gun which operates on the recoil system, with a simplified representation of the gas operated and blowback systems. In the MG 42, the bolt is driven forward by the recoil spring when the trigger is depressed. The bolthead drives a cartridge into the barrel chamber and is locked in position by the locking piece. A further small movement forward by the bolt (red arrow) fires the round. The barrel and the bolt recoil and the locking piece releases the bolthead. The cycle is then repeated. A flash hider is fitted to the barrel and, for stability, the gun is mounted on a bipod.

Oerlikon

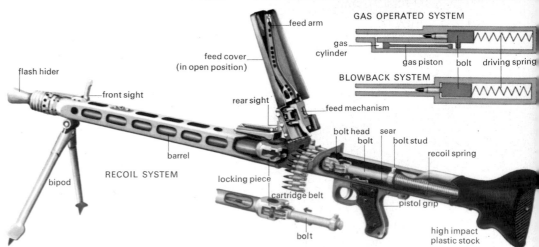

GAS OPERATED SYSTEM

BLOWBACK SYSTEM

RECOIL SYSTEM

Labels: feed arm, gas cylinder, gas piston, bolt, driving spring, feed cover (in open position), rear sight, feed mechanism, flash hider, front sight, bolt head, bolt, sear, bolt stud, recoil spring, barrel, locking piece, cartridge belt, pistol grip, bipod, bolt, high impact plastic stock

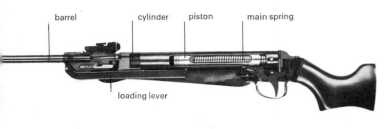

barrel    cylinder    piston    main spring

loading lever

Cooper Bridgeman

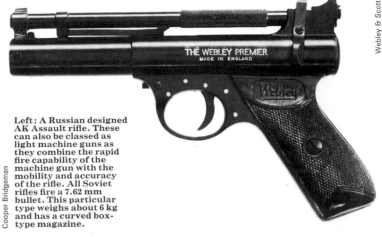

THE WEBLEY PREMIER
MADE IN ENGLAND

Webley & Scott Ltd

**Left: A Russian designed AK Assault rifle. These can also be classed as light machine guns as they combine the rapid fire capability of the machine gun with the mobility and accuracy of the rifle. All Soviet rifles fire a 7.62 mm bullet. This particular type weighs about 6 kg and has a curved box-type magazine.**

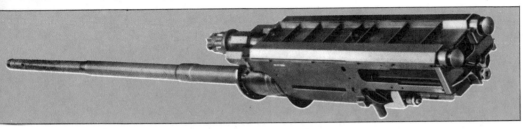

Oerlikon

**Top left: A cutaway diagram of an air rifle. Air guns are weapons in which the force for propelling the bullet (or pellet, as it is more commonly called) is derived from compressed air or gas. The gun is 'primed' by compressing the main spring. This is attached to the piston which fits snugly into the cylinder.**

**Above: An air pistol. With air pistols, a more compact design is required. Here, the barrel is mounted above the piston and cylinder arrangement. To prime the pistol, the barrel is released at the rear and pushed round in an arc. The barrel is connected to the piston via a linkage arm and compresses the spring.**

**Above: An Oerlikon 30 mm aircraft cannon. This is a high-performance cannon which operates on the revolver principle. It is basically designed for installation in tactical aircraft and has an effective range of about 2000 m. Its rate of fire is 1,350 rounds/minute and it has a high muzzle velocity of 1,050 m/sec.**

**Below: An 81 mm Mortar. These have a range exceeding 1.6 km (one mile) although they are usually used for lobbing shells over hills and other obstacles at close quarters. The barrel is smooth and they are muzzle loaded with finned projectiles. As such, mortars stand in a class of their own but are related to artillery.**

Peter Russell/Spectrum

The magazine was in the butt and the whole weapon was light and handy, and it set the pattern which has been followed by most manufacturers since.

### Machine guns

Towards the end of the First World War the Germans produced the first *sub machine gun*, a two-handed, light shoulder gun which fired pistol ammunition from a box magazine containing 30 or more bullets. The Italians did the same in a slightly different and less practical way, and the Americans followed with a larger and heavier version which became the famous, or infamous, 'Thompson' sub machine gun.

From the very beginnings of gun-making there were dreams of a gun that could fire continuously. This could never be done with muzzle-loaders, and it was not until the metal cartridge case came into general use that inventors got to work to make the first *machine gun*. Doctor Gatling produced the first practical model to be made in quantity, a gun consisting of six rifle barrels grouped around a spindle and rotated by hand. Each barrel had a bolt which was opened and closed by a cam-way as the barrels turned. Ammunition dropped in at the top of the circle from a gravity hopper. As the barrel went round the bolt closed, fired when at the bottom and opened again to eject the spent case on the way up.

The Gatling gun was heavy and clumsy and it was not long before single-barrelled machine guns appeared. The best was the invention of another American, Hiram Maxim. He used a single water-cooled barrel and fed the ammunition in with a long cloth belt, each round in a pocket sewn into the belt. His mechanism was complex, but immensely robust. The system used the force of recoil to provide the energy, as in the Borchardt pistol. Maxim's design first appeared in 1882 and was instantly successful. It was adopted all over the world and used by both sides in both World Wars. The British Army, for example, changed it slightly and called it the Vickers gun, and it is still in service

with many armies.

In France, a machine gun was developed which used the pressure of the propellant gas to drive the mechanism. This was the Hotchkiss gun, and the principle of gas operation is the most popular today in all countries. A small hole about half-way down the barrel taps off a little of the propellant gas and conducts it through a tube to a piston. This piston is connected to the bolt and a suitable delay is arranged so that the bullet has left the barrel before the breech opens. Most machine guns fire at about 600 rounds per minute, or 10 shots per second.

Machine guns generate enormous quantities of heat when they are fired and the chief difficulty for the designer is cooling the barrel. Maxim and some others used a water jacket, but this is heavy and vulnerable and modern guns are all cooled by air. This often means having a removable barrel, which can be taken off to cool down while another is fitted.

### Field guns

As the rifles and pistols improved and advanced, so also did the cannons and heavy guns. Breech-loaded field guns gave immensely greater power to any army, and rifled guns enabled cylindrical, pointed shells to be fired. These shells carried a far greater load of explosive than the old circular ball. Smokeless powders appeared in the 1880s and 1890s and these were so much more powerful than gunpowder that it became necessary to use some sort of recoil absorber, otherwise the guns could not be restrained when they fired. This gave rise to a completely new technology of buffering heavy shocks and in its turn enabled yet more powerful guns to be built.

Modern field guns weigh about four tonnes, fire a shell weighing around 20 kg (40 lbs), and have a range of about 16 km (10 miles). They have complicated firing mechanisms and recoil-absorbing gear. The barrels are made from the very highest grade of steel, and they are very expensive.

79

# Explosives

When wood is burnt on a fire, compounds in the wood slowly combine with oxygen and release heat, light and gases. This process is known as *combustion*. With some substances, however, this combustion takes place very rapidly with the sudden release of heat, light and gases and this is called an *explosion*.

The destructive effect of explosives is largely attributable to the rapid and violent release of gases and where this occurs in a confined space, such as in a bomb, the effect is greatly increased. Thus, a small quantity of petrol vapour and air does not produce much of an explosion when it is ignited in the open, but within the cylinders of an internal combustion engine these gases are produced at a pressure of about one million newtons per square metre (several hundred pounds per square inch) and so drive the piston down. Yet even these explosive forces within an internal combustion engine are trivial compared with those produced by modern high explosives. For example, some of the bombs dropped during the Second World War generated at the moment of detonation a pressure of about 3,500,000,000 N/m² (500,000 psi).

## Classification of explosives

Explosives are broadly defined as substances which can undergo rapid combustion, and may be in either solid, liquid or gaseous form. But there are basically two classifications: 'high' and 'low'.

With the *low* explosives, combustion spreads through the material at relatively slow speeds up to 400 m/sec (1,300 ft/sec). With these types of explosives, however, the burning speed increases with pressure which is why their destructive power is enhanced when they are placed in a confined space. This relatively slow combustion is often termed *deflagration* and low explosives are sometimes referred to as *propellant explosives* because they tend to push or propel objects rather than shatter them. They are useful as propellants for shells and rockets.

*High* explosives, on the other hand, undergo extremely rapid combustion and in a completely different way to low explosives. When a high explosive is set off, the combustion sets up a supersonic shockwave or *detonating wave* that travels through the material at between 2,000 and 9,000 m/sec (approximately one to six miles per second). The shockwave disrupts the chemical bonds of the substance, and so initiates combustion as it proceeds—this rapid reaction is known as *detonation*.

High explosives need no container as the shockwave velocity is independent of pressure. The shockwave pressure is, however, extremely high—up to 100 tonnes/cm² (600 tons/sq inch)—and tends to shatter anything in its path. Consequently, they are used in bombs and artillery shells and for blasting in mines.

There are three factors which determine the effectiveness and safety of an explosive: power, velocity of detonation and sensitivity to detonation.

*Power* is measured by the quantity of gas produced by a given weight of the explosive. This is compared with the volume produced from the same weight of picric acid (picric acid is an explosive used as a standard) which is given a rating of 100. Thus, if the relative rating of the test sample is over 100 it is a more powerful explosive than picric acid. For example, PETN, the high explosive in *cordtex* (a detonating cord with industrial and military applications), has a power rating of 166.

*Speed of detonation* is measured directly as a speed (in metres per second or feet per second, for example). Nowadays, this is measured electronically.

Measuring an explosive's *sensitivity to detonation* is based on the fraction of material that will explode when struck and how this relates to the force which is applied. Some extremely insensitive materials will only explode locally and not propagate through the whole explosive when struck. Again, picric acid is used as the standard and given a sensiti-

Left: Preparing charges for blasting at a quarry face. The holes are drilled deep and positioned along the line of the required fault. Firstly, a detonator is placed at the bottom of each hole and then black powder is poured into the holes. Finally, a small amount of sand is carefully placed in the hole to act as a plug. Because the charges must be detonated simultaneously, electrical fuzes are used and these are connected together in series.

Right: With the charges prepared, the detonator leads are taken to this generator.

Below: An explosion in a stone quarry using the benching technique.

K. Hackenberg/ZEFA

Dr. W. C. G. Baldwin

Left: The operating panel of the Biazzi-type glycerine nitrator. Glycerine is fed from the extreme right into the large nitrating vessel (centre right) where it is added to a mixture of *oleum* (super-strong sulphuric acid) and nitric acid. The mixture is stirred mechanically by paddles powered from above. The nitro-glycerine is then fed to the mushroom-shaped gravity separator in the middle. The nitro-glycerine floats above the acid, is collected at the top and fed to the three washers further to the left.

Right: One type of machine used for packaging nitro-glycerine powders.

Dr. W. C. G. Baldwin

**QUARRYING**

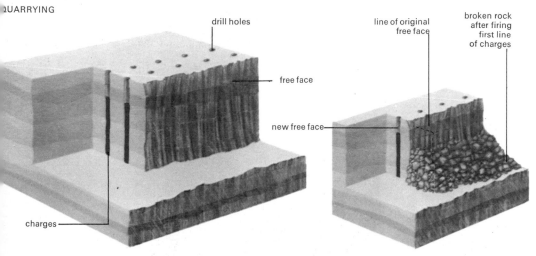

drill holes

line of original free face

broken rock after firing first line of charges

free face

new free face

charges

**Above: Where sequential blasting is required it may be advantageous to use slow-burning time fuzes. Such a fuze is shown here. Where several are to be lit in sequence, some warning must be given to the operator when the detonation is due. To achieve this, an ingredient is added to the fuze which produces a red flash one minute before the explosive is detonated.**

**Left: A lorry for the transportation of *prilled* ammonium nitrate (in the form of ball-bearings about 2 mm in diameter). This is mixed with about 5% oil and fed by pump to the required location such as the shot holes drilled into the ground in quarry blasting.**

**Above: How drill-holes are positioned for blasting in a stone quarry. The method is known as benching. Each bench may be 15 to 20 m high. The holes are placed about 4 m back from the face and spaced about every 4 m. The exact positioning will depend on the nature of the rock and its intended purpose. This will also determine the type of explosive used. High explosives will fragment rocks suitable for road chippings. Low explosives are used for large masonry blocks.**

**Left: Explosives are often used in civil engineering. This explosion near Kazakhstan in the USSR helped to excavate a basin for an ice-skating rink.**

vity rating of 100. Explosives with a sensitivity rating of less than 100 are more sensitive, unstable and unsafe.

## Types of explosive

Gunpowder was the first of all explosives and is still used in many types of fireworks. Although gunpowder had been used by the Chinese for thousands of years in fireworks and as a propellant in a primitive type of military rocket fired from a leather launcher, it was unknown in Europe until the mid-thirteenth century. The first European to make written reference to gunpowder was the English monk Roger Bacon who described its potentialities as a military weapon in his book *De Secretis Operibus Artis et Naturae* (The Secret Works of Art and Nature) published in 1245.

Today, gunpowder consists of 75 per cent potassium nitrate (saltpetre), 15 per cent charcoal and 10 per cent sulphur and when burned it releases about 3,000 times its own volume in gases. Its explosive action is due to the charcoal and sulphur burning in the oxygen released by the saltpetre. Gunpowder is classified as a low explosive.

Black powder, or blasting powder as it is often called because of its early use in quarries, is really a minor development of gunpowder. By reducing the saltpetre content, the rate of combustion is slowed down thus making it more suitable for quarrying building-stone where shattering is not required. It was once used as a propellant in firearms and artillery pieces, but it suffered from the disadvantage that it released enormous amounts of thick smoke which not only betrayed the position of the gunner but also interfered with his aim. Gunpowder and black powder ceased to be used as military explosives with the invention of the smokeless powders based on nitro-cellulose.

One of the landmarks in the development of explosives was guncotton—the first useful high explosive. It was compounded by the German chemist Christian Schönbein in 1845. Guncotton was originally made by treating cotton fibre with strong sulphuric and nitric acids, but this was found to be a rather unstable compound. Today, it is made by treating paper or wood shavings with sulphuric and nitric acids and for that reason is generally called nitro-cellulose. Nitro-cellulose has a sensitivity rating of 23 when dry and about 120 when wet. Depending on its preparation, its final state (for example, whether it is wet or dry) and its blending with other ingredients, nitro-cellulose can be used as either a high or low explosive. As a low explosive it was once used as a propellant for artillery shells.

In 1846, Ascanio Sobrero, Professor of Chemistry at Turin Institute of Technology, discovered nitro-glycerine. This is an extremely powerful explosive—it releases 12,000 times its own volume of gas when exploded, has a power rating of 160 and a detonation speed of 7,750 m/sec (25,426 ft/sec). Nitro-glycerine is made by dripping glycerine slowly into strong sulphuric and nitric acids. For some years after it was first compounded, it was too dangerous to handle as it could be set off by mere shaking or rough handling. It had a sensitivity rating of only 13.

In 1886, the Swedish chemist Alfred Nobel discovered that if nitro-glycerine was mixed with a kind of clay called kieselguhr it became a semi-solid substance with the consistency of cheese which could be rolled into sticks. Nobel named his improved nitro-glycerine *dynamite*. Although dynamite is a less powerful explosive than the original nitro-glycerine, it is relatively safe to handle and responds only to sharp and heavy impact. In much of the dynamite used today, ammonium nitrate replaces a large proportion of the nitro-glycerine, while in place of the absorbent kieselguhr, wood-pulp mixed with sodium nitrate is used as a safety factor. Because of dynamite's convenience and cheapness, it is extensively used for quarrying.

Picric acid was first prepared by Woulfe in 1771 by the nitration of phenol. Although it is a powerful explosive comparable with nitro-cellulose and nitroglycerine, it is much less sensitive and for over a hundred years it was found difficult to detonate. By 1888, however, it had replaced gunpowder as a shell-filling with a mercury fulminate cap as a detonator. Picric acid is of little use today except as a standard.

Because of their devastatingly shattering effects, high explosives constitute the explosive elements in the shells and bombs used in warfare. The high explosive most commonly used in both world wars, for example, was trinitrotoluene, better known as TNT. This has a power rating of 95, a detonation speed of 7,000 m/sec and a sensitivity rating of 110. Another important explosive is pentaerythritol tetranitrate or PETN. This has a power rating of 166, a detonation speed of 8,100 m/sec and a sensitivity rating of 40.

RDX, also called *Hexogen* or *Cyclonite*, is a very powerful explosive (power rating 167) discovered by a German called Henning in 1899. It also has one of the highest detonation speeds at 8,400 m/s, and a sensitivity rating of 55.

## Detonators

One of the characteristics of high explosives is that they are not easily set off or exploded by themselves, either by heat, flame, friction or impact. Indeed, some explosives merely burn fiercely when ignited but do not explode.

Consequently, high explosives need some method or substance to initiate their explosion. These initiators are called primary explosives or *detonators* and work by creating a high pressure shockwave which triggers the main explosive. Examples of primary explosives are mercury fulminate, lead azide, copper

acetylide, silver acetylide, nitrogen sulphide, fulminating gold, nitrogen chloride, tetracene, lead styphnate and mixtures of chlorates with red phosphorous or sulphur.

To obtain complete combustion of the main explosive and consequently the maximum destructive effect from it, a quantity of a powerful but moderately sensitive high explosive is used to boost or reinforce the detonating or primary explosive. This booster is called an *intermediary charge*. The more sensitive explosives, with values around 20 are used as the primary charge. The impulse from this can set off the intermediary charge (with a sensitivity of about 60) which in turn will initiate the shockwave in the main (high) explosive. For example, to detonate TNT (sensitivity 110), a detonating cap with a mercury fulminate primary (sensitivity 8) and a tetryl intermediary charge (sensitivity 70) may be used.

## How explosives work

Although the mechanisms of combustion differ widely between deflagrating and detonating explosives, the chemical processes involved are essentially the same. During an explosion, oxygen is rapidly consumed and because this cannot be readily obtained from the air the explosive

*Spectrum*

Above: Positioning charges to remove a large tree stump with laterally spreading roots. The charges are usually placed under the largest roots. Electrical fuzes are used because the charges must be detonated together.

Right: Demolishing a tall factory chimney with explosives. If

correctly placed, only a small amount of explosive is required.

Below: A general purpose bomb designed to explode after penetrating the upper floor of a building. The firing pin and primer are screwed into contact with the booster charge by the propeller as the bomb falls through the air.

Above: Unblocking a canal with explosives. Unlike quarry explosions, which are accompanied by large amounts of dust which hide the hot expanding gases, in this photograph the fireball can be clearly seen. It gives an impression of the temperature of the liberated gases. Much of an explosion's destructive effect, however, is due to the inrush of air immediately after detonation.

Right: The British Army demolishing Gillhall House—a seventeenth century stately home. The charges are placed at the base of the house and ignited simultaneously using electrical fuzes for maximum effect.

*Syndication International*

must incorporate its own supply. For this reason explosives include chemicals such as ammonium nitrate which are rich in oxygen.

Nitrogen compounds are used extensively in explosives because of their chemical instability. Indeed, an explosive might be described as an unstable substance which undergoes a complete transformation within a very short period of time—in other words, a mixture of substances which are in unstable equilibrium. This equilibrium is upset when the mixture is ignited or detonated.

As combustion proceeds through the material, the originally large molecules of the explosive are converted into a large number of smaller molecules (gases) and heat is released. Initially, these gases are confined in a small volume at a high temperature and therefore exert a tremendous pressure.

In low explosives, combustion takes place throughout the whole material but not instantaneously. The hot gases under high pressure that are generated accelerate the total combustion until the container ruptures. With high explosives, however, no container is required. Nearly all the combustion takes place on the front of the detonating wave as it travels through the material. Thus, the combustion *spreads through* the material, albeit in a very short time—no more than a few millionths of a second.

### The blast wave

As the gases expand into the air they set up a blast or pressure wave that travels in all directions at speeds up to 335 m/sec (1,100 ft/sec). This pressure wave forces away the surrounding air and any other objects in its path. There is, however, a secondary effect. In the vicinity of the explosion, where the air has been displaced, a partial vacuum is created into which air rushes to reestablish normal atmospheric pressure.

Although the pulling effect of the vacuum is weaker than the pressure wave, it lasts longer. As a result, objects which have been merely weakened by the initial pressure wave are further damaged and sometimes completely demolished by this secondary effect. That is why windows some distance from a blast may actually be sucked towards the source of the explosion rather than away from it.

### Applications

Rather unexpectedly, figures show that more explosives are employed for peaceful purposes than were ever used in warfare. For example, vast quantities are used in mining, quarrying and demolition. Without explosives to cut through or loosen rock and hard ground, the boring of tunnels and the building of canals would be almost impossible.

Carefully controlled explosions of small charges are used for cutting heavy steel and for forming metals into required shapes. In this latter application, called *explosive forming*, the sheet of metal is placed over the open end of a die mould and together they are enclosed in a sealed chamber containing an explosive charge. When the explosive is detonated, the gases force the metal into the die where it is shaped. A similar technique is used for the cold-welding of dissimilar metals. Explosive forming can also be used for compressing powdered metals into dies to form solid shapes.

Above right: East German border guards placing explosives along the East/West border in the Harz mountains. Although explosives are the stock-in-trade of all modern armies, more are used for peaceful purposes. It is also true, however, that many of the major advances in explosives technology throughout the centuries have resulted from military experience.

Left: A percussion fuze with mercury fulminate primary and a booster (or intermediary) charge. Detonators are classed as either *igniferous* (heat producing) or *disruptive* (producing shockwaves) depending on which initiates the main explosion.

HAND GRENADE

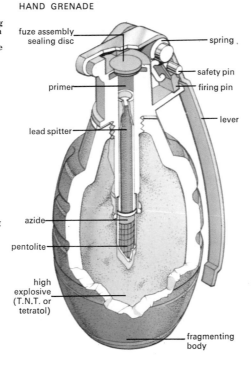

fuze assembly sealing disc
spring
safety pin
primer
firing pin
lead spitter
lever
azide
pentolite
high explosive (T.N.T. or tetratol)
fragmenting body

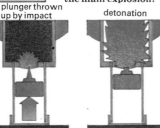

plunger thrown up by impact

detonation

fulminate of mercury

firing pin

plunger

safety pin

Above: The basic mechanism of a hand grenade. When the lever is released, the spring tensioned firing pin strikes the time fuze primer. This triggers the time fuze which finally sets off the primer, intermediary charge and main explosive. Time fuzes or an electric current are the main methods for setting off detonators.

Left: This lump of iron, left at the bottom of a demolished blast furnace, is to be fragmented using explosives. Holes are being cut in the iron with a thermic lance into which the explosive charges can be placed. In this particular case, high explosives are necessary.

# Warships and Submarines

The development of the modern warship began in the middle of the nineteenth century, when the first steam-driven, armour-plated warships went into service. Until this time, the navies of the world were equipped with wooden-hulled sailing ships armed with rows of cannon. Ships of this type had ruled the seas for centuries, but they became obsolete in a matter of only a few years.

Armour-plated ships were first developed in response to the use of explosive shells. In November 1853, in a naval battle between Russia and Turkey, Russian ships destroyed seven Turkish frigates in the Black Sea, and attacked the town of Sinop. Three thousand Turks died in the battle, but only 40 Russians. The Russian success was largely due to their use of explosive shells instead of the ordinary solid cannonballs.

This dramatic demonstration of the ineffectiveness of unprotected wooden hulls caused a major change in warship design. Armour plating was now essential and the new ships were fitted with steam engines as well as sails to compensate for their greatly increased weight.

The first armoured warship was the French frigate *La Gloire*, designed by Dupuy de Lôme and built in 1859. It had a wooden hull protected by 120 mm (4.72 in) thick iron armour plate. Its displacement was 5,600 tonnes. At the same time the British Royal Navy was building the warship *Warrior*, under the direction of Isaac Watts, which was the first armoured warship built entirely of iron. Construction began in 1859 and it was launched in 1861. Soon after completion the *Warrior* was fitted with two of a new type of naval gun which had a rifled bore for greater accuracy.

Breech-loading guns, which could be re-loaded and fired more quickly than the muzzle-loading guns, were installed on the *Hercules* in 1867, a vessel which had armour from 152 to 248 mm (6 to 9.75 in) thick. After the *Warrior* and the *Hercules* came a long contest between advances in the effectiveness of guns and advances in armour design, from which the 'belt and battery' system evolved. This system used thick armour to protect a battery of heavy guns placed amidships, but allowed the 'belt' of armour around the hull to be reduced in thickness at the less vulnerable regions near the ends of the ship.

As naval guns became larger and more powerful, the armament of the ships was concentrated in this central battery. However, it was later decided that it was better to place the large guns on revolving turrets, widely separated around the vessel, so that a single shell could not put all the guns out of action, as was possible when they were all grouped together. The rotating turrets enabled the guns to be fired to either side of the vessel and, in addition, the guns could be aimed without have to turn the whole ship. HMS *Devastation*, 1873, was the first turret battleship without sail, laying down the design principles for the future battleships.

On 28 May 1905, the Japanese navy

*Imperial War Museum*

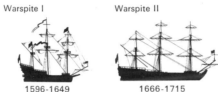

Warspite I
1596-1649

Warspite II
1666-1715

The eight Royal Navy ships that have had the name *Warspite*. The first, launched in 1596, displaced 648 tonnes and was armed with 36 guns. The first steam-powered *Warspite*, launched in 1884, displaced 8,400 tonnes, followed in 1913 by a 27,000 tonne ship. The eighth is a nuclear submarine.

Above: The *Dreadnought*, launched in 1906, which set new standards of armour and fire power. It was also the first turbine-powered battleship; the 18,420 kW (24,700 hp) produced by its four Parsons steam turbines gave it a speed of over 21 knots. Its displacement was 22,500 tonnes.

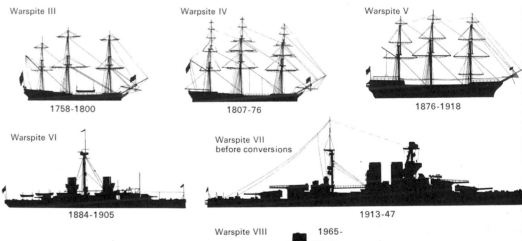

Warspite III
1758-1800

Warspite IV
1807-76

Warspite V
1876-1918

Warspite VI
1884-1905

Warspite VII
before conversions
1913-47

Warspite VIII    1965-

COI

Left: The commissioning ceremony of the nuclear powered fleet submarine HMS *Warspite*, when it formally went into service with the Royal Navy. It is 87 m (285 ft) long and 10 m (33 ft) wide, and displaces 4,500 tonnes when submerged. Its underwater speed is 30 knots and it is armed with torpedoes.

Right: A guided missile cruiser of the Russian Navy, now possibly the most powerful navy in the world. The first guided missile cruisers were converted from conventionally-armed ships, the first purpose-built guided missile cruiser being the 14,000 tonne, nuclear-powered, USS *Long Beach*, launched in July 1959.

**HMS BRISTOL**
1  Laundry
2  Anti-submarine mortar
3  Helicopter flight deck
4  Sea Dart missiles
5  Mess decks
6  Missile control radar
7  Funnels for gas turbines
8  Surface search radar
9  Engine rooms
10  Funnel for steam turbines
11  Air search radar
12  Ikara control radar
13  Ikara missiles
14  4.5 in gun

Left: The American warship USS *Alabama*.

Above: The Type 82 guided missile destroyer HMS *Bristol*, which displaces 6,000 tonnes and is 154.5 m (507 ft) long and 16.8 m (55 ft) wide. It is driven by steam and gas turbines, and is used to test Sea Dart and Ikara missile systems. The Sea Dart is radar-guided, with a range of over 30 km (19 miles); the Ikara is a kind of small, radio-controlled plane that carries a homing torpedo. The Ikara flies near its target, and then releases the torpedo, which homes in on the sounds made by the target.

defeated a Russian fleet at the Battle of Tsushima Strait. An analysis of this battle led Admiral Fisher to design a new type of battleship for the British Navy. He concluded that what was needed was a heavily-armoured ship, armed with large guns capable of accurate fire over a long distance. The ship he designed was the *Dreadnought*, fitted with ten 305 mm (12 in) guns and 280 mm (11 in) armour. The *Dreadnought* was launched in 1906, having been built in only a year, and its armour and fire power set the pattern for the battleships of other nations.

The Washington Naval Treaty of 1921, which limited the displacement of capital ships to 35,000 tonnes, had a great effect on warship design. It meant that Britain could no longer build massive warships like the *Hood*, completed in 1920, which had a displacement of 42,000 tonnes and carried eight 380 mm (15 in) guns. This restriction on the size of warships, together with limitations of the numbers of warships each nation was allowed to have, effectively prevented Britain from being the dominant naval power in the world.

The major naval powers continued building battleships, subject to the treaty limitations, but the Second World War showed that such ships were no longer really effective, as their big guns were no defence against torpedoes and aircraft. The last British battleship was the *Vanguard*, completed in 1946, and the principal ships of the Russian and American navies are now the aircraft carriers.

Another class of warship, similar to the battleship but smaller, is the cruiser. Cruisers are fast and were used to patrol

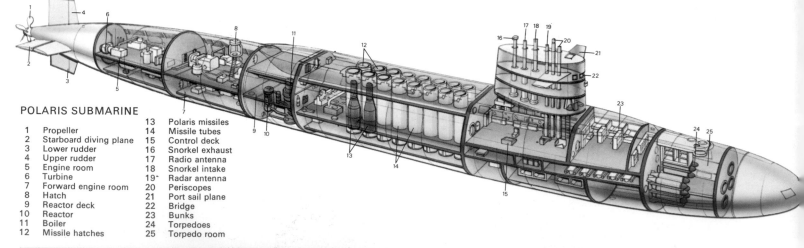

## POLARIS SUBMARINE

| | | | |
|---|---|---|---|
| 1 | Propeller | 13 | Polaris missiles |
| 2 | Starboard diving plane | 14 | Missile tubes |
| 3 | Lower rudder | 15 | Control deck |
| 4 | Upper rudder | 16 | Snorkel exhaust |
| 5 | Engine room | 17 | Radio antenna |
| 6 | Turbine | 18 | Snorkel intake |
| 7 | Forward engine room | 19 | Radar antenna |
| 8 | Hatch | 20 | Periscopes |
| 9 | Reactor deck | 21 | Port sail plane |
| 10 | Reactor | 22 | Bridge |
| 11 | Boiler | 23 | Bunks |
| 12 | Missile hatches | 24 | Torpedoes |
| | | 25 | Torpedo room |

Left: A royal Navy task force on manoeuvres in the English Channel in 1975. The vessels shown here are, from left to right, the frigates *Tartar*, *Londonderry*, *Rothesay* and a Leander class frigate. The helicopter on *Tartar* is a Westland Wasp, which is an anti-submarine helicopter.

Above: A cutaway of a nuclear submarine equipped with Polaris nuclear missiles. The Polaris missiles can be launched from under the water, and have a range of 4,500 km (2,800 miles). The latest versions carry multiple warheads. This submarine is also armed with conventional torpedoes.

Below: The Lockheed Corporation are building Deep Submergence Rescue Vehicles (DSRVs) for the US Navy. These vehicles are designed to rescue crew members from damaged submarines at depths of about 1,220 m (4,000 ft). Operated by a crew of two, they can rescue 24 men at a time.

shipping routes, typical armament being 152 mm (6 in) or 203 mm (8 in) guns and displacement ranging from 4,000 to 12,000 tonnes, with thinner side armour than that used on battleships. Modern cruisers are armed with guided missiles.

### Destroyers

Destroyers are smaller than cruisers, but fast and well-armed. In the First World War they were used to attack the enemy battle fleets with torpedoes and to prevent the enemy flotillas from attacking merchant convoys or naval vessels. They also acted as a screen against possible submarine attack. In the Second World War destroyers were fitted with anti-aircraft guns, anti-submarine depth charges and greatly improved submarine detection equipment.

The thinly-armoured guided missile destroyer (GMD) has become one of the most important surface vessels. The British County class destroyers are an example of this kind of warship. They have a displacement of over 6,000 tonnes and are powered by both steam turbines and gas turbines. Their armament consists of two 114 mm (4.5 in) guns, plus Seacat, Seaslug and Exocet guided missiles which can be used against aircraft or surface targets. In addition, each ship carries a Lynx helicopter, armed with homing torpedoes, for anti-submarine work.

Modern destroyers such as these are very expensive because, as well as having costly propulsion and weapons systems, they also have many features not fitted to earlier types. These features include reversible-pitch propellers, stabilizers, and the special closing and washing-down facilities needed for protection against

nuclear fall-out. A modern destroyer can provide long and close range anti-aircraft cover for the fleet, and it can defend surface forces against a ship attack. They may also act as radar stations to direct aircraft attacks and they can be used to hunt and destroy submarines.

### Frigates

Frigates are fast vessels originally used for fleet reconnaissance work. The frigates used in the Second World War for convoy escort were characterized by a single gun main armament, with no torpedo tubes but with a powerful battery of anti-aircraft guns. Corvettes, smaller than frigates but with anti-submarine weapons and detection equipment, were also used for convoy escort. Post-war development was aimed at producing three principal types of frigate, namely anti-submarine, anti-aircraft and aircraft direction. Designs capable of fulfilling all of these roles, the general purpose frigates, were later introduced.

Modern frigates, such as the British 'Broadsword' class, often have a greater displacement than the destroyers used in the Second World War and may carry more hitting power than some battleships of that period. The armament used on the new frigates includes surface-to-air, surface-to-surface and anti-submarine missiles, anti-submarine torpedoes, guns, and torpedo-carrying helicopters.

### Aircraft carriers

The idea of using a ship as an aircraft carrier began before the First World War —the first aircraft take-off from a ship happened on 14 November 1910, when Eugene Ely flew a Curtiss biplane from a

platform built on the bows of the USS *Birmingham*. In January of the following year, Ely was the first to land a plane on a ship, in this case on a platform on the after-deck of the USS *Pennsylvania*.

During the Second World War the aircraft carrier took over from the battleship as the heart of the naval battle force. After the war the introduction of jet aircraft resulted in several modifications to carrier design. The higher take-off and landing speeds required by jet aircraft led to the introduction of steam-powered catapults to accelerate the jets along the deck at take-off. The carriers were fitted with angled flight decks to enable aircraft to take-off along the angled section while others were landing on the straight section.

The Royal Navy will shortly have three modern 'Invincible' class carriers — with a displacement of 19,500 tonnes and powered by gas turbine engines — carrying Sea Harrier fighters, Sea King Helicopters and Sea Dart surface-to-air missiles.

The US Navy has a fleet of modern carriers, including the nuclear powered *Enterprise*, with a displacement of 83,350 tonnes and a flight deck measuring 335.6 m (1,101 ft) by 76.8 m (252 ft). Recent advances have led to ships of the marginally larger *Nimitz* class.

### Fast patrol boats

The first coastal motor boats (CMBs), were developed by Thorneycrofts in England in 1916, and were powered by petrol engines which gave them a speed of over 30 knots. They were armed with torpedoes and later versions were equipped for minelaying work. American motor launches developed during the First World

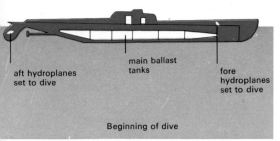

aft hydroplanes
set to dive

main ballast
tanks

fore
hydroplanes
set to dive

Beginning of dive

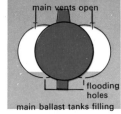

main vents open

flooding
holes

main ballast tanks filling

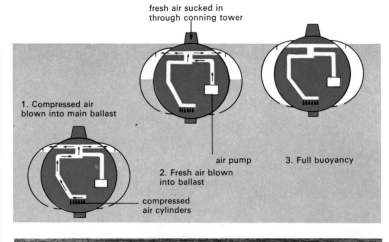

fresh air sucked in
through conning tower

1. Compressed air
blown into main ballast

2. Fresh air blown
into ballast

air pump

3. Full buoyancy

compressed
air cylinders

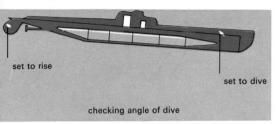

set to rise

set to dive

checking angle of dive

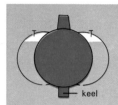

keel

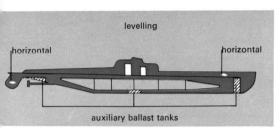

levelling

horizontal

horizontal

auxiliary ballast tanks

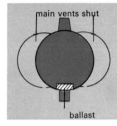

main vents shut

ballast

**Above:** Submarines dive by flooding the main ballast tanks with water and setting the hydroplanes to the 'dive' position. Once a sub is submerged, the rear hydroplanes are re-set to control the dive angle, and when it is at the desired depth it is levelled by flooding small internal ballast tanks.

**Above right:** A submarine surfaces by using its hydroplanes to bring it close to the surface, then following the procedure shown here. It begins blowing the water out of the ballast tanks with compressed air, and as the conning tower leaves the water it sucks in fresh air to finish the process.

**Right:** The *Dat Assawari*, a modern frigate of the Libyan Navy built by Vosper Thorneycroft in Britain. Modern frigates have displacements of up to about 5,000 tonnes.

**Below:** The Polaris missile room in the nuclear submarine HMS *Resolution*.

War were used for anti-submarine work.

During the Second World War, small, fast coastal craft were widely used as harbour defence launches, motor torpedo boats and motor gun boats. Modern patrol boats are powered by gas turbine engines and are capable of speeds of over 50 knots, some of the faster craft being hydrofoil boats.

## Minesweepers

Minesweepers have non-magnetic hulls built from glass-reinforced plastic, aluminium or wood—this means they do not trigger off mines which are activated by the magnetic disturbance caused by a metal hull passing near them. Magnetic mines are exploded by trailing a cable, carrying a pulsating electric current, from the stern of the minesweeper. Acoustic mines, triggered by sound waves created by the engines and propellers of a nearby ship, are detonated by a noise generator which is towed behind the minesweeper.

## Submarines

Despite many attempts to build submarines, from the seventeenth century onwards, real naval interest in submarines did not begin until the early twentieth century, but submarine development proceeded rapidly once the major navies began to build them. Most early subs used battery-powered electric motors to propel them while submerged, with petrol or steam engines to drive them on the surface and generate power to recharge the batteries. The role of the petrol and steam engines was soon taken over by the diesel engine, and the diesel/electric system is still used on all sub-

**Above: The Aircraft Direction Room of the aircraft carrier HMS Ark Royal.**

**Right: The US Navy's Enterprise, the world's first nuclear-powered aircraft carrier, which was launched on 24 September 1960. The ship's turbines produce about 223,710 kW (300,000 hp), giving it a cruising speed of about 33 knots. The larger aircraft are F-4 Phantom fighter-bombers and the smaller ones are A-4 Skyhawk light attack bombers. The aircraft are kept in hangars below the flight deck, and their wings can be folded so that they take up less space in the hangars. The ship is armed with anti-aircraft missiles instead of guns.**

**Above: Assault vessels leaving the dock at the stern of an assault ship. These vessels are used for ferrying troops and light equipment ashore.**

**Below: A Boeing Sea Knight anti-submarine helicopter lands on the helicopter deck of an assault ship, as a light assault vessel**

enters the dock below it. Assault ships can also carry Harrier vertical take-off jets, and large assault vessels capable of carrying tanks, self-propelled guns and other heavy equipment. The ships themselves are armed with guided missiles and anti-aircraft guns for self-defence.

**Above: HMS Brave Borderer, a fast patrol boat of the Royal Navy, travelling at over 50 knots. The first fast patrol boats, built in 1916, were coastal motor boats and had a speed of about 30 knots. They were armed with torpedoes, as is the modern boat shown here, and later versions were equipped for minelaying work. During the Second World War small, fast coastal craft were widely used as harbour defence launches, motor torpedo boats and motor gun boats. Modern patrol boats are powered by gas turbine engines and some of them are fitted with hydrofoils. Many are equipped with anti-aircraft and anti-ship missiles as well as guns and torpedoes.**

marines except nuclear vessels.

Submarines are fitted with pairs of *hydroplanes*, horizontal rudders rather like small wings, whose angles can be altered so as to direct the vessel upwards or downwards as it moves forwards under the thrust from its propeller. When a submarine dives, it opens valves which admit sea water into its *ballast tanks*, thus reducing its buoyancy, and the hydroplanes are angled to direct it downwards. To surface again, the hydroplanes are angled so as to direct it upwards, and when it is just below the surface the water is blown out of the ballast tanks by compressed air to restore its buoyancy and enable it to float normally on the surface.

The development of the *periscope* enabled submarines to travel inconspicuously just below the surface yet still see what was going on there. Another development which aided this was the *schnorkel* (also called a *snorkel* or *snort*), a retractable arrangement of vent pipes which allowed the vessel to draw in fresh air while at periscope depth. This allowed the sub to run at periscope depth on its diesel engines, the schnorkel system supplying the engines with air and removing their exhaust fumes.

The first nuclear-powered submarine was the USS *Nautilus*, which made its first run under nuclear power on 17 January 1955. The nuclear power plant uses heat from a nuclear reactor to raise steam to drive its propulsion turbines, and also to drive a turbogenerator which generates the electricity needed by the vessel. Exhaust steam from the turbines is condensed, and the water is returned to the reactor for re-use.

U.S.S. *Will Rodgers* (dived displacement 8,250 tons) was commissioned in April 1967. The 41st Fleet Ballistic Missile submarine authorised by U.S. Congress, she is 425 feet long and manned by two crews alternating every two months.

Dirck Halstead/Contact/Colorific

# Rockets and Missiles

Of all those confusing and remote doctrines of the classroom, Isaac Newton's Third Law of Motion must surely rank among the most well remembered. This 300-year-old law stating that 'every action must have an equal and opposite reaction' has maintained a dramatic significance on world events through its most direct application—the rocket.

A rocket is simply a device or vehicle propelled by the expulsion of a stream of matter (usually gas) from it. The emerging surge of matter imparts an equal and opposite force to the vehicle itself. The inflated balloon or the garden hose nozzle are everyday examples of the principle—both come to rather eccentric (unguided) life when released. The escaping jet of air or water generates a *reactive thrust*.

A rocket vehicle does not fly, but maintains travel under impetus. A thrown ball continues until air resistance (or *drag*) and gravity overcome its projected force. Likewise, a rocket will continue to ascend for a little while after its engine cuts out, and then the combination of drag and gravity will slow it so that it falls back to Earth in an arc corresponding to that of its ascent. This is called a *ballistic* course or trajectory and can be used as a means of delivering a warhead from one part of the Earth to another in the shortest possible time.

The more a rocket accelerates and the higher the speed attained, the farther it will be 'thrown' before it falls back to Earth. Eventually it will reach a speed where its fall will take it constantly beyond the Earth's curvature and it will continue to fall around the Earth for ever, or until slowed by rocket thrust or fringe atmospheric particles. It is then in orbit. The minimum speed necessary for this is nearly 7,925 metres per second (26,000 ft/sec.). In this application the rocket is usually called a *launch vehicle*.

## Rocket development

The rocket owes its development largely to the needs of war. Its first known use was to provide power assistance to the arrows and spears of the thirteenth century Chinese against the Mongols who, in turn, developed it for use against the Arabs, who then introduced it warmly to the French Crusaders. Brought to Europe, the rocket was used by the French against the British at Orleans in 1429.

The emergence of the more accurate cannon reduced the rocket's military value for 300 years until the late eighteenth century, when British troops fighting in India found themselves once again on the receiving end of fiery salvos. This time they took notice, and the early nineteenth century saw extensive efforts, notably by Sir William Congreve and later by William Hale, to produce effective war rockets. Their work led to a naval bombardment weapon, to marine distress and rescue rockets, and to the

Above: The Russian rocket pioneer Konstantin Tsiolkovsky (1857-1935), working on a model of one of his rocket designs.

Below: A model of the West German ORTAG rocket, a low-cost vehicle designed to burn diesel oil and nitric acid.

Left: A Titan/Centaur rocket of the kind used to carry the Viking missions to Mars. The rocket is 48.8 m (160 ft) tall, and consists of two solid-fuel boosters, a US Air Force Titan III, and a NASA high-energy Centaur final stage. The lift-off thrust of the boosters is 2.4 million pounds.

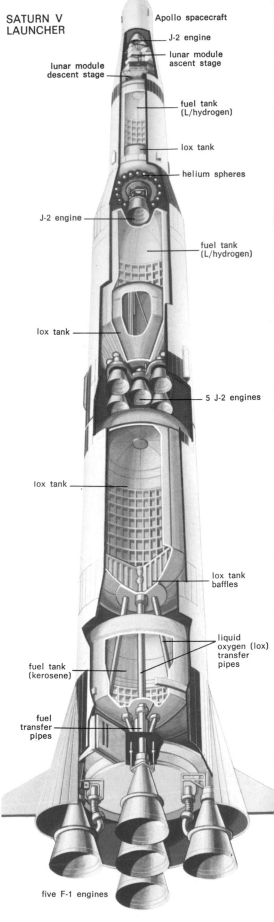

SATURN V LAUNCHER

- Apollo spacecraft
- J-2 engine
- lunar module ascent stage
- lunar module descent stage
- fuel tank (L/hydrogen)
- lox tank
- helium spheres
- J-2 engine
- fuel tank (L/hydrogen)
- lox tank
- 5 J-2 engines
- lox tank
- lox tank baffles
- liquid oxygen (lox) transfer pipes
- fuel tank (kerosene)
- fuel transfer pipes
- five F-1 engines

Above: The Saturn V rocket which was used by the Apollo Moon missions. The first stage was powered by five kerosene/liquid oxygen (lox) F-1 engines, and the subsequent stages, including the Apollo spacecraft itself, were powered by liquid oxygen/liquid hydrogen J-2 engines.

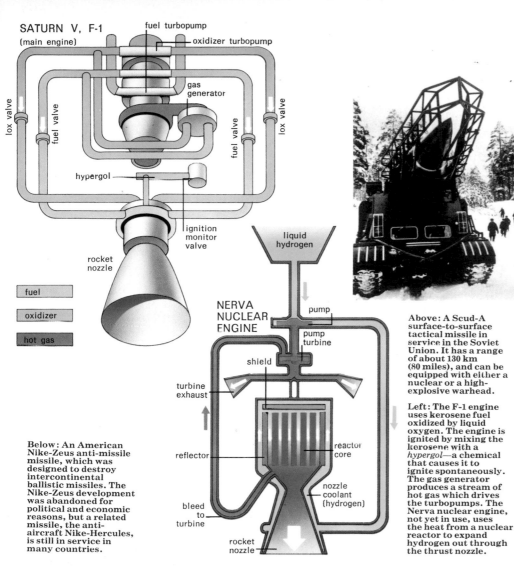

SATURN V, F-1
(main engine)

fuel turbopump
oxidizer turbopump
gas generator
lox valve
fuel valve
fuel valve
fuel valve
lox valve
hypergol
ignition monitor valve
rocket nozzle

fuel
oxidizer
hot gas

NERVA NUCLEAR ENGINE

liquid hydrogen
pump
pump turbine
shield
turbine exhaust
reflector
reactor core
nozzle coolant (hydrogen)
bleed to turbine
rocket nozzle

**Below:** An American Nike-Zeus anti-missile missile, which was designed to destroy intercontinental ballistic missiles. The Nike-Zeus development was abandoned for political and economic reasons, but a related missile, the anti-aircraft Nike-Hercules, is still in service in many countries.

**Above:** A Scud-A surface-to-surface tactical missile in service in the Soviet Union. It has a range of about 130 km (80 miles), and can be equipped with either a nuclear or a high-explosive warhead.

**Left:** The F-1 engine uses kerosene fuel oxidized by liquid oxygen. The engine is ignited by mixing the kerosene with a *hypergol*—a chemical that causes it to ignite spontaneously. The gas generator produces a stream of hot gas which drives the turbopumps. The Nerva nuclear engine, not yet in use, uses the heat from a nuclear reactor to expand hydrogen out through the thrust nozzle.

crude anti-airship missiles of the First World War.

The birth of modern rocketry, however, is generally associated with Russia's Konstantin E. Tsiolkovsky (1857-1935) who, as early as 1883, began expounding on the potential and means of using rockets as launch vehicles. In 1929 Russia became the first nation to offer official, albeit military, status to rocket research. In Germany the theories of Hermann Oberth stimulated the formation of the celebrated Society for Space Travel (VfR), itself succumbing in the mid-1930s to the opposition of the Nazi party. Military work absorbed some of its members, notably Wernher von Braun, whose efforts led to the world's first ballistic missile—the V-2. In the US, Robert Goddard independently covered much pioneering work in practical research.

As well as the V-2, used against Britain in 1945, small tactical missiles, fired by aircraft or from ground batteries, were used with reasonable effect in the Second World War. Since then the missile has really come into its own. The growth of the Cold War in the 1950s gave rise to the *strategic* missile, the intercontinental carrier of nuclear bombs. America delayed its development programme slightly to await the perfection of the compact hydrogen bomb, and the consequent reduction in launcher size. Russia, however, went straight ahead with the construction of large missiles to carry the massive atom bombs. Soviet scientists saw, too, that the same missile could place a smaller payload in orbit—and in October 1957, Sputnik 1 soared into space.

**Left:** A battery of Nike surface-to-air missiles erected and ready to be fired. Nike missiles can be deployed either at fixed launch sites, as they are here, or carried on mobile launchers.

**Right:** Many long-range missiles are launched from underground 'silos'. The US, for example, houses its Minuteman III intercontinental ballistic missiles in silos 24.4 m (80 ft) deep. The Minuteman III can be equipped with MIRV (multiple independently-targetable re-entry vehicle) warheads, which contain several separate nuclear warheads that spread out to attack several targets at once.

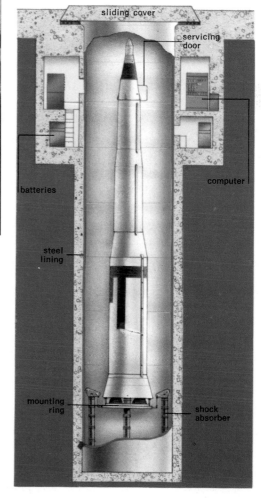

sliding cover
servicing door
batteries
computer
steel lining
mounting ring
shock absorber

America's belated response four months later was due not just to the deliberate 'missile lag' but also to an inter-service rivalry over launch vehicle development, of which the winner, the US Navy, had far from the best programme in hand. Later, as the Thor, Atlas and Titan missiles became obsolete they formed the core of the development of 'medium' launchers, while the diminutive Scout and the mighty Saturn rockets were civilian programmes.

## Specific impulse

The fundamental key to rocket propulsion is still Tsiolkovsky's *Ideal Rocket Equation* ('Ideal' because it ignores atmospheric drag) which says that total increase in vehicle velocity is equal to the exhaust velocity times the natural logarithm of the *mass ratio* (launch weight divided by empty weight). The greater the required acceleration, the higher must be either or both of the exhaust velocity and the mass ratio. Mass ratio can be improved by minimizing structural weight so that fuel burn-off plays a maximum part in allowing speed to increase. The exhaust velocity can be improved by increasing the efficiency of the *propellant* (fuel mixture).

Propellant efficiency is defined as the number of pounds of thrust that can be developed per second out of each pound of fuel (using a maximum efficiency engine). It is called the *Specific Impulse* (Isp) and the units in which it is measured are called *seconds*. Obviously, the faster the gases are emitted the greater the value of thrust per second, so that high speed/low volume tends to be more efficient than the reverse. There is thus a direct relationship between Isp and exhaust velocity, and an Isp of about 102 seconds provides an exhaust velocity of 1 km/sec. As a result, the higher the rated Isp, the lower the fuel mass needed for any specific acceleration, or the greater the acceleration obtainable from any given fuel mass.

Today's chemical propellants have a relatively low Isp and therefore present a severe weight penalty. Without the techniques of *staging* it would be impractical to accelerate a payload to orbital velocity. Any increase in propellant mass to prolong acceleration reduces the *rate* of acceleration—and therefore cancels out the value of the extra propellant. The extra mass can be used more effectively, however, if it is placed in separate tanks and given its own engine, forming an upper stage. It then becomes an extra rocket launched at altitude. In the vacuum of space, the Isp is measurably increased and the smaller mass needs only a small and less thirsty engine to maintain acceleration.

Guidance systems vary according to the degree of accuracy required. A general environment-measuring satellite intended for an orbit of 560 km (350 miles) will not suffer from a moderate variation from its course, provided that it can be accurately tracked. A pre-programmed autopilot would probably provide adequate positioning, while engine cut-out at the required velocity is obtainable by radio signal or pre-determined fuel supply. For pin-point aiming of a missile, or the injection of a deep-space probe into interplanetary trajectory, a very much higher degree of accuracy is required. A sophisticated

Above: The BAC Rapier is a close-range surface-to-air missile system. The missile is guided to its target by radio signals from the tracker's computer.

Right: The US Army's Davy Crockett is one of the growing number of portable battlefield missiles now in use, and it can be equipped with either a nuclear or a high-explosive warhead.

Below: A Polaris A-3 strategic nuclear missile launched from a submarine. The Polaris has a range of 4,630 km (2,875 miles), and is equipped with multiple nuclear warheads. It has two stages, each of which is powered by a solid-propellant rocket motor.

Right: A prototype Air Launched Cruise Missile (ALCM) being launched from the weapons bay of a B-52G bomber. The ALCM is a new breed of small, cheap and very accurate nuclear missile.

Below: One of the most widely-used forms of rocket is the *sounding rocket*, a small, lightweight vehicle, usually solid-fuel propelled, used for scientific experiments in the upper atmosphere. This diagram shows some of their many uses.

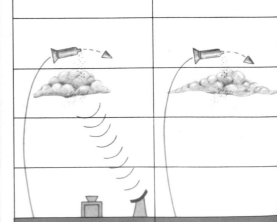

| Wind measurement: clouds of alkali metals are released in the atmosphere and tracked by radar. | Rainmaking: clouds are « seeded » with dry ice to make them release their moisture. |

## T4 ION ENGINE

- electrons
- flow of neutralized ions
- neutralizer cathode supplies electrons to neutralize the ions
- discharge chamber
- electromagnet producing magnetic field
- keeper anode
- plasma arc
- mercury atom
- hollow cathode
- mercury ions
- accelerator grid
- main anode
- electron trajectories
- mercury vapour feed
- main ionization region

**Above: The Russian Mig-25 Foxbat, equipped with AA-6 Acrid air-to-air missiles mounted under its wings.**

**Left: The T4 ion engine designed for use on a European satellite. Its thrust is obtained from the stream of neutralized ions expelled through the accelerator grid.**

**Above: The US Navy's F-14 Tomcat fighter is equipped with the Phoenix air-to-air missile system, which can track up to 24** separate targets at once, and attack six of them simultaneously. The radar-guided missiles have a range of over 160 km (100 miles).

| Atmospheric temperature and pressure information radioed to ground station by instruments in the rocket and in separated instrument package. | Electrical and magnetic properties of the upper atmosphere measured by instruments in nose cone. | Cosmic rays detected by geiger counters. | Atmospheric absorption of solar radiation measured by infra-red spectrometers. |
|---|---|---|---|

altitude in kilometres
250
200
150
100
50
0

inertial guidance system is now usual in which gyroscopes sense minor variations from the programmed path and correct them by vectoring the main thrust.

This can be backed up by ground-based navigation and control. A short-range combat missile may often be wire-guided, an operator 'flying' it by sending corrective signals along a wire that is drawn out behind. Others are controlled by radio signals, with visual directions supplied to the operator by a television camera in the nose of the missile. Still others have automatic homing devices using radar, infra-red or visual contact.

### Rocket engines

A basic characteristic of the modern rocket is its ability to operate independently of atmosphere. Rocket propulsion consists of burning a chemical in a confined space and allowing the gases to escape through a restricted nozzle. As oxygen must be present for combustion, a large supply of oxidizer must be carried. In modern liquid-fuel engines the fuel, such as kerosene or liquid hydrogen, and the oxidizer, now often liquid oxygen, are pumped separately into a small combustion chamber.

Solid-fuel rockets are also in common use for their simplicity and reliability, powering most missiles and acting as auxiliary boosters and integral stages on many launch vehicles. Solids are basically power-packed squibs, the charge being a mixture of a dry fuel and a dry oxygen-rich chemical (polyisobutane, for example, and ammonium perchlorate). Disadvantages include high weight—the rocket is, in effect, one large combustion chamber; the fact that the fuel has a lower Isp than liquids; and a lack of controllability except in burn rate, which is determined by the shape of the propellant grain or of the core cavity.

Many other means of generating thrust are now being identified, some within technology's present grasp, others merely options for the future. Much work has been done in Russia and America on nuclear engines which, if unsuitable for Earth launchings because of contamination risks, could at least provide the hard acceleration needed for a quick orbital insertion or fast interplanetary flight.

In a very different category are low-thrust systems which develop minute thrust in relation to engine weight and are therefore suitable only for overcoming inertia, rather than gravity. They do, however, offer extremely high Isp ratings. Already test flown is the *electrostatic* or *ion* engine which isolates ions from the fuel (mercury or caesium) and accelerates them electrically to produce thrust. The thrust is tiny (about 1/1,600 lb), but the fuel consumption is very low and the craft could attain otherwise impossible speeds merely by accelerating slowly for months on end.

Still on the drawing boards is the electromagnetic or *plasma* rocket, in which an electric arc is used to convert hydrogen to a charged plasma (a gas-like stream of particles) which can then be accelerated out by a magnetic field. Even more exotic is the idea of the *photon* rocket which, in theory, will provide thrust from a concentrated beam of light —the exhaust velocity being, of course, the speed of light.

The U.S. Pershing 2
tactical nuclear missile
is highly accurate,
compact and mobile. The
missile and its mobile
launch trailer can be
air-lifted to a war zone.

94

# Spaceflight

Space activities are generally divided into two categories: manned and unmanned spaceflight. Major design differences as well as different operational roles distinguish the two categories. Unmanned craft, such as Earth satellites, also fall into various subgroups according to their intended purpose. The main groups cover space sciences, space applications, military support and interplanetary exploration. Manned craft have, to date, been devoted to such a limited range of objectives that they cannot be compared operationally with the unmanned vehicles, although most tasks performed by unmanned craft have at times been attempted on manned missions.

The majority of space activities have been confined to a small sphere of space enclosing the Earth and broadly termed Earth orbit. Orbit is achieved when the speed of a body produces a momentum that balances the force of gravity and therefore continues literally to fall round the Earth. An almost infinite variety of orbits is obtainable from a permutation of factors such as the *altitude*; the *velocity*, which, by Kepler's laws, is dependent on the altitude; the *inclination*, which is the angle the orbit makes with the equator; and the *eccentricity* or *ellipticity* which is the degree by which the shape of the orbit differs from circular. All these factors can be adjusted to give the right orbit for the particular scientific mission.

Orbital speed at low altitudes of about 190 km (120 miles) is about 4,755 m/sec (15,600 ft/sec). Acceleration pushes the orbit higher and, if speed is increased to about 10,670 m/sec (35,000 ft/sec) it will raise the orbit to the distance of the Moon. This is the method used for lunar travel. Arrival speed is invariably too high for orbital capture by lunar gravity, and so a braking rocket must be fired to slow the craft and achieve orbit, and then fired again if a soft landing is required, there being no atmosphere to slow the craft.

Return flights require an escape velocity of only about 2,377 m/sec (7,800 ft/sec) to overcome the low gravity. Apart from landing missions, lunar orbit has also been used for lunar surface photography as an 'anchor' for a few satellites devoted to certain types of cosmic science.

For interplanetary travel, a spacecraft must break out of Earth orbit and enter an elliptical orbit around the Sun which will intersect with that of the destination planet. Initial speed required for this is about 11,580 m/sec (38,000 ft/sec). Missions to Venus are launched 'backwards' in relation to the Earth's motion around the Sun, so that their relative speed is slower and they drop towards the Sun. Missions to Mars and the outer planets are launched ahead of the Earth for the opposite effect.

Known as a *Hohmann ellipse*, this technique reduces the power required from the launch vehicle, and so although it is not the fastest route, it permits the use of much smaller and cheaper launch vehicles. It also requires specific positioning of the departure and destination planets at launch, usually near the period of closest approach. Such approaches occur at short and infrequent intervals, and the associated launch opportunities are called 'launch windows'. For Venus this occurs every 583 days, and Mars every 280 days.

Journeys to the more remote planets have been shortened by a *gravity swing-by* technique. America's Mariner 10 reached

Left: Valentina Nikolayeva-Tereshkova, the first woman to make a spaceflight. Her Vostok-6 spacecraft, launched from Baikonur cosmodrome in Central Asia on 16 June 1963, made a total of 48 orbits during its 70 hour 50 minute flight, covering a distance of 1,970,990 kilometres (1,224,084 miles).

Below left: The first man in space was the Soviet cosmonaut Yuri Gagarin (1934-1968). His 108 minute flight, during which he made one complete orbit of the Earth in his Vostok-1 spacecraft, took place on 12 April 1961. In this picture, Gagarin is talking to Soviet rocket designer Sergei Korolyev.

Below: This multiple exposure shows the launch tower dropping away as the American Gemini-10 lifts off on 18 July 1966. Gemini-10, which used a Titan launch vehicle, was crewed by John Young and Michael Collins, and successfully docked with an Agena target vehicle orbiting at 298 km (185 miles).

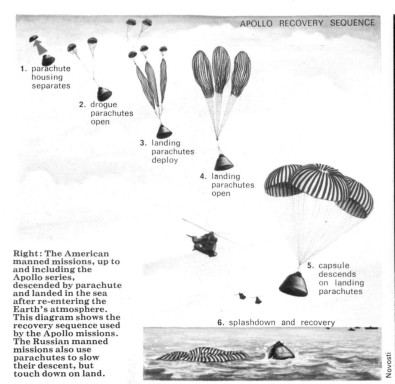

APOLLO RECOVERY SEQUENCE

1. parachute housing separates

2. drogue parachutes open

3. landing parachutes deploy

4. landing parachutes open

5. capsule descends on landing parachutes

6. splashdown and recovery

Novosti

**Right:** The American manned missions, up to and including the Apollo series, descended by parachute and landed in the sea after re-entering the Earth's atmosphere. This diagram shows the recovery sequence used by the Apollo missions. The Russian manned missions also use parachutes to slow their descent, but touch down on land.

Photri

**Above:** Russia's Luna 16, an unmanned vehicle which in September 1970 travelled to the Moon, collected samples of soil, and returned them to Earth for analysis.

**Right:** Lunokhod 2, the second of Russia's remotely-controlled lunar exploration vehicles, was landed at the edge of the Sea of Serenity on 16 January 1973. Lunokhod 2's equipment included: 1, directional antenna; 2 and 8, tv cameras; 3, photoreceptor; 4, solar panel; 5, magnetometer; 6, laser reflector; 7, astrophotometer; 9, soil analysis unit; 10, telephotometers; 11, soil mechanics probe. The vehicle covered a total distance of 37 km (23 miles). It is planned to send a similar machine to explore the surface of Mars.

**Left:** Apollo 15 astronaut James Irwin with the electrically-driven Lunar Roving Vehicle, which enabled the astronauts to explore a wider area of the Moon than they could cover on foot. In the background is Mount Hadley.

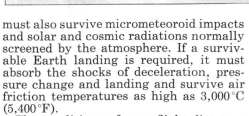

Novosti

Mercury in 1975 by flying close to Venus and using the force of that planet's gravity to accelerate and re-direct the spacecraft to its destination. Likewise Pioneer 11 was boosted by Jupiter's gravity as it flew by on its way to Saturn.

## Spacecraft

The term 'spacecraft' usually applies to any self-sustaining, active device operating for extended periods beyond the Earth's atmosphere. Spacecraft designed to leave Earth orbit and explore planets or adopt solar orbits of their own are known as *space probes*. Their designs vary considerably according to their particular destination, duration of mission and objective—whether they are supposed to fly-by, enter orbit or release a landing craft. The operational and environmental demands placed on these craft has led to their development into some of the most sophisticated robots yet devised.

The general design of a spacecraft is dominated by three main considerations —intended purpose of the mission, launch vehicle compatability and, usually most important, weight reduction. The peculiarities of its operational life require a spacecraft to protect and support its payload over a wide range of extreme conditions. At launch it may experience acceleration forces 10 to 15 times that of gravity, atmospheric pressures which fall rapidly from that at sea level to a vacuum, plus heavy vibration.

In space it meets a considerable range of temperatures according to its position and attitude in relation to the Sun, and must also survive micrometeoroid impacts and solar and cosmic radiations normally screened by the atmosphere. If a survivable Earth landing is required, it must absorb the shocks of deceleration, pressure change and landing and survive air friction temperatures as high as 3,000 °C (5,400 °F).

The conditions of spaceflight dictate a basically common complement of subsystems. Unmanned craft consist of a simple open-frame structure to which subsystems are individually attached in separate boxes, or a sealed container enclosing most of the systems together. Manned spacecraft, with their need for living and working quarters for their crews, demand a very large sealed structure, usually large enough for the subsystems to be distributed widely in and around it.

The basic elements of any spacecraft consist of power supply, temperature control, communications, data-processing, stabilization and attitude control equipment and, if required, navigation and propulsion systems and even a computer. Power is usually supplied by panels of solar cells which convert the Sun's energy to electricity. As far from the Sun as Mars, solar arrays are efficient

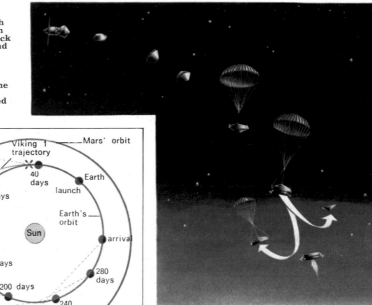

Left: Testing one of the Surveyor lunar landing probes, which made soft landings on the Moon and sent back television pictures and scientific data. The first of the seven Surveyor probes was launched on 30 May 1966, and landed on the Moon on 1 June. The final one was launched on 7 January 1968.

VIKING 1 - INTERPLANETARY TRAJECTORY

Mars

Viking 1 trajectory

Mars' orbit

40 days

Earth launch

80 days

120 days

Earth's orbit

Sun

arrival

160 days

280 days

200 days

240 days

Photri

Left: David R. Scott standing in the hatch of the Apollo 9 command module. The Apollo 9 mission, from 3 to 13 March 1969, was an Earth-orbital mission designed to test the rendezvous and docking procedures of the command/service module and the lunar module. This picture was taken from the lunar module.

Below: A simulated picture of a Pioneer probe passing the Moon on its way from Earth to the outer planets. The first Pioneer programme was a series of probes intended to investigate the Moon, but it was not a success. The second, successful, series has been investigating the solar system.

Above: The Viking 1 and 2 Mars probes each consisted of two sections, an *orbiter*, which went into orbit around the planet, and a *lander*, which descended to the surface. This diagram shows the interplanetary trajectory of Viking 1 and the descent sequence of the lander.

Below: The complete EVA spacesuit weighs 113kg (250lbs), but when it is pressurized, it actually supports much of its own weight. The Displays and Controls Modules on the front of the suit include a microprocessor with a buzzer and light to warn of any malfunction. It also displays the trouble and its cure on a screen.

Photri

Photri

enough to be kept manageably small, but beyond Mars the Sun's strength attenuates to unusable levels and radioactive isotope-powered thermoelectric generators (RTGs) were used on the two Pioneer probes to Jupiter.

Short-life craft, notably the early satellites and some of the Soviet lunar probes, carry only simple chemical batteries. In all other cases, however, the generated raw power is conditioned and stored in batteries before delivery to components. Most spacecraft require between 100 W and 500 W. Large solar arrays developed for high-power comsats (communications satellites) can produce 1.5 KW. Some US manned spacecraft—the Apollos and later Geminis—depended on fuel cells in which hydrogen and oxygen were processed to generate electricity, supplying drinking water as a by-product.

Temperature control is often the most challenging element of a spacecraft, involving the appropriate distribution of cooling and heat with minimal power use. Some craft now use controllable louvres to exploit the Sun's heating. Rotation of the craft, or positioning of reflective thermal blankets and sunshields, keeps temperatures down.

Numerous techniques, some ingenious, include relative positioning of hot- and cold-running components, heat sinks and direct electric heating.

Communications involve several essential links between controllers and craft, each link operating at a different frequency through its own type of aerial. One receives commands from Earth, while another feeds out telemetry data reporting on the condition of the various subsystems. Finally there is the mission data, the information which the spacecraft is sent to collect. Most Earth satellites use simple non-directional aerials, but at planetary ranges, and even from the Moon, probes must concentrate the available power into highly directional signals if they are to be readable on arrival, hence the large, parabolic

Photri

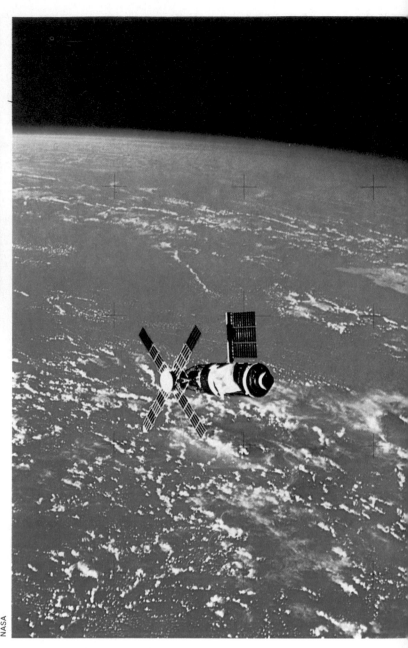

NASA

dish-shaped aerials which characterize most interplanetary craft.

Even then there is such a heavy flow of information that some form of data processing becomes necessary. Normally this involves equipment which can selectively sample the telemetry or payload data on a command from Earth or from an on-board sequencer. Earth satellites often have to select data and store it on tape recorders while out of sight of a control station, and transmit it all on the next pass.

Like an aircraft, most spacecraft need to be able to change attitude at will and to keep stable at any particular attitude. Attitudes and navigational positions in space are identified by light sensors graded to specific objects such as the Sun, the Earth's horizon or, for interplanetary craft, the conveniently positioned bright star Canopus. Attitude is changed either by small gas jets or inertial wheels aligned along all three axes, both methods using reaction to turn the craft. Stabilization can be maintained most simply by spinning the entire spacecraft to create gyroscopic forces which keep it stable. For more accurate stability a system of three gyroscopes is required.

Many satellites spend their operational lives in the orbits into which they were first launched. Any manoeuvring, however, means that a rocket motor must be carried. For example, if recovery is intended, then the craft must have a braking rocket. Geostationary satellites are first launched into elliptical orbit with apogee (highest point) at 35,900 km (22,300 miles). On board is a solid-fuel *apogee-motor* which is fired at apogee to

**Above: During the Apollo-Soyuz Test Project (ASTP) in July 1975, an American Apollo spacecraft docked in Earth orbit with a Russian Soyuz vehicle. This picture shows one of the American astronauts, Vance D. Brand, in the docking passage connecting the two vehicles.**

**Above right: Skylab, the American space station which was put into Earth orbit on 14 May 1973. Shortly after lift-off, Skylab's meteoroid shield and one of its solar cell arrays broke away, and the damaged area was covered with aluminized plastic by the astronauts who docked with the station on 25 May.**

European Space Agency

98

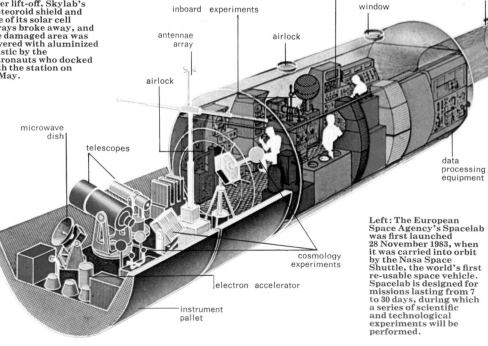

display equipment

inboard experiments

window

airlock

antennae array

airlock

airlock

microwave dish

telescopes

data processing equipment

cosmology experiments

electron accelerator

instrument pallet

**Left: The European Space Agency's Spacelab was first launched 28 November 1983, when it was carried into orbit by the Nasa Space Shuttle, the world's first re-usable space vehicle. Spacelab is designed for missions lasting from 7 to 30 days, during which a series of scientific and technological experiments will be performed.**

**Above: Examples of the
packages of food
carried on spaceflights,
and their equivalent in
conventional food. The
dehydrated foods are
reconstituted by means
of a water gun.**

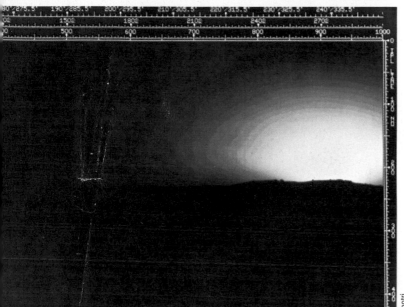

**Left: Sunset on Mars,
20 August 1976,
photographed by the
Viking 1 lander. The
layered effect of the
light is due to the
camera scanning action.**

**Below: The proposed
Spacelab mission cycle.
The Shuttle Orbiter,
carrying the Spacelab,
takes off using its
three main engines and
two boosters. At 43 km
(27 miles) the boosters
separate and return to
Earth by parachute for
re-use. At 113 km
(70 miles) the external
fuel tank separates and
burns up in the
atmosphere. The Orbiter
then remains in orbit
while the experiments
are performed, and
finally re-enters the
atmosphere and glides
back to Earth.**

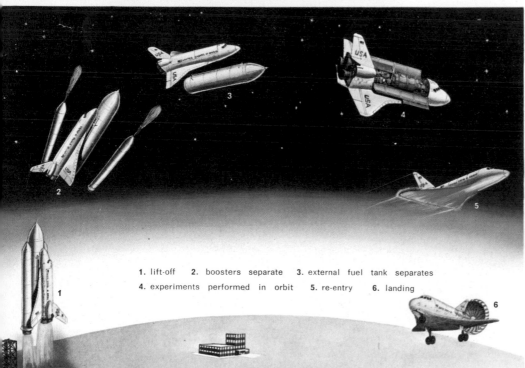

**1.** lift-off  **2.** boosters separate  **3.** external fuel tank separates
**4.** experiments performed in orbit  **5.** re-entry  **6.** landing

circularize the orbit. Missions that
might require numerous manoeuvres
must carry a liquid-fuel engine which
can be stopped and started at will.

A few satellites and most modern
probes have some form of automatic
control system. Generally this is just a
simple sequencer which converts particular signals into necessary sequences
of actions. More sophisticated craft
have varying sizes of computer. At their
most advanced level, such as those used
by Mariner 10, these are programmed not
only to correct minor faults but also to
perform the entire planned mission without reference to Earth should command
reception fail.

## Space Shuttle

Manned spaceflight has been revolutionized with the introduction of the *Space
Shuttle* — the world's first re-usable
spacecraft. The craft consists of an
*orbiter*: a cross between a conventional
rocket and a jet airliner. For launching,
the orbiter is stood 'on end', dwarfed by
the huge fuel tank which supplies its main
engines. Additional boost is provided at
launch by two solid-fuel rocket motors,
placed one either side of the external fuel
tank. The rocket motors and fuel tank are
all jettisoned before the orbiter is placed
in orbit — the rocket motors being
recovered.

For landing, the orbiter first fires
thruster motors to slow down and drop
out of orbit. Then it pitches nose up, so
that the underside which is protected
takes the full heat of re-entry as it hits the
atmosphere. The landing is unpowered —
the orbiter returns to earth as a 100-tonne
glider, landing on its special runway and
(almost) ready for service in space again.

Early flights of the Space Shuttle were
used to gain experience and to test systems, but the spacecraft is not designed
simply to satisfy the interests of pure
scientific research. It will supply
commercial services to companies that
now have an interest in space.

One major function is the launch of satellites. The orbiters are little more than
large space-going trucks, and behind the
astronaut 'drivers' there is cargo space for
several types of satellite. In orbit, the
doors of the cargo bay swing open, and an
astronaut uses a remote-controlled arm to
pick out the required satellite and toss it
into space. Repair and retrieval of satellites is also possible.

One mission, planned for early 1984,
involved a space walk by an astronaut to
attend the broken-down Solar Maximum
Mission (SMM) spacecraft which up to
1980 provided a wealth of information on
solar flares. Sometimes, roadside repairs
will be possible on such satellites; in other
cases, the satellite will have to be tethered
to the Shuttle's manipulator arm, and
pulled back into the cargo bay.

A wide range of experiments will be
carried out in future years as the Shuttle
carries laboratory modules forming
Spacelab into orbit. This unique
laboratory, operated by scientists rather
than astonauts, might be used, for
example, to operate a furnace to make new
types of alloy, that cannot easily be
produced under the gravitational pull of
Earth. Other experiments that make the
most of the weightless environment of
Spacelab may include the processing of
super-pure drugs and vaccines, or
watching the behaviour of cancerous cells. 99

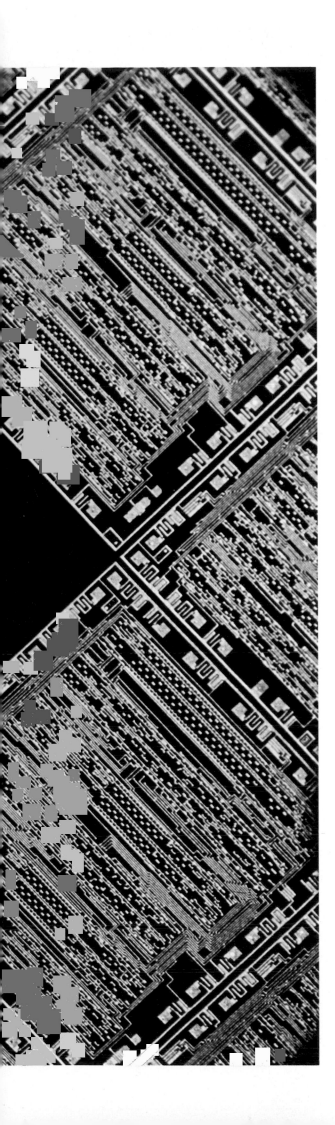

# Applied Technology

Tiny chips of crystalline silicon (the central test chip is 4mm square) are used as semiconductors, such as transistors, rectifiers and solar batteries. Silicon can deal with large amounts of power without overheating.

# Mechanics

The science of mechanics deals with the effects of forces—anything from the force needed to make a knife cut an apple to the massive forces of gravity which keep the planets in orbit around the sun. A force is an influence which acts on an object to alter its position, its speed or its direction of travel, or to create pressure or stress within it. Forces themselves are invisible, but their effects can be measured and so their size and direction can be calculated.

One of the most important natural forces is the force of gravity, and the weight of an object is a measure of the downward pull exerted on it by the earth's gravity. The mass of an object, which is often confused with its weight, is a measure of the amount of matter it contains and is independent of the earth's gravity.

When more than one force acts on an object, the overall effect or *resultant* of these forces can be calculated by drawing a *vector* diagram. Each force is represented by a line called a vector, which is drawn in the direction in which the force acts and whose length is proportional to the size of the force. The vector diagram is drawn in such a way that a resultant line is produced, whose length and angle represent the size and direction of the resultant force.

There is often no resultant force, however, even with several forces acting on the object. This happens when the forces are balanced or cancel each other out, for example when two equal forces are pulling in opposite directions. When there is no resultant force the object is said to be in *equilibrium*.

### Stress and strain
When a force is applied to an object which is moving or free to move, it will try to alter the object's motion in some way. If the object is fixed, however, the force will try to deform it in some way (stretch it or compress it, for instance), a situation which the object will naturally try to resist.

Internal resisting forces are set up within the object, acting in the opposite direction to the applied force to counteract it. The object is then in a state of *stress*; this will be *tensile* stress if the external force is pulling on the object, *compressive* stress if the load is pushing on it, or *shear* stress if there are two or more external forces acting on it in opposite directions but not in line with each other.

Stress is calculated by dividing the value of the external force by the area of the cross-section of the object. *Strain* is a numerical ratio which gives an indication of the effect of such a force on an object. It is found by dividing the change in the length of the object (when subject to the stress) by its original length.

Up to a certain point, this change in length is directly proportional to the size of the force or load producing it, and when the load is removed the object will return to its original length. This ability of an object to return to its original length is known as its *elasticity*—all materials have some degree of elasticity.

The relationship between load and deformation was first demonstrated by Robert Hooke in 1667. The behaviour of a spring is a good example of what is known as Hooke's Law (which applies to all materials, and not just springs). If a weight is hung on a spring it will stretch by a certain amount, and if the load is doubled the spring will stretch twice as much. The stretching is proportional to the load; in other words strain is proportional to stress.

The spring continues to stretch until a point is reached where it has been stretched so far that it will not return to its original length when the load is removed. This point, where strain is no longer proportional to stress, is known as the *elastic limit*.

Once the elastic limit has been passed, the spring will stretch further and further until it eventually breaks.

Hooke's work was taken a step further in 1807 by Robert Young, who found that provided the elastic limit is not exceeded, stress divided by strain gives a certain value or *constant*. The value of this constant, known as Young's Modulus of Elasticity, varies from one material to another. Flexible materials, for example, have lower values than rigid ones.

### Pressure
Pressure is the amount of force acting on each unit of area, and so it is expressed in terms such as kilograms per **square** metre (Kg/m$^2$) or pounds per **square** inch (lb/in$^2$ or psi). Reducing the area on which a force acts increases the pressure it exerts; increasing the area reduces the pressure. A knife needs less force to make it cut if it is sharp than if it is blunt, because the area of the cutting edge is smaller and so the pressure required to make it cut can be produced with a smaller force.

In the case of a knife, the area on which the force acts is kept as small as possible so that the maximum pressure can be obtained. On the other hand it is sometimes necessary to increase the area to minimize the pressure. For instance, vehicles designed to work over soft sand or marshy ground have wider tyres than road vehicles, so that by spreading the weight of the vehicle over a larger area the pressure exerted on the ground is lower and the wheels will not sink in.

### Speed, velocity and acceleration
Forces not only produce stress and pressure. They may also act on an object to make it move, or to alter its motion if it is already moving.

The speed at which an object is travelling is the distance it travels in a specified time, such as the number of miles per hour or metres per second. The measurement of speed does not involve consideration of the direction of travel, but any measurement of velocity does. Velocity is the speed of an object in a specified direction.

Acceleration is defined as the rate of change of velocity with time and, as velocity involves both speed and direction, a change in either or both of these is an acceleration. A train increasing its speed as it travels along a straight length of track is accelerating, and so is a train moving at a constant speed as it goes around a curve.

If an object is increasing its velocity by, for example, 10 metres per second

Right: A spring balance gives a direct measurement of weight and it will show a different weight for the same object at the top of a mountain than at sea level. This is because at the mountain top the object will be further from the centre of the Earth, so the pull of gravity will be less than at sea level—as predicted by the universal law of gravitation.

Left: The pull of gravity acts on every particle within an object, and if all the tiny weight forces of these particles were replaced by one large force it would act down through a point called the centre of gravity. This point is not necessarily within the material of the object. In the case of this vase, for example, it is a point in the space inside it.

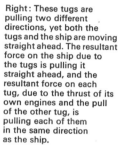

Right: These tugs are pulling two different directions, yet both the tugs and the ship are moving straight ahead. The resultant force on the ship due to the tugs is pulling it straight ahead, and the resultant force on each tug, due to the thrust of its own engines and the pull of the other tug, is pulling each of them in the same direction as the ship.

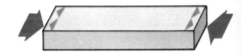

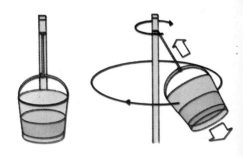

Weight is a measure of the pull of gravity on an object. This pull was explained by Newton in his universal law of gravitation. It states that the force between two bodies (such as the Earth and an object on it) is directly proportional to the product of their masses and inversely proportional to the square of the distance between them.

Left: Unlike the spring balance, which measures a weight by the extent to which it stretches the spring, the beam balance compares the unknown weight with a known weight or weights. It will give the same measurement at a mountain top as it will at sea level because the change in the pull of gravity affects both weights equally. They still balance despite their change in weight.

Left: This weightlifter is lifting a bar carrying 80 kg (176 lb) of weights. In lifting the weights he is doing work against gravity. If he lifts them 2.2 m (7.2 ft), he will have done 80 x 2.2= 176 m.kg (1269 ft.lb) of work. This is in addition to the work done in lifting the bar itself and in raising the weight of his own body from a crouched position.

Left: The load hook is positioned so that the load's centre of gravity is in line with the helicopter's. If it was in front or behind it would tend to tilt the craft.

Right: A tower crane can lift a greater weight when the load trolley is near the tower. This is because the load is then exerting less leverage than it would at the end of the jib.

Right: When a barge is being towed along a canal by two ropes, one on either side, the resultant force can be calculated by drawing a parallelogram, two adjacent sides of which represent the size and direction of the two pulling forces. The size and direction of the resultant is found by measuring the length and angle of the diagonal of the parallelogram.

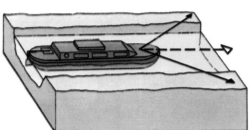

Left: The geodesic dome is made up of metal tubes arranged in triangles. The triangle was chosen as the basic unit of the framework because its shape cannot be altered without physically bending any of the tubes. Other shapes, such as squares or pentagons, can be altered by changing the angles between the tubes, so they are more liable to collapse.

Far left: When an object such as a bar is subject to forces pushing in from each end, internal forces are set up to resist them and the bar is then said to be in a state of compression.

Left: When the applied forces are pulling on the bar, the internal forces act inwards to resist the pull, and the bar is then in a state of tension.

Right: If water leaks from three holes in a tank of water, it will spurt out fastest from the lowest hole. This is because there is more pressure driving it—since pressure in a liquid increases with depth. It is the weight of liquid above a given point which creates the pressure. Thus, conversely, nearer the surface the pressure of liquid will be less.

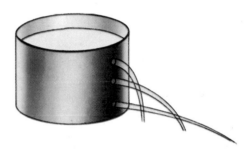

Left and Right: Two examples of friction, the resistance force which opposes the motion of two surfaces sliding over each other. The scorched paint-work of the Apollo capsule is the result of the heat generated by air friction when the craft entered the atmosphere. The smoke from the car's tyres is due to friction caused by wheelspin during acceleration.

Left and right: A rocket taking off illustrates Newton's laws of motion. First, it will not move or change direction unless acted on by a force, in this case the reaction to the engine thrust; second, its acceleration is proportional to the force applied; third, every action (the engine thrust) produces an equal but opposite reaction (the motion of the rocket).

Left: A bucket of water, swung round on a rope, is travelling in a circle and so continuously changing direction. It is said to be accelerating all the time, because acceleration is a change in either speed or direction. The force producing this acceleration is the tension in the rope which is preventing the bucket from flying off in a straight line. This is called the centripetal force. The value of this force is the square of the speed of the bucket divided by the radius of the circle around which it is travelling. The tendency of the bucket to fly off in a straight line is the centrifugal force, equal in size but opposite in direction to the centripetal force. This is holding the water in the rotating bucket despite it being almost horizontal.

Left: A picture of a hurricane in the South Pacific taken from the Skylab orbital laboratory. The rotation of the earth causes a deflection of the winds blowing over it—to the right in the northern hemisphere and to the left in the south. This effect (known as the Coriolis force) makes hurricanes spiral clockwise in the south and anti-clockwise in the north.

(m/sec) every second, its acceleration is written as 10 m/sec/sec or 10 m/sec². 

Velocity, acceleration, time and distance are brought together by the three equations of motion, providing the acceleration remains constant during the specified time. These deal with initial velocity (u), final velocity (v), acceleration (a), distance travelled (s) and time (t).

The first equation, v=u+at, enables us to calculate the final velocity from the initial velocity, the acceleration, and the length of time the object was accelerating. The second, s=ut+½at², gives the distance travelled when the initial velocity, the acceleration and the time are known.

The third equation, v²=u²+2as, allows the final velocity to be calculated from the initial velocity, the acceleration, and the distance travelled. In each of these equations, of course, any one of the quantities involved can be calculated if all the others in the equation are known.

### Acceleration due to gravity
The force of gravity causes falling objects to accelerate as they drop, and in theory this acceleration is approximately 981 cm/sec² (32 ft/sec²). In practice, however, falling objects are slowed down by air resistance and so a steel ball falls much faster than a feather.

An object falling freely from a great height does not continue accelerating until it hits the ground, because it eventually reaches a speed at which the upward force of the air resistance equals the downward pull of gravity. When this happens the object stops accelerating and falls at a fairly constant velocity known as its *terminal velocity*.

The terminal velocity an object can attain depends on its size and shape. A person falling from an aircraft without a parachute is unlikely to achieve a terminal velocity greater than about 225 kph (140 mph). In a vacuum, of course, there is no air resistance and so any falling object will continue accelerating until it hits something.

### Momentum and inertia
The inertia of an object is its reluctance to move when it is stationary, or to change its direction or speed once it is moving. The amount of inertia a body possesses depends on its mass, the larger the mass the greater the inertia. In the case of a rotating object such as a flywheel, it is a quantity called the *moment of inertia* which must be considered.

The moment of a force is its turning effect about a given point. This is found by multiplying the size of the force by the perpendicular distance between its line of action and the point.

For example, a girder projecting from a wall, has a weight of 4 kg hanging on it at a distance of 2 metres from the wall. The moment of the weight about the point where the girder is fixed to the wall is 4×2=8 kg.m (kilogramme-metres).

The moment of inertia therefore takes account of not only the mass but also its distance from the point about which it is rotating. The further the mass is from its centre of rotation, the larger its moment of inertia. This means that a flywheel has a larger moment of inertia if it is made with a thick rim and thin spokes than if it were a solid disc of the same weight and diameter, because most of its mass is at the edge, away from the centre of rotation.

The *momentum* of an object is the product of its mass and its velocity, and a small, fast-moving object may have the same momentum as a large, slow-moving one. For example, a mass of 1 kg moving at 100 m/sec has the same momentum as a mass of 100 kg moving at 1 m/sec. In both cases the same amount of force would be required to change the momentum of each one equally.

The momentum of an object due to its rotation, its *angular momentum*, is found by multiplying its moment of inertia by its *angular velocity*. Angular velocity is the angle the object rotates through in a given time, and is commonly measured in radians per second. A radian is approximately 57.3°.

### Potential and kinetic energy
Work is performed when a force acts on something to produce motion, and it is defined as the product of the force and the distance moved. The capacity to do work is termed *energy*. There are two kinds of energy in mechanics which are called *potential energy* and *kinetic energy*.

An object possesses potential energy because of its position, and kinetic energy because of its velocity. If a stone weighing 2 kg is lifted to a height of 10 metres, the work needed to do this (force×distance) is 20 m.kg (metre kilogrammes); this is stored in the stone in the form of potential energy, also 20 m.kg. When the stone is allowed to drop, this energy can be turned back into work by, for example, dropping the stone on to a stake to drive it into the ground.

When the stone is half way to the ground (at a height of 5 metres), its potential energy (weight×height) is now only 10 m.kg, half what it was before. As it has not yet done any work, its total energy must still be the same, and so half its original potential energy must have been converted into another form of energy. This other form is kinetic energy, which it now possesses because it is moving.

When it reaches the ground all its potential energy will have been converted into kinetic energy and when it hits the stake this energy will be released as work, to push the stake into the ground. The kinetic energy of an object of a mass m travelling at a velocity v is ½m×v².

The conversion of potential energy into kinetic energy follows the *Law of Conservation of Energy*, which states that energy cannot be created or destroyed, only converted from one form into another.

### The uses of mechanics
The study of machines is an essential part of many areas of science and technology. In civil engineering, for example, before a building or a bridge can be built the designers must calculate the stresses likely to occur within the structure, to ensure that the materials used will not be overloaded and collapse during use.

When a vehicle is being designed—whether it is a car, a locomotive or a space rocket—its weight, its planned top speed and the acceleration required must be decided so that the power needed from the engine can be calculated. In fact the basic principles of mechanics are involved in any consideration of the design or performance of any kind of structure or machine.

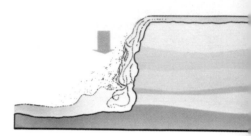

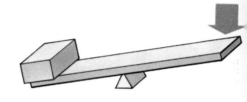

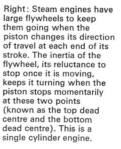

Left: A seventeenth-century piledriver. Pulling on the rope G drew the lever E downwards, turning the pulley wheel. This wound up the rope and lifted the block A, giving it potential energy. When the rope was released the block fell back down, turning its potential energy into kinetic energy, which was released as work to drive the pile into the ground.

Right: Steam engines have large flywheels to keep them going when the piston changes its direction of travel at each end of its stroke. The inertia of the flywheel, its reluctance to stop once it is moving, keeps it turning when the piston stops momentarily at these two points (known as the top dead centre and the bottom dead centre). This is a single cylinder engine.

Left: This waterwheel is turned by the force of the water flowing under it. This force acts near the edge of the wheel and produces a turning effect called a torque. Multiplying the value of the force by the distance between its point of action near the edge of the wheel and the centre of rotation at the axle, gives the value of the torque.

Left and right: The force of the wind pushes the sails of a windmill round, producing four torques on the shaft carrying the sails. This mill has four sails, the torques on each opposing pair of sails combining to form what are known as couples. A couple is formed when two forces, acting in opposite directions, act on directly opposite points about an axis.

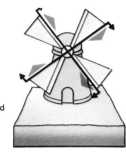

Left and right: The water at the top of a waterfall has a certain amount of kinetic energy because it is moving. It also has potential energy because of its height from the bottom of the fall. As it drops over the edge it starts losing potential energy because its height is decreasing, and gaining kinetic energy as it picks up speed. At the bottom, all its energy is kinetic.

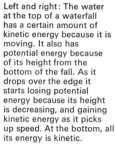

Left: The effect or moment of a force acting at a distance from a pivot is the product of the size of the force and the distance from the pivot. Thus a force of 10 kg exerted on the handle of a crowbar, 0.5 m from the pivot, will produce a force of 100 kg at the other end of the bar if it is 0.05 m from the pivot. The total moment on each side of the pivot is always equal.

Left: If an effort of 2 kg exerted on one side of a lever lifts a load of 4 kg on the other, the lever has a mechanical advantage of 2 (calculated by dividing the load by the effort). The work done by each side of the lever is the same because the effort moves twice as far as the load; thus the lever has a velocity ratio (distance moved by effort divided by that moved by the load) of 2.

Left: A simple lever which has the load and effort on opposite sides of the pivot or fulcrum is called a first order lever. A lever which has both load and effort on the same side of the pivot is a second order lever. A pair of nutcrackers is in fact a pair of second order levers joined at a common pivot. In both orders the effort is further from the pivot than the load.

Left: Sugar tongs are third order levers, the load being further from the pivot than the effort. The load is therefore less than the effort.

Right: An example of seventeenth-century mechanical engineering. This machine for raising water from a well uses several basic mechanical devices, such as levers, gears and cranks.

Left: Gears are devices which are used to transmit rotational motion. If a gear has twice as many teeth as the one it is driving, the driven gear will turn twice as fast as the driving gear. In other words the gear ratio is 2:1. The driven gear turns in the opposite direction to the driving gear. For example, in this illustration the large gears turn the opposite way to the small one.

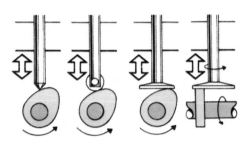

Left: Cams are used to turn rotational motion into reciprocating motion—that is up and down or back and forward. Cams are mounted on shafts and act upon cam followers. These follow the profile of the cam rising as the high point of the cam comes round and falling back as it passes. Shown here are four common types of cam follower in general use.

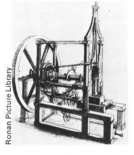

Left: A machine, designed by Sir Marc Isambard Brunel in the late eighteenth century, for cutting slots in blocks of wood used in ship-building. Born in France in 1769, Brunel was a prolific inventor and a civil engineer, as was his son Isambard Kingdom Brunel who designed railways, ships and bridges. Sir Marc died in London in December 1849.

Left: In a pulley system the velocity ratio is equal to the number of pulleys, providing all pulleys are of equal diameter. 'Work' must be done to overcome friction and lift the lower pulley block itself, and the efficiency of a system is work output divided by work input. The efficiency equals the mechanical advantage divided by the velocity ratio.

Right: The crank is a means of converting reciprocating motion into rotary motion. As the piston moves to the right the connecting rod, which is attached to the wheel, moves down and to the right and turns the wheel clockwise. When the piston moves to the left the wheel end of the rod moves up and then to the left, so keeping the wheel turning.

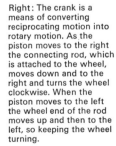

Right: The swing of a pendulum is due to gravity accelerating it on its downward swing and decelerating it on its upward swing. Because acceleration due to gravity does not depend on the mass of an object, the time a pendulum needs to complete one swing depends on its length and not its mass. The motion of a pendulum is called simple harmonic motion.

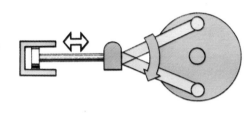

Left: The collapse of the Tacoma Narrows bridge, Washington, in 1940. Gusts of wind started it swinging, and it reached such a rate that it tended to keep moving even when the wind dropped. At this rate of swing, which is called the resonant frequency of the bridge, such severe stresses were set up within it that it literally shook itself to pieces.

# Machine Tools

Machine tools, power-operated machines which shape articles to any desired form by the action of mechanically-controlled cutting tools, played an essential part in the Industrial Revolution and are vital to modern industry. As well as greatly simplifying the manufacture of individual items, the use of machine tools permits the making of large numbers of identical articles at a low cost.

The earliest machine tool was the lathe, which is known to have been used by the Egyptians in the third century BC, by the Etruscans in about 700 BC, and possibly in Mycenae in around 1200 BC. Water-driven saws, boring machines and hammers were invented in the Middle Ages, and Leonardo da Vinci produced designs for several types of machine tool.

The machine tools in use in the late eighteenth century were essentially little different from those of the Middle Ages, but by 1850 their designs had improved radically and they were, in principle, the same as their modern counterparts. As the Industrial Revolution progressed, the need for more and better machine tools to facilitate the manufacture of such items as textile machinery and steam engines grew considerably. In their turn, machine tools benefited from the new technologies they helped to create.

For example, James Watt was able to develop his improved steam engine because John Wilkinson's cylinder-boring machine, invented in 1775, was capable of boring cylinders to the close tolerances required by the design. Watt's engines could drive rotating shafts, which earlier steam engines could not do satisfactorily, and this rotary motion was soon employed to drive, via belts and pulleys, new forms of machine tools.

By far the greater part of machine tool development in the first half of the nineteenth century took place in England and the US. Most of the general-purpose machine tools of the present day, such as boring, planing and shaping machines, the powered lathe, and tooling such as taps and dies for cutting screw threads, were developed in England during this period. By the middle of the century, however, the US had become the world leader in machine tool design.

The rapid expansion of the US economy created a scarcity of skilled labour, and this prompted the production of machine tools capable of high output rates which needed a minimum of labour to operate them. Among these were the automatic lathe, and the turret lathe which had several tools mounted on a rotatable turret, so that a series of machining operations could be carried out on a workpiece simply by rotating the turret to bring the appropriate tool into operation. This meant that a sequence of operations could be performed on a single machine without the need to replace the cutting tool between each operation.

The interchangeable system of manufacture, known in the nineteenth century as the 'American System', was pioneered in the US by Eli Whitney and others. This system was the origin of today's mass-production techniques, and it was based on the idea of assembling articles from standardized components.

Michael Holford

Alfred Herbert Ltd

Alfred Herbert Ltd

Left: A lathe built in 1810 by Henry Maudslay (1771-1831). Maudslay was a pioneer of precision engineering, and the screw-cutting lathes that he built were capable of producing screws of high accuracy that were sufficiently uniform to be interchangeable. Machines capable of producing large numbers of virtually identical components were essential to the development of mass production techniques.

Below: Some of the types of machining action used by machine tools. In the pressing action shown here (*blanking*), the punch cuts a disc of metal from the sheet by forcing it through the hole in the die.

Above: When metal parts are being machined, as on this turret lathe, streams of *cutting fluid* are directed on to the cutting points to dissipate the heat generated and provide lubrication. This protects both the tools and the machined part and reduces the chance of breakage. The fluids are usually oil-based.

Below: The mass production of cluster gears for automobile gearboxes. At the top of the picture a gear has just been cut by a rapidly-rotating cutter, which is itself shaped like a large gear. This type of machine, known as a *gear shaper*, is widely used for rapid and economic gear production.

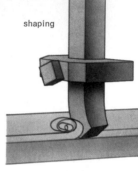

shaping

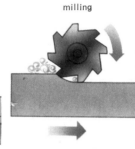

milling

drilling

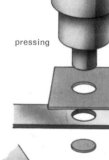

pressing

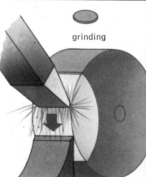

grinding

Below: *Grinding* is the removal of metal from a component by the action of a rapidly-rotating abrasive wheel. One of the commonest abrasive materials used in the grinding wheels is Carborundum, synthetic crystals of silicon carbide (SiC) formed by fusing a mixture of silica and carbon in an electric furnace.

Rolls Royce

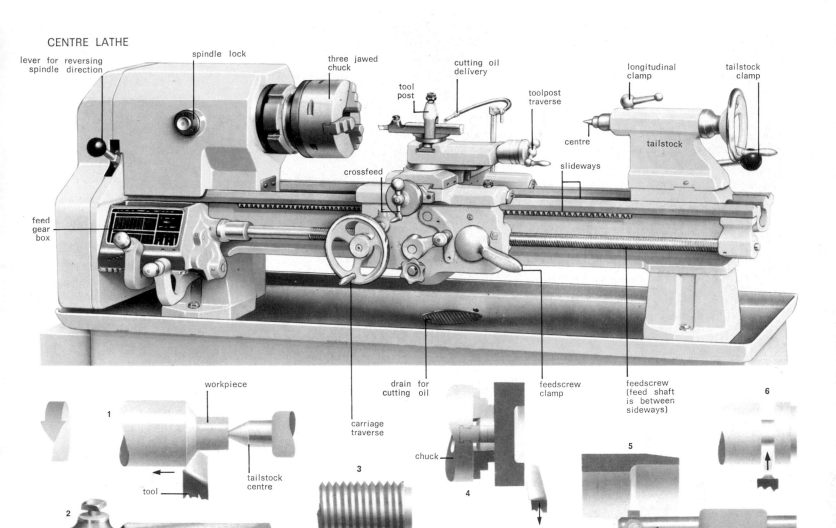

lever for reversing spindle direction

spindle lock

three jawed chuck

cutting oil delivery

tool post

toolpost traverse

longitudinal clamp

tailstock clamp

centre

tailstock

slideways

crossfeed

feed gear box

workpiece

drain for cutting oil

feedscrew clamp

feedscrew (feed shaft is between sideways)

6

tailstock centre

tool

carriage traverse

chuck

5

1

2

3

4

**Above:** A centre lathe, and some of the cutting operations that can be done on it: 1. straight cutting; 2. a tool holder and cutting tool; 3. thread cutting—speed of workpiece and motion of tool determine thread pitch; 4. facing off—cutting a flat face on the end of the workpiece; 5. boring—tool advances within rotating workpiece, cutting inner surface; 6. cutting a machined component from the unmachined bar. A lathe of this type, in common with most other machine tools, would be driven by an electric motor.

**Below:** Turning the barrel of a large gun.

## Lathes

The basic type of lathe is the *centre lathe*, which is used for operations such as machining or *turning* cylindrical components and for cutting screw threads on them. The workpiece is rotated horizontally while the cutting tool is drawn along it by the *feed* mechanism of the machine.

On a typical centre lathe, the workpiece is held in a chuck mounted on the *headstock* at the left-hand end of the machine. The headstock contains the gearing which transmits the drive from an electric motor to the chuck. At the other end of the machine is an adjustable *tailstock* which can be used to support the right-hand end of a long workpiece during turning.

The cutting tool is clamped in a *tool-post* mounted on a *carriage* assembly, which moves on slideways along the *bed* of the lathe between the headstock and the tailstock, and is driven along the bed by a *leadscrew*. A workpiece can be drilled longitudinally by fitting a drill bit to the tailstock in place of the pointed *centre* which it normally carries.

On *turret lathes* and *capstan lathes*, the tailstock is replaced by a turret assembly, usually hexagonal, to which several different tools can be fitted. This means that several operations, such as drilling and thread-cutting, can be performed in sequence by *indexing* (rotating) the turret to bring each tool on it into operation in turn. The turret of a capstan lathe is mounted on a short slide, which is carried on a base that can be positioned at a convenient point on the bed. On a turret lathe, however, the turret is mounted directly on a saddle which moves along the bed itself.

Other types of lathe include the *vertical borer*, a large machine which operates vertically instead of horizontally and is used for boring and turning large castings, and the *automatic bar lathes*, which machine components from long bars of metal fed in through the hollow chuck spindle of the headstock and held in place by the chuck. As each component is finished it is separated from the bar, which is then fed forward into the machine ready for the next component to be machined from it.

## Milling machines

*Milling machines* are used for metal-shaping operations such as cutting grooves and slots. Unlike a lathe, on which the workpiece is rotated while a stationary tool is brought into contact with it, a milling machine uses a rotating tool which cuts the metal away while the workpiece is moved beneath it. When the workpiece is moved in the opposite direction to that in which the teeth of the cutter are moving when they contact it, the action is known as *up-cutting*. If the teeth and the workpiece are moving in the same direction, the milling action is *down-cutting*.

Milling machines can be divided into two general classes: those on which the cutter is mounted on a horizontal spindle and is shaped rather like a wheel with cutting teeth around its edge, and those on which the spindle is vertical and the cutter is roughly cylindrical with teeth cut into its sides and often on its end. Some of the vertical machines have an *offset* milling head which can move the spindle in an arc while it is rotating the

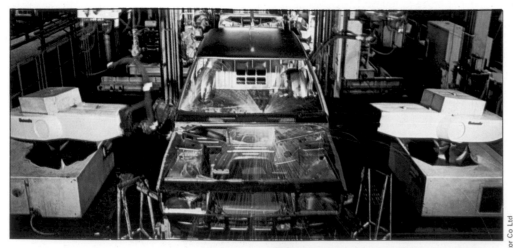

Above and below: Two types of robot machinery at work in a modern car manufacturing plant. The one above is more or less a 'playback' unit, that is, one which simply remembers everything it has been taught and can repeat it perfectly. The one shown below is the simplest of all and can only follow electric tracks; it has no sensory 'eyes', no 'hands' and no ability to carry out a complicated process.

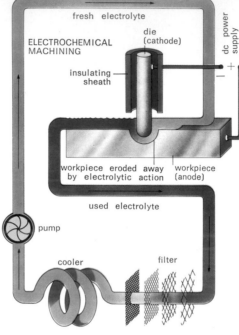

Above: In the *electrochemical machining* (ECM) process a current is passed between a die and the workpiece through a suitable electrolyte. Metal from the workpiece combines with the electrolyte to form ions, which are carried away by the electrolyte. The workpiece is thus eroded away, the shape of the eroded area corresponding to the profile of the die.

Below: A complete ECM machine.

tool. This means that the machine can cut irregularly-shaped holes if required.

*Jig bores*, also known as *mill bores* or *boring mills*, are large, versatile milling machines. The horizontal spindle can be moved up or down and in or out, and the workpiece can be moved in the same way as on an ordinary milling machine. They are used for machining large workpieces, such as heavy machinery castings.

### Shapers and planers

Shapers and planers are used to remove metal from flat surfaces. On a shaper, the workpiece is held stationary, and the cutting tool is driven across it by a mechanical or hydraulic ram. The tool is lifted clear of the workpiece during the return strokes. Planers are much larger than shapers, and so can handle larger workpieces. On a planer, the tool is stationary and the workpiece is held on a reciprocating table that moves it backwards and forwards beneath the tool.

### Other machine tools

The machine tools mentioned above are only a few of the multitude now in use. Others include drills, grinders, machines for cutting gears, and *machining centres*. A machining centre is a machine tool which carries a wide range of tools that enable it to carry out, under automatic control, a sequence of operations such as drilling, thread-cutting and milling.

Many specialized machines have been developed for production-line work where high output rates are required. These units comprise a series of *machine stations*, each of which is tooled up to perform a specific machining function such as drilling or milling. The component to be machined, such as an engine's cylinder block, is passed automatically to each station in turn until the complete sequence of operations has been completed.

One of the automatic control systems for machine tools is known as *numerical control*. The instructions for the machine tool, such as tool positions, cutting speeds and operating sequences, are recorded as numerical and symbolic codes on a storage medium such as paper tape, punched cards or magnetic tape. The coded instructions are read by a control unit, which activates the machine functions in accordance with the instructions. The use of numerical control means that machine tools can be programmed to operate at their most efficient, with a consequent reduction in production times and cost.

The most advanced form of machine control is the *industrial robot* — an arm-like device, capable of movement like a human arm, and equipped with a 'hand' that can pick up and manipulate components or work with various tools such as spray guns or arc-welding torches. A robot is taught how to do its job by a human operator, who will employ a form of *tracer control*.

This particular type of control system involves the use of a template or a three-dimensional model of the component to be produced. A mechanically or electrically driven probe is moved around the template or model, following its contours. As the probe moves, a servomechanism makes the cutting tool move in exactly the same way, so that the workpiece is machined to the same shape as the model or template.

**ELECTROCHEMICAL MACHINING**

fresh electrolyte

die (cathode)

dc power supply

insulating sheath

workpiece eroded away by electrolytic action

workpiece (anode)

used electrolyte

pump

cooler

filter

# Welding

Welding is the joining together of two pieces of metal by means of heat, pressure, or by a combination of both. Early examples of welding include a forge-welded headrest which belonged to the Pharaoh Tutankhamun and was made in about 1350 BC, and a hammer-welded gold sheet produced in Ireland in about 1000 BC. An early example of a joint made by brazing, which is a similar process to welding, is a decorated copper panel made in Mesopotamia before 3000 BC.

## Gas welding and cutting

*Gas welding* is a common form of welding in which the surfaces to be joined are melted, usually together with a *filler metal*, by the flame from a torch burning a mixture of oxygen and a fuel gas such as acetylene or propane. The oxygen and the fuel gas are fed to the torch from separate cylinders, and flame temperatures of around 3,000°C (5,430°F) are produced.

Oxy-acetylene torches are also used for cutting through materials, particularly ferrous metals such as steel or cast iron. When ferrous metals are being cut, the cutting process involves not only a melting away of the material by the high temperature of the flame, but also a certain amount of actual burning of the metal because of its strong chemical affinity for the oxygen in the gas jet. In addition to this chemical reaction there

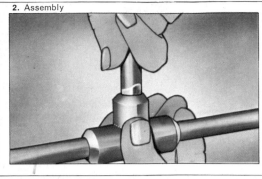

1. Application of flux

2. Assembly

3. Soldering

**Above:** Soldering three copper tubes to a tee-joint. The ends of the tube are coated with flux, and then the tubes and joint are assembled. Each tube is then soldered into place by heating with a blowtorch and applying the solder wire, which melts and is drawn into the join.

**Below:** Four important welding processes: gas, submerged arc, plasma-arc and laser welding.

**Right:** In *reflow soldering*, an electrode is placed on either side of the joint, then an electric current is passed between them and through the joint, heating the joint so that the solder melts. The third probe in this picture is a thermocouple that controls the current flow.

**Below:** Repairing the bucket of an excavator by gas welding.

BFI Electronics Ltd

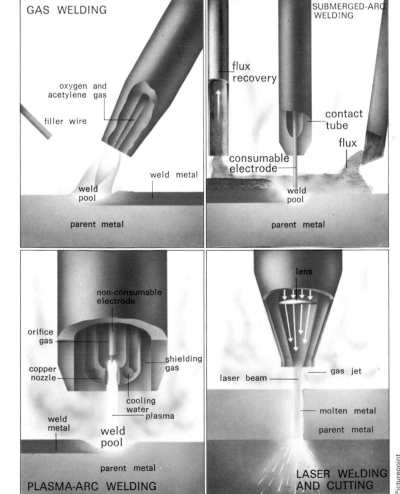

GAS WELDING

oxygen and acetylene gas

filler wire

weld pool

weld metal

parent metal

SUBMERGED-ARC WELDING

flux recovery

contact tube

flux

consumable electrode

weld pool

parent metal

PLASMA-ARC WELDING

non-consumable electrode

orifice gas

copper nozzle

shielding gas

cooling water

plasma

weld metal

weld pool

parent metal

LASER WELDING AND CUTTING

lens

laser beam

gas jet

molten metal

parent metal

Picturepoint

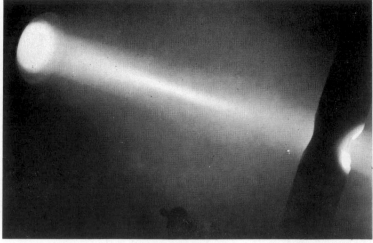

Above: Two cylindrical components being joined by *friction welding*. One component is rotated at high speed, and then pressed against the other, which is held stationary. The resulting friction generates a great deal of heat, which melts the ends of the components. When sufficient melting has occurred, the fixed component is released so that it can rotate with the moving one, and the joint then cools and solidifies.

Right: A joint produced by *explosive welding*, in which components are forced together by explosives and the heat and pressure of the impact welds them together.

Above: Electron beam welding, which is carried out in a vacuum chamber, uses the energy contained in a beam of electrons to generate the heat required to melt the metal. This picture shows a 25 kW beam melting through a 3.8 cm (1.5 in) thick tube made of stainless steel.

Below: An electron beam welding unit. Electrons from an electron gun, 1, pass through a focusing system, 3, on to the workpiece, which is carried on a servo-controlled trolley, 5. A vacuum system is connected to the side of the chamber, 4, and the operator can view the workpiece through an optical system, 2.

ELECTRON BEAM WELDING

is an extremely important mechanical eroding effect produced by the kinetic energy of the flame, which blows molten material and oxidized metal away from the cut.

## Brazing

Gas torches are also used in *brazing*, a process in which the metals to be joined are heated to above about 400°C (750°F) and a non-ferrous filler metal is melted into the junction between them. The filler metals used in brazing have lower melting points than those of the metals that they are used to join.

Brazing in its simplest form is carried out using an oxy-fuel gas torch similar to that used for oxy-acetylene welding. *Silver-alloy* brazing, one of the most common forms, is used in the silverware industry and for making joints where strength and resistance to shock are required, such as in the joining of band-saw blades. The filler metals used contain from 10 to 80 per cent of silver, with 50 to 15 per cent copper and 40 to 5 per cent zinc. They are often known as *silver solders*, but they should not be confused with the metals used for *soft soldering*, the type of soldering used for making connections in electronic circuits. The silver solders melt at between about 700 and 875°C (1,290 and 1,600°F), whereas soft solders melt at around 200°C (390°F) or even less.

Brazing can also be carried out by heating the workpieces, together with the filler metal, in a gas-fired or electrical furnace, or by immersing them in a bath of molten salt. Whichever method is used, however, it is imperative that the surfaces to be joined are completely clean. They must be degreased, and any oxide or scale must be removed chemically or mechanically. The cleaned surfaces must then be protected by a film of *flux*, a material which prevents the formation of a film of oxide on the surfaces during the brazing. One of the oldest and most commonly used flux materials is *borax*, which is hydrated sodium borate ($Na_2B_4O_7.10H_2O$). In certain instances the filler metal must also be protected by a coating of flux.

## Arc welding

In *arc welding* the heat required is produced by an electric arc struck between an electrode and the workpiece. One of the most versatile forms of this is *manual arc welding*. The electrode holder is connected to one terminal of a power source, such as a motor-driven generator, a transformer or a transformer-rectifier, and the workpiece is connected to the other terminal. The electrode is typically about 36 or 46 cm (14 or 18 in) long, consisting of a filler metal wire core coated with a layer of flux.

The power is turned on, and the end of the electrode is brought to the workpiece so that an electric arc is struck between them. The heat generated by the arc melts at the join and at the tip of the electrode, and metal and flux from the electrode are drawn across the arc to the workpiece.

Manual arc welding equipment is, in general, inexpensive and portable, and can be used in a workshop or out of doors, for example in a shipyard or on a construction site. It is, however, limited in some respects; for instance, because each electrode is relatively short, only small lengths of weld can be made with each one, necessitating frequent stopping and starting.

A process designed to overcome many of the limitations of manual arc welding is the *gas metal arc* process, which includes $CO_2$ welding and *metal inert gas* welding. Instead of using a short length of wire coated with flux, the electrode wire is fed from a continuous roll, and the join is shielded from the oxidizing effects of the atmosphere by surrounding it with a suitable gas or gas mixture.

In this process, the electrode wire passes through a heavy-duty welding gun and is surrounded by gas supplied from a cylinder. An arc is then struck between the wire and the workpiece, and a droplet of molten metal forms on the end of the wire. This drop is detached

Above: In plasma-arc welding, the arc ionizes a jet of gas to form a very hot stream of *plasma* that is directed on to the workpiece. The nozzle of the gun concentrates the arc and plasma into a very narrow stream, and this results in very high arc temperatures of up to 30,000°C (54,000°F).

Above right: A plasma-arc cutting machine. Two arcs are produced by plasma-arc cutting and welding torches: one, the *non-transferred* arc, is within the nozzle and creates the initial ionization of the gas; the other, the *transferred* arc, is carried in the plasma jet to the workpiece.

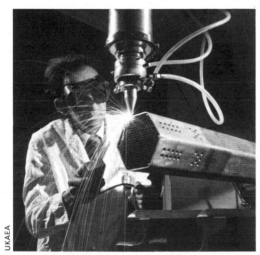

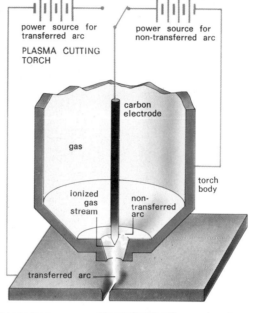

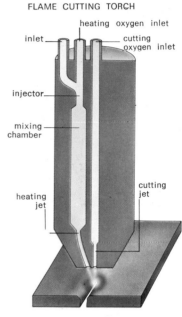

PLASMA CUTTING TORCH

power source for transferred arc

power source for non-transferred arc

carbon electrode

gas

ionized gas stream

non-transferred arc

torch body

transferred arc

FLAME CUTTING TORCH

heating oxygen inlet

inlet

cutting oxygen inlet

injector

mixing chamber

heating jet

cutting jet

Left: Using a laser beam cutter to trim the outer skin of a nuclear fuel canister without damaging the interior structure.

Above: Sectional drawings of the nozzles of a plasma-arc cutting torch, left, and an oxygen-fuel gas cutting torch.

from the electrode and transferred to the workpiece by the arc, drops of metal being formed and transferred at a rate of about 200 times per second.

The gases used include argon, helium, and argon-helium mixture (for metal inert gas welding) and carbon dioxide for $CO_2$ welding. The inert gases give a better weld finish than that produced with a carbon dioxide shield, but their cost is much higher. This difference can be overcome by using a tubular electrode filled with flux instead of a solid electrode wire. This flux-cored wire can be used, depending on the composition of the flux, with a carbon dioxide shield or with no gas shield at all.

The flux-cored wire enables higher rates of metal deposition to be achieved with a lower heat input, thereby reducing the risk of distortion of the workpiece. A further advantage of these 'gasless' flux-cored wires is that when welding in exposed positions, such as on a bridge or on the top of an oil rig, there is no gas shield to be blown away.

Another process using a continuous wire electrode is *submerged arc welding*. This process is carried out with one or more welding heads mounted on special carriages, and a hopper placed just in front of the electrode deposits a layer of flux on the workpiece. The arc is struck beneath this loose blanket of flux, hence the name of the process.

Other important forms of arc welding are *tungsten inert gas* welding and *plasma-arc* welding. In tungsten inert gas welding, heat is produced by an arc struck between a non-consumable tungsten electrode and the workpiece. The electrode, arc, weld pool, and the adjacent heated areas of the workpiece are protected from contamination by a stream of gas such as argon or helium.

The process is best suited to the welding of thin materials, and although many of its applications are for the production of *autogenous* welds (where the workpiece is welded by melting together just the two abutting surfaces without a filler), some now involve the use of a separate filler wire which is fed into the weld pool by hand. Tungsten inert gas welding is finding an increasing number of applications in areas such as nuclear engineering and the aerospace industry.

Plasma-arc welding is similar to tungsten inert gas welding, but the arc used is constricted by a narrow nozzle just beneath the electrode. This has the effect of concentrating the arc and of increasing the velocity of the gas flow, which also passes through the nozzle. The gas becomes a stream of electrically-charged atoms (or *ions*) which is known as a *plasma*, and temperatures as high as 30,000°C (54,000°F) may be reached. The process can be used with very thin as well as thick materials, and the high arc temperatures allow a wide range of metals to be welded, including stainless steel, aluminium and titanium. The plasma-arc principle is also used for the cutting of sheet metals.

## Resistance welding

The heat for *resistance* welding is produced by an electric current which is passed through the workpiece. Much of the heat generated is dissipated by the water-cooled electrodes used, so that the melting is confined to the area of the joint. Major applications of *resistance spot welding* include the production of car bodies and of domestic equipment such as washing machines.

*Resistance seam welding* is an extension of spot welding, but the pieces to be welded are joined by continuous seams of welding rather than by a series of spot-welds. The electrodes which pass the current through the workpiece are in the form of a pair of wheels, as opposed to the two rods used in spot welding. Typical applications include the welding of the gutter channels on to car roof panels, and the production of tubes.

Rolls Royce Ltd

Plascut Ltd

UKAEA

# Telephone and Telegraph

The technology of telecommunications is concerned with the transmission and reception of information using electricity and electromagnetic waves (such as light and radio waves). It involves many different disciplines from electrical engineering to electronics, signal analysis and information theory. The information itself may be printed news, speech, television pictures or telegraphic messages.

## The early telegraph

The basic components of a telegraphic system, such as sources of direct (dc) current (batteries), electromagnets (solenoids) and current-carrying metal wires, all existed by about 1830. Of the numerous designs invented during this period, many were concerned with methods for displaying the characters (letters, numbers and punctuation) at the receiver after their transmission in an electrical form.

One of the most important telegraph systems of the nineteenth century was that invented in America by an artist called Samuel Morse. The Morse telegraph was attractive because of its simplicity—requiring only one wire (and a return) for the transmission of any character. Each character was represented by a combination of two simple signals: a dot (short burst of current) and a dash (a current of longer duration). The complexity of each coded character was chosen according to its frequency of use. Thus, for example, the most common English letter, 'e', is a single dot, while an 's' is three dots and an 'o' three dashes. The international distress call 'SOS' is simply · · · — — — · · ·.

## Automatic telegraphy

The speed and accuracy of the Morse system was determined by the operator's skill rather than any technical limitations of the apparatus itself, and with the growth of telegraphic traffic, ways of using existing telegraph lines more efficiently were sought.

Michael Holford

Bell Labs

Frequency division multiplexing

**Top:** A replica of a 19th-century Morse telegraph receiver.

**Above:** *Frequency division multiplexing,* a method of sending more than one message simultaneously down a single wire by superimposing each one on to a different carrier frequency, was first suggested by Elisha Gray in the late 19th century. These diagrams show a carrier wave (top) and a carrier wave modulated by a Morse code signal of one dot and three dashes; this gives one short and three long pulses.

ITT

**Above:** Bell's telephone transmitter (left) and receiver (right) which on 10 March 1876 carried the first sentence ever spoken over a telephone. The sentence, spoken by Bell to his assistant Thomas Watson, was 'Mr Watson, come here; I want you.'

**Left:** A teleprinter produces electrical pulses, based on a 5-unit code, which represent the various characters typed by the operator. These pulses are transmitted to the receiving teleprinter, which decodes them and types out the message.

**Right:** This chart shows the international code used for punched paper tape telegraphy, plus the Morse code. The patterns of holes in the tape code mean either letters, or other characters and instructions, depending on whether they were preceded by a 'letters' or a 'figures' code.

| combination nos | Figures & symbols | 5 | 4 | 3 | 2 | 1 | letters | Morse Code |
|---|---|---|---|---|---|---|---|---|
| 1 | — | | | | • | • | A | •— |
| 2 | ? | • | • | | | • | B | —••• |
| 3 | : | | • | • | • | | C | —•—• |
| 4 | who are you | | • | | | • | D | —•• |
| 5 | 3 | | | | | • | E | • |
| 6 | (optional) | | • | • | | • | F | ••—• |
| 7 | (optional) | • | • | | • | | G | ——• |
| 8 | (optional) | • | | • | | | H | •••• |
| 9 | 8 | | | • | • | | I | •• |
| 10 | bell | | • | | • | • | J | •——— |
| 11 | ( | • | | • | • | • | K | —•— |
| 12 | ) | • | | | • | | L | •—•• |
| 13 | . | • | • | • | | | M | —— |
| 14 | , | | • | • | | | N | —• |
| 15 | 9 | • | • | | | | O | ——— |
| 16 | 0 | • | | • | • | | P | •——• |
| 17 | 1 | • | | • | • | • | Q | ——•— |
| 18 | 4 | | • | | • | | R | •—• |
| 19 | | | | • | | • | S | ••• |
| 20 | 5 | • | | | | | T | — |
| 21 | 7 | | | • | • | • | U | ••— |
| 22 | = | • | • | • | • | | V | •••— |
| 23 | 2 | • | | | • | • | W | •—— |
| 24 | / | • | • | • | | • | X | —••— |
| 25 | 6 | • | | • | | • | Y | —•—— |
| 26 | + | • | | | | • | Z | ——•• |
| 27 | carriage return | | • | | | | | |
| 28 | line feed | | | | • | | | |
| 29 | letters | • | • | • | • | • | | |
| 30 | figures | • | • | | • | • | | |
| 31 | space | | | • | | | | |
| 32 | all space | | | | | | | |

Punched paper tape code and Morse code

Telephone exchange systems, showing the transition from hard wired stage (left) through integrated circuits (mid 1970's) to large scale integration (late 1970's). The exchange on the right has a capacity 16 times greater than the hard wired circuit.

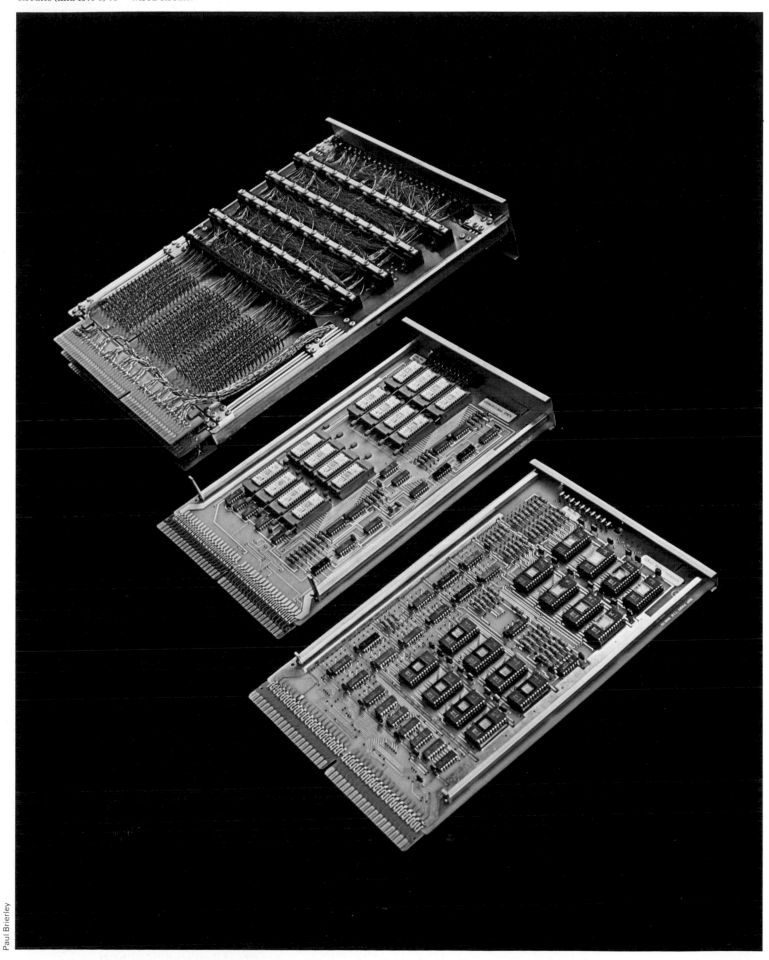

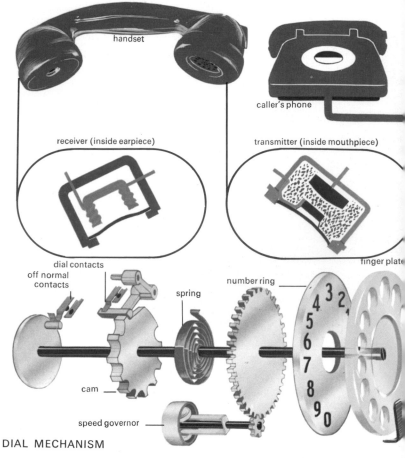

Charles Wheatstone provided a simple solution to this problem by designing a mechanical Morse sender which converted messages, stored in the form of holes punched in paper tape, into electrical pulses. At the receiver, an inker recorded these pulses on another reel of paper. The speed limitation of this device was determined solely by the reading and recording speeds of the terminal equipment. Whereas an expert Morse operator could send only 30 to 35 words a minute, the paper tape system could transmit at speeds up to 600 words per minute.

**The telephone**
Although others before him had succeeded in using electricity to transmit sounds and musical notes over a wire, in 1876 Edinburgh-born Alexander Graham Bell was the first to patent a device capable of sending and receiving recognisable words. While the device worked well as a receiver, its performance as a transmitter was less successful.

An improved transmitter was developed almost simultaneously by Edison and Hunnings in 1878. This was the *carbon granule transmitter*. The modern version consists of an aluminium alloy diaphragm which is attached to a dome-shaped piece of carbon, anchored in such a way as to be free to move in and out of another cup-shaped piece of carbon, filled with carbon granules. Electrical connections are made to the carbon electrodes at the front and back and the current flows from one, through the granules, to the other. The rapid changes of air pressure set up by speech cause the granules to be alternately compressed and released, so altering their electrical resistance. The current flowing through the granules thus fluctuates in the same way as the air pressure, so that the original sound can be faithfully reproduced at the distant end.

Bell's original earpiece worked on the principles of a combined permanent magnet and electromagnet acting on an iron diaphragm. A similar system is used in modern receivers, in which a thin metal diaphragm is made to vibrate by variations in the magnetic field of an electromagnet. These variations are set up by the varying electrical current carrying the incoming voice signal.

**Telephone exchanges**
The first telephone exchange opened in Connecticut, USA, in 1878, followed a year later by the first European exchange in Coleman Street in the City of London.

**Above:** A telephone with its casing and handset removed. One of the two bell gongs, and part of the electromagnet that operates the hammer which strikes the gongs, are visible below the dial.

**Right:** These diagrams show a simplified telephone mouthpiece and earpiece, and an exploded view of a dial mechanism. The cam opens and closes the dial contacts to produce the dialling pulses as the dial returns to its rest position.

DIAL MECHANISM

The earliest exchanges were all manual, with operators physically placing and removing plugs to complete circuits. The first automatic telephone exchange was installed at La Porte, Indiana, USA, in 1892. It was based on a system invented in 1889 by Almon B. Strowger, an irascible American undertaker irritated by inefficient operators.

An automatic exchange is simply a set of apparatus to which all the telephones in a neighbourhood are connected, with a switching network that will interconnect any two of them. Interconnection is achieved by a series of signal pulses, transmitted by the dial mechanism of the sender's telephone, which control the switching network.

Strowger's invention consisted of a metal arm, rather like a windscreen wiper, which was driven around a series of numbered contacts (arranged in a semi-circular form) by the dial pulses. The modern version of this *selector* is a two-motion type which first moves the wiper vertically to select one of ten sets of contacts, and then sweeps it in a horizontal arc to select one of the ten individual contacts in that set.

When dialling the first digit of a telephone number, say six, six pulses are sent to a *first selector* in the exchange. This makes the wiper move vertically to the contacts on the sixth level—corresponding to all telephones beginning with the number six. At this point it is necessary to find a *second selector* for handling the second telephone digit. To do this, the first selector wiper moves in a horizontal arc 'searching' for a free contact (and thus a free second selector). If the next digit dialled is 'two' the second selector wiper moves up to level two and then sweeps horizontally until a free third selector is found (corresponding to all telephone numbers beginning with 62). This third selector deals with the third digit (vertical

**Above:** A rear view of the inside of a loudspeaking telephone unit. This type of telephone puts the incoming speech through an amplifier and loudspeaker, and has a microphone at the front to pick up the user's voice. The handset is provided for use when confidential calls are being made.

**Below:** A telephone with a pushbutton dial instead of the conventional rotary type. The electronic unit shown next to it is the circuitry which produces the dialling pulses and transmits them to the exchange, leaving a pause between each set of pulses to allow the exchange equipment to operate.

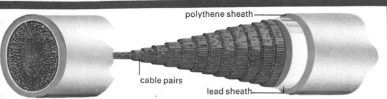

local exchange

The series of drawings along the top of this page and the following pages shows the route taken by an overseas telephone call, and details of some of the types of telephone cables used.

The local exchange (left) puts the call through to the trunk exchange (right) to which the international circuits are connected. The trunk exchange then routes the call to its destination country.

international trunk exchange

repeater

multipair cable

ltipair cable

polythene sheath

cable pairs

lead sheath

Above: The cables to which individual telephones are connected, and some connecting small local exchanges, are of the *multipair* type. Large multipair cables serving an area's telephones may contain up to 4,800 pairs of wires. The large cable is successively split off into smaller ones

serving smaller groups of subscribers, and these smaller cables eventually terminate at *distribution points*. From these points, single-pair cables run to the subscribers' telephones. Multipair cables have aluminium or copper alloy conductors, insulated with paper or polythene.

Right: Submarine telephone cable stored in the cable tanks of the cable-laying ship the CS *Mercury*, operated by Cable & Wireless Ltd. Fully laden, the *Mercury* can carry up to 1,930 km (1,200 miles) of cable, plus submarine repeater units. It can lay the cable at speeds of up to 5 knots.

STROWGER EXCHANGE SYSTEM
dialling 7649

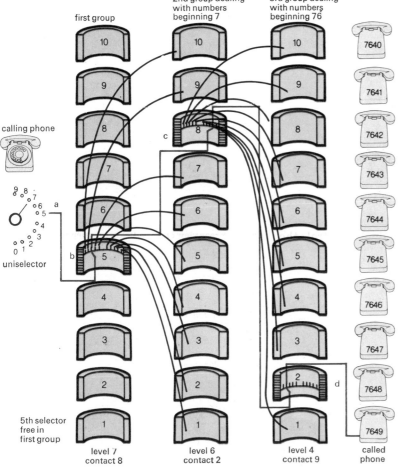

first group

2nd group dealing with numbers beginning 7

3rd group dealing with numbers beginning 76

calling phone

uniselector

5th selector free in first group

level 7 contact 8

level 6 contact 2

level 4 contact 9

called phone

7640
7641
7642
7643
7644
7645
7646
7647
7648
7649

Right: A uniselector switch used in Strowger exchange equipment. Each subscriber's phone has its own uniselector in the exchange; when the subscriber picks up the handset of the phone, the central part of the selector rotates so that the contacts it carries step around the fixed contacts, which are connected to other sets of selectors in the exchange, until it finds a set which is not in use. When a free set has been found, the dialling tone is transmitted to the subscriber's phone.

Below: Some of the complex wiring used in telephone exchanges to link up the various sections of the equipment. The wires are made of copper, with plastic insulation which is colour-coded. This makes it easier to identify a particular circuit when equipment is being installed, tested or repaired.

Above: The operation of a Strowger exchange. When a caller lifts the handset, the uniselector to which the phone is connected *a*, finds a free first selector, *b*. Other equipment then sends a dialling tone back to the phone, and the number required can then be dialled. If the first digit dialled is

a '7', the first selector steps up to level 7, to which a 2nd selector group, which deals with all numbers beginning with 7, is connected. In this case, it finds that the 8th selector in that group, *c*, is free, and connects the call to it. When the '6' is dialled, this selector steps to level

6, which is connected to a 3rd group that deals with numbers beginning '76'. Finding the 2nd selector of this group, *d*, free, selector '*c*' connects with it. Dialling the final two digits steps selector '*d*' up to level 4 and round to contact 9, which is connected to the wires leading to phone 7649.

international trunk exchange

repeater

coaxial cable

submarine coaxial cable

Submarine coaxial cable

insulation    steel core

centre
conductor    outer
conductor

Multicore coaxial cable

coaxial core :
centre
conductor
insulation
outer
conductor

steel
screening
tape

control
pair

lead
sheath

polythene
sheath

fibre optic link

signal → modulator → laser source

signal ↑

demodulator

photodiode

optical fibre
diameter 0.1 mm
core diameter 0.05 mm

modulated
light beam

**Left:** At the country of destination for an overseas call, the trunk exchange linked to the international cable routes the call to the local exchange (right) serving the called number.

The groups of digits dialled by the caller route the call as follows: dialling the USA from London, for example, '010' connects the caller (via the local exchange) with the international trunk

exchange. A further '1' routes the call to the USA, and the next three digits route it to the city required, such as '305' for Miami. The remaining digits set up the final connection via the local exchange.

This diagram shows the principles of a new telecommunications technology called *fibre optics*, in which information is modulated onto a light beam transmitted along thin glass fibres.

**Above:** Light is a form of electromagnetic radiation. It has a very much higher frequency than radio or microwaves, but it can be modulated in a similar fashion. In a fibre optic system, the light from a laser is modulated by an information signal such as a telephone conversation. The

modulated light is beamed into the inner core of the fibre, which has a higher refractive index than the outer cladding layer. The light is reflected from side to side along the fibre by the core/cladding interface which acts as a sort of pipe to carry the light along. At the receiving end,

a photodiode produces an electrical output signal when the light strikes it, and this signal is demodulated to reproduce the original signal.

**Below:** This experiment simulates the passage of a laser beam along a fibre optic link, so that its attenuation can be measured.

movement) and fourth digit (horizontal movement) and at this point the required telephone is interconnected.

A *uniselector* precedes the first selector, and this hunts for a free first selector. Consequently, no selector 'belongs' to a particular telephone but can be allocated to one for the duration of the call. This reduces the amount of equipment necessary in an exchange—the only equipment which does belong to each telephone is the uniselector, and this is relatively simple and cheap. If at any stage a free selector cannot be found, or if the telephone sought is in use, an 'engaged' tone is transmitted to the sender.

Since Strowger's invention, other switching systems have been developed, some of them electro-mechanical and others electronic. In the electronic exchanges the switching is performed by electronic circuits which are faster, more compact and less prone to failure than electro-mechanical systems such as Strowger or the 'crossbar' system widely used in many countries.

## Multiplexing techniques

If one pair of wires were necessary for every telephone conversation going on in the world then we would either be queuing to use the phone or the world would be a veritable maze of copper wires. These problems are avoided by the use of transmission methods known as *multiplexing*. These methods allow us to transmit hundreds and sometimes thousands of conversations along one pair of wires.

One common multiplexing method, *frequency multiplexing*, uses a similar technique to that used in radio transmission, where it is necessary to be able

**Above left and above:** Drawings of submarine and land *coaxial* cables. Coaxial cables can carry signals of a much higher frequency than can multipair cables, so multiplexing techniques employing high frequency carrier waves can be used on coaxial circuits. A submarine cable such as this one would be capable of carrying up to 4,000 simultaneous telephone calls. The multicore land coaxial cable shown here could carry up to 16,200 telephone circuits, using carrier frequencies of up to 12.5 MHz with repeaters spaced at intervals of 2 km (1.24 miles). The paper-insulated control pairs are used for system control purposes.

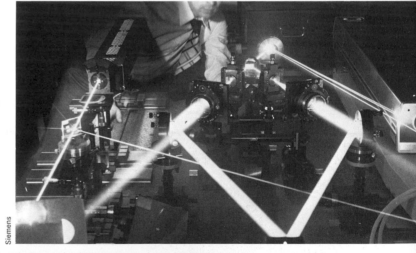

Siemens

Julian Barnard/John Watney

**Left:** One of the services provided by most telephone systems is the 'speaking clock'. The time announcements are put together from phrases recorded in tracks on a rotating, magnetically-coated drum. The drum is 'read' by sets of pick-up heads controlled by timing cams.

**Right:** The Transaction Telephone is used for automatic verification of credit card transactions. Two cards are inserted into the machine: a dialling card which instructs it to dial the computer at the credit company's data centre, and the customer's credit card. The amount of the transaction is entered via the keyboard.

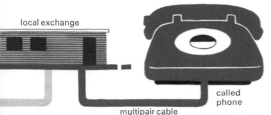

local exchange

called phone

multipair cable

Below: The crossbar system, like Strowger, is electro-mechanical, but faster and more reliable. Crossbar switches have contact assemblies arranged in a grid pattern. Connections are made by electromagnets which make a row of input contacts intersect with a column of output contacts.

pulse code modulation

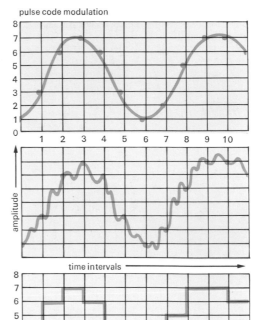

amplitude

time intervals

Left: The principles of *pulse code modulation* (PCM). This is a system for transmitting information so that it arrives with a minimum amount of distortion caused by electrical 'noise' — unwanted voltages picked up as it passes through the system. The first graph shows the waveform of the original signal.

This is how the original wave might look after being transmitted in an unmodulated form. The instantaneous values are the same, but it is very distorted. A wave reconstructed from a PCM signal would be free from this distortion, being based only on the instantaneous values.

This graph shows how the modulator measures the amplitude of the wave at regular intervals, and then produces electrical pulses whose amplitudes correspond to those of the original wave at those intervals. At the receiving end the demodulator uses these pulses to reconstruct the original wave.

Left: A communications station in the United Arab Republic. A large number of information channels can be carried by microwaves, and they are widely used instead of cable transmission systems. Because microwaves travel in straight lines and cannot bend around obstructions or over the horizon, the transmitter and receiver must normally be in 'line of sight' of each other. This can be overcome by beaming them up to a satellite, which then re-transmits them to distant stations, or by *tropospheric scatter,* bouncing them off the layers of air in the lower atmosphere. The large dish shown here is for satellite communications.

to distinguish one signal from the hundreds of radio signals received by an aerial. This is achieved by a process known as *modulation*, whereby every broadcast is superimposed on a unique 'signature tone' or *carrier frequency*. At the radio receiver, a particular broadcast is obtained by selecting its associated carrier frequency and *demodulating* the incoming signal.

The use of carrier frequencies enables the capacity of a telephone network to be greatly increased. Between exchanges, for example, where the communications traffic is most dense, each conversation to be transmitted can be modulated on to a unique carrier frequency and at the receiving end a demodulater can extract any one of the conversations to the exclusion of all the others.

### Frequency and bandwidth
The most important frequencies making up speech lie between 400 and 4,000 Hz, and if these are present the words and the person speaking them are recognizable. Thus a telephone line (and the associated transmitter and receiver) must be capable of handling these frequencies without losing too much of their strength (amplitude).

Unfortunately, a simple pair of telephone wires impedes high frequency alternating currents more than lower frequencies—a situation exacerbated by long distances. Consequently, the frequency bandwidth which the wires can handle decreases with distance. With a simple telephone conversation, this can be overcome by attaching inductive filters to the line which 'boost' the higher frequencies of the electrical signal. When, however, a modulated signal is transmitted down a telephone line other techniques must be sought.

When a speech signal, with frequencies from 400 to 4,000 Hz, is modulated on to a carrier frequency (which is much higher and beyond the audible range), the whole signal is moved up to the region of the carrier frequency. For example, if the carrier frequency is 100,000 Hz then the modulated signal occupies a bandwidth of 8,000 Hz about the 100,000 Hz mark (that is from 96,000 to 104,000 Hz). This presents a problem in telecommunications because ordinary wires will not handle such high frequencies.

Two inventions eventually came together to overcome the problem of transmitting high frequency modulated signals over long distances—these were the *coaxial cable* and the *telephone repeater*.

Modern coaxial cables will handle frequencies up to 10 MHz (10 million Hertz). If each signal occupies a bandwidth of 8,000 Hz about its own carrier frequency then approximately 1,000 different conversations can be transmitted along it.

However good a cable is, it will still attenuate (reduce) signals over long distances. To overcome this, amplifiers were developed which could be placed periodically along the cable to boost the signals—these are called *repeaters*. As low frequency currents (and especially dc) are attenuated less than high frequency ones, it was found to be possible to power all the repeaters on a cable from the terminal exchanges by passing direct current along the cable.

# Radio

The invention of radio, at the end of the nineteenth century, marked the beginning of the era of mass communications. It was soon possible to broadcast the details of events, as they happened, directly to people's homes, and to communicate directly with ships at sea or moving aircraft. The development of radio also paved the way for the advent of television, which has had an even greater impact on home entertainment. Military operations have been affected by radio, and space exploration, both manned and unmanned, would be impossible without it.

Radio waves are a form of *electromagnetic radiation*, which consists of a combination of alternating electric and magnetic fields. Radio waves travel at the same speed as light, and the peaks of the waves are the points at which the values of the electric and magnetic fields are at their maximum.

The *frequency* of a radio wave is the number of times per second that these fields reach a maximum in one direction, reverse to a maximum in the other direction, and then return to the original maximum. The distance between two successive maximum values in the same direction is known as the *wavelength* of the wave, and the higher the frequency of a wave the shorter its wavelength.

Radio waves range from the very low frequency (VLF) waves having wavelengths of between 1,000 km and 10 km, up to the very high microwave frequencies which have wavelengths of from 1 m down to less than 1 mm.

## The invention of radio

The existence of electric and magnetic fields was first recognized by Michael Faraday in 1845. Faraday's concepts were taken up by James Clerk Maxwell, who went on to predict the existence of electromagnetic radiation and calculated that electromagnetic waves could travel through space at the speed of light.

The German physicist Heinrich Hertz devoted much time to the study of Maxwell's theory—although it was generally not accepted by other scientists at that time—and in 1887 he succeeded in demonstrating the generation, transmission and reception of electromagnetic waves. He produced his waves by making a spark jump across a small gap in a loop of wire. A similar loop, with a small gap in it, was placed nearby, and when the spark was created in the first loop, a spark also appeared at the gap in the second. The current flowing in the first loop had created electromagnetic waves, which radiated away from the loop and were picked up by the second loop, causing a current to flow in it.

The work of Hertz was studied by researchers in many countries. Sir Oliver Lodge in England, Alexander Popov in Russia, Edouard Branly in France and Augusto Righi in Italy are among the most notable of these. Their work ·on methods of generating and detecting radio waves was studied by Guglielmo Marconi, who took out the first patent for wireless telegraphy in June 1896.

Marconi began his experiments in 1894, constructing a transmitter and receiver

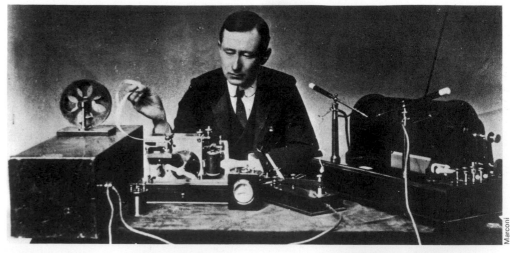

Above: Guglielmo Marconi (1874-1937), the son of an Italian father and an Irish mother, was only 22 years old when he patented the first wireless telegraph in 1896. He was a joint recipient of the Nobel Prize for physics in 1909, and received other honours from both Britain and Italy.

Right: This 1927 radio is a *superheterodyne* receiver. It contains circuits which mix the modulated signal with an unmodulated one to produce a lower, intermediate frequency signal. This signal is then demodulated to produce the audio frequency signal that is used to drive a speaker or headphones.

Above: George Bernard Shaw broadcasting from a studio in Plymouth, England, in 1929. The microphone is contained within the 'meat safe' housing; it comprised a flat aluminium coil mounted within the field of an electromagnet and held in place by cotton wool pads covered in petroleum jelly.

Below: A 'crystal set', a popular form of cheap radio during the 1920s. The crystal set had a coil and a variable capacitor for tuning, and a silicon or germanium crystal which, when contacted with a wire probe called a 'cat's whisker', demodulated the signal by rectifying it.

Right: Radio waves can be transmitted considerable distances around the earth because the electrically-charged layers in the upper atmosphere, known collectively as the *ionosphere*, reflect them back down to distant receivers. The ionosphere is a series of layers, known as D, E, $F_1$ and $F_2$, consisting of ionized gas molecules with free electrons which were liberated when the molecules were ionized by the action of solar radiation. The height at which radio waves are reflected depends on their frequency, and the highest frequencies are not reflected at all. At night, the $F_1$ layer merges with $F_2$.

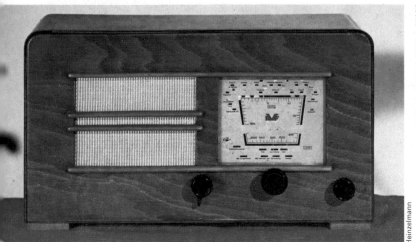

Left: The 'Heinzelmann' radio of 1948 was the German Grundig company's first product. It was supplied initially in kit form, but no valves were provided; customers were advised to buy the valves from army surplus stores.

Right: Low and very low frequency radio waves can travel around the earth in the region between the earth's surface and the ionosphere. This region acts as a kind of natural waveguide for waves of these frequencies. Short wavelength, high frequency waves, with frequencies up to 30 MHz, are bounced around the world between the ionosphere and the surface.

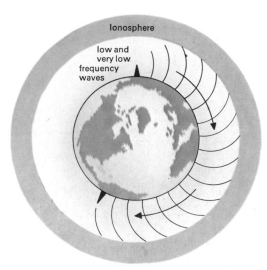

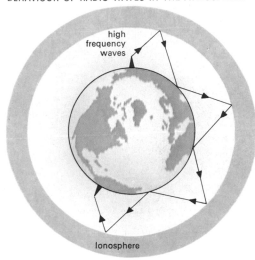

BEHAVIOUR OF RADIO WAVES IN THE ATMOSPHERE

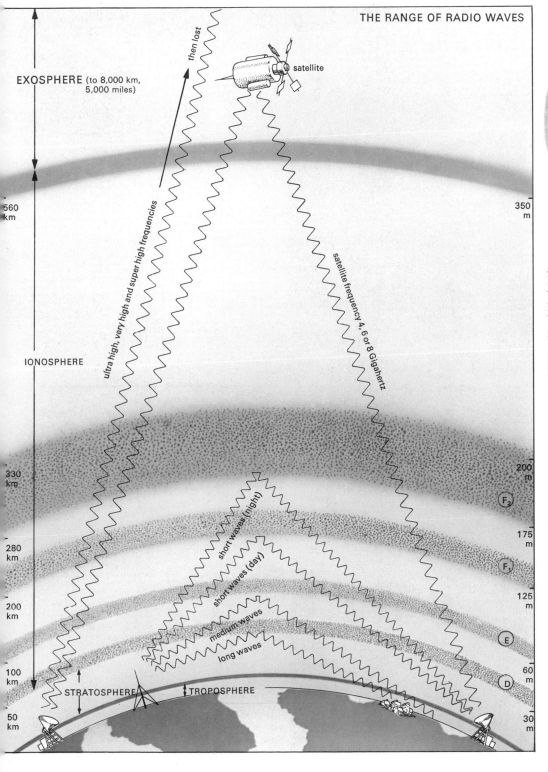

THE RANGE OF RADIO WAVES

at his father's villa near Bologna, Italy. His receiver was a detector of the 'coherer' type, invented by Branly, in which metal powder inside a glass tube stuck together when magnetized by a spark appearing across a gap in the adjacent aerial circuit. When the powder stuck together it allowed a current to be passed through it, and this current operated a telegraph receiver. By transmitting Morse Code signals in the form of pulses of radio waves, similar pulses of electric current were made to flow in the coherer and so the message was recorded by the telegraph receiver connected to it.

## Post Office backing

Marconi approached the Italian government for backing, but they were uninterested and so he went to England, where Sir William Preece, the Engineer in Chief of the Post Office, put full facilities at his disposal. His system was successfully operated between the Post Office headquarters and the Thames Embankment in 1896, and the following year a 13 km (8 mile) circuit was set up across the Bristol Channel.

By removing the spark gap from the aerial circuit to a closed circuit—which acted as a reservoir of energy—long trains of waves were produced and very soon distances of several hundred miles could be covered. After building links to the Isle of Wight and to France, in 1901 Marconi successfully transmitted the first transatlantic signal, an 'S' in Morse Code, from Poldhu in Cornwall to St John's in Newfoundland.

The Marconi system only transmitted telegraphic messages in the form of pulses of radio waves, and it was not until 1906 that a method of transmitting speech was developed. This method was the work the Canadian physicist Reginald Fessenden, who invented the technique of *modulating* radio waves.

Fessenden used a continuous signal or *carrier*, with the speech signal superimposed on it in such a way that the amplitude of the waves varied with the variations in the speech signal. At the receiver, these variations in amplitude were used to produce a varying electrical signal which corresponded to the original signal with which the carrier was modulated. This signal was then amplified and put through a loudspeaker to reproduce the original sounds.

This method is known as *amplitude modulation* (AM), and it is the modulation technique used for long, medium and short wavelength radio broadcasts. One major drawback to AM radio, however, is that the wave can be modulated by unwanted electrical signals such as those produced by thunderstorms and some types of electrical equipment. This means that the signal can arrive at the receiver modulated not only with the original signal but also with these unwanted ones, which produce the background noise or 'static' often heard on AM radio.

A solution to this problem of static interference was found in 1939 by Edwin Armstrong in the US. Instead of using the sound signal to vary the amplitude of the carrier wave, he used it to vary its frequency. The signal produced by the receiver varied according to the variations in the frequency of the incoming carrier wave. This method is known as *frequency modulation* (FM), and it is used for transmissions in the higher frequency wavebands such as the VHF (very high frequency) band and the microwave bands.

Static interference still creates variations in the amplitude of FM signals, but as the receiver only responds to variations in the frequency of the signal these amplitude variations do not affect the reproduced sound.

## Tuning

When a radio is tuned to a particular station, its tuning section is set to accept only the carrier frequency of that station. The tuning circuit contains, in its simplest form, a coil and a capacitor that together constitute a *resonant circuit*, one that offers very little impedance to a current whose frequency is the same as the *resonant frequency* of the circuit. This resonant frequency is determined by the values of the inductance of the coil and the capacitance of the capacitor.

The capacitor in a simple radio tuning circuit is variable, and when the tuning knob is turned the value of the capacitor is altered, so altering the resonant frequency of the circuit. The radio will now be tuned to the station whose frequency is the same as the new resonant frequency of the circuit.

Radio transmitters operate by amplifying the modulated signal and applying it to the transmitting aerial from which the radio waves are emitted. At the receiving end, the radio waves coming into contact with the aerial create tiny currents in it which are then passed through the tuning stage, demodulated, and amplified. Finally, the signal is played through the loudspeaker to reproduce the

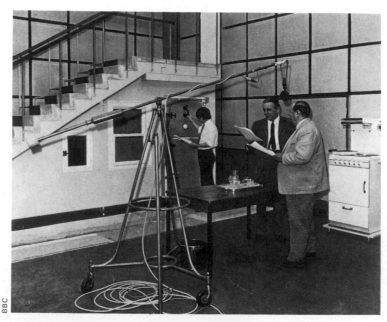

BBC

Cable & Wireless

**Above: A studio control booth. The signals from the studio, on the other side of the glass screen, pass through the control console** before being sent to the transmitter.

**Below: Part of the output stage of a large radio transmitter.**

Marconi

Left: Actors rehearsing an episode of a radio serial. The studio is equipped with various items for producing sound effects, including three types of stairs; two types of window; a door with a knocker, bell, latch, three types of lock and a bolt; and kitchen equipment including a stove.

Below: Radio waves are either *amplitude modulated* (AM) or *frequency modulated* (FM). In both cases, the variations in the modulated carrier wave correspond to the variations in the original sound signal. In the case of AM, the wave's amplitude varies; in that of FM its frequency varies.

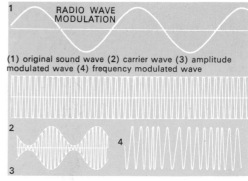

RADIO WAVE MODULATION

(1) original sound wave (2) carrier wave (3) amplitude modulated wave (4) frequency modulated wave

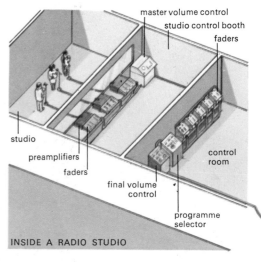

master volume control
studio control booth
faders
studio
preamplifiers
faders
final volume control
control room
programme selector

INSIDE A RADIO STUDIO

**Above: A studio and control room arrangement. The studio has its own control booth where the signals from its microphones are amplified and then combined, using faders to adjust their relative volumes. The combined signal is then sent to the control room, which controls the output from several** studios, before going on to the transmitter.

**Right: At the transmitter, the carrier wave is modulated with the signal from the studio then transmitted. The receiver retrieves the sound signal from the modulated wave and plays it through the loudspeaker.**

Left: A portable radio, and below it a stereo receiver and its loudspeakers. Stereophonic broadcast signals contain sub-signals that are used by the receiver to sort out the separate sound channels. Each channel is then amplified separately and fed to its speaker.

broadcast sound.

An aerial transmits and receives radio waves most efficiently when its length is the same as the wavelength of the waves it is handling. This is usually quite feasible with a single frequency radio transmitter or receiver using the shorter wavelengths. An aerial will also operate quite effectively when its length is an even sub-multiple, such as a half or a quarter of the wavelength, and in many cases this may be more convenient. However, aerials designed to handle a wide range of wavelengths, such as those in domestic radio sets, cannot be accurately matched to all the wavelengths and so a loss of efficiency is unavoidable.

## Broadcasting

The wavelengths of all radio stations are determined in accordance with the rules laid down by the International Telecommunications Union. These rules are intended to prevent transmissions from one station interfering with those from another. For stations not transmitting to other countries, the most widely used frequencies are between 150 and 550 kHz (long wave), 550 and 1660 kHz (medium wave) and 87.5 and 100 MHz (VHF). Most overseas broadcasts use the 2.2 to 30 MHz region of the short wave band. Amplitude modulation is used for long, medium and short wave broadcasts, and frequency modulation for the VHF transmissions.

The VHF frequencies (30 to 300 MHz), together with the UHF (ultra high frequency, 300 to 3,000 MHz) band, are also used for two-way radio systems such as those used by aircraft, ships, the armed forces, the police, and other operators such as taxi services.

The lower end of the long wave band, below about 100 kHz, plus some of the very low frequency band (3 to 30 kHz), is used for marine communications, radio navigational aids, and for long-range military communications.

Microwaves are radio waves with frequencies between 1,000 MHz (or 1 gigahertz, abbreviated 1 GHz) and 300 GHz. They are widely used in telecommunications because they can be modulated in such a way as to enable them to carry, for example, up to about 1,000 simultaneous telephone conversations on a single carrier wave.

Microwaves cannot be handled in the same way as lower frequency radio waves, because at frequencies above 1 GHz a current cannot be passed along a cable from one point to another, such as from the modulator to the transmitter, without it radiating all its power away or losing it due to capacitive effects. Instead of using cables, microwave transmitters use *waveguides*, hollow tubes which channel the microwaves from their source to the aerial. The aerial is a dish-shaped structure, and the microwaves are beamed into the centre of it so that it reflects them away in a narrow, straight beam.

Microwave receiver aerials are of similar construction, with the dish serving to reflect the incoming beam into the open end of a waveguide situated at the focus of the dish. In addition to their use in ordinary telecommunications networks, microwaves are used for space vehicle communications links and are the type of radio waves employed by radar systems.

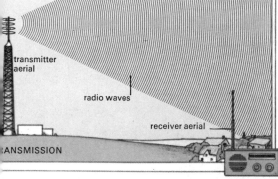

transmitter aerial

radio waves

receiver aerial

TRANSMISSION

Above: The signal applied to the transmitter aerial creates the radio waves which spread out in all directions. When they are picked up by the receiver aerial they set up a corresponding signal in it.

Right: A two-way radio.

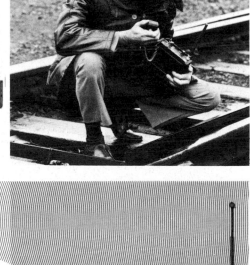

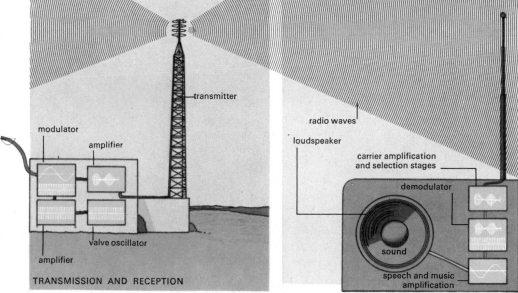

modulator

amplifier

transmitter

valve oscillator

amplifier

radio waves

loudspeaker

carrier amplification and selection stages

demodulator

sound

speech and music amplification

TRANSMISSION AND RECEPTION

# Cameras and Film

The first photograph was taken as long ago as 1826, by the French engineer J. N. Niépce (1765-1833). Niépce died before he could perfect his process, but his work was carried on successfully by his partner, L. J. M. Daguerre (1787-1851). Daguerre produced a photographic plate coated with light-sensitive silver iodide, and his process, known as the *Daguerrotype* process, was what made photography a commercial proposition.

The earliest cameras were very simple. A lens at one side of a box threw an image on to the box's opposite wall, where the photographer would have his light sensitive plate. The other essential was a means of controlling the exposure time. A top hat could be used just as well as any more elaborate device: it covered the lens until you wanted to take the picture. By taking it off the lens for a few minutes, you admitted light into the camera. After a suitable length of time, you replaced the top hat and the exposure was complete.

The improvement which, more than any other, brought photography within everyone's reach was the invention of film, first introduced by George Eastman in 1889. Although glass plates and single sheets of film are still used for special purposes or for studio work, the use of lengths of film, giving 12, 20 or 36 shots in rapid succession, is practically universal.

The 'top hat' aspect has also changed. Instead of many minutes' exposure, modern films usually need just a few milliseconds; but a complete range from perhaps 1/1000 sec to a minute or longer may be required. The *shutter* which achieves this has to be designed so that no part of the frame area receives more exposure than any other part.

The easiest way to accomplish this is to put the shutter at a point where it is completely out of focus—as close to the lens as possible. Most modern lenses have several components, so if a camera has a non-interchangeable lens the shutter can actually be located inside the lens, between the components. It consists of two sets of thin metal blades or leaves, which are pivoted so that one group moves out of the light beam to start the exposure and the other moves in to end it. The timing of these actions is done simply by the tension in the spring which causes them to move. The shutter is usually *cocked*—tensioning the spring—when the film is wound on.

If the camera has an interchangeable lens, however, it is most likely to have a *focal plane shutter*. This consists of a pair of blinds which move across the frame immediately in front of the film. As long as the blinds move together, all parts of the film will be exposed equally. By changing the distance separating the blinds, rather than their speed, different exposure times are possible.

## Choosing the lens

Today, lenses range from simple plastic ones for mass-produced cameras to interchangeable multi-element ones costing as much as or even more than the camera they fit. A very wide range of lenses are

Radio Times Hulton Picture Library

**Above: A replica of a camera used by William Fox-Talbot (1800-1877), who invented the negative/positive photographic process. His photographs were taken on paper impregnated with silver chloride, which gave negative images when developed. Positive prints were then made from the negatives.**

**Right: A cutaway drawing of a modern 35 mm single lens reflex (SLR) camera. These cameras have interchangeable lenses, and built-in exposure meters. The exposure meter shows the user whether or not sufficient light is entering the lens for a satisfactory image to register on the film.**

SLR CAMERA

cocking lever
shutter release
shutter speed control
frame counter
main spring
self timer
film transport sprocket
film take-up spool

250 mm (10 inch) TELEPHOTO LENS
focusing
depth of field scale

diaphragm setting ring
helical focusing
rear 3 ele

Spectrum

**Left: A Kodak 'Brownie' box camera, an easily-operated camera that was very popular in the 1950s. The main lens is the large one in the centre, and the two smaller ones are the viewfinder lenses, one for use with the camera upright and the other with the camera on its side. It took eight shots per roll of film.**

**Below: A Mamiya twin lens reflex camera, with a light meter (right) and two pairs of interchangeable lenses. Unlike an SLR, where the main lens is also the viewfinder lens, this type of camera has separate main and viewfinder lenses, so both must be changed if a different focal length is needed.**

Photri

Agfa-Gevaert

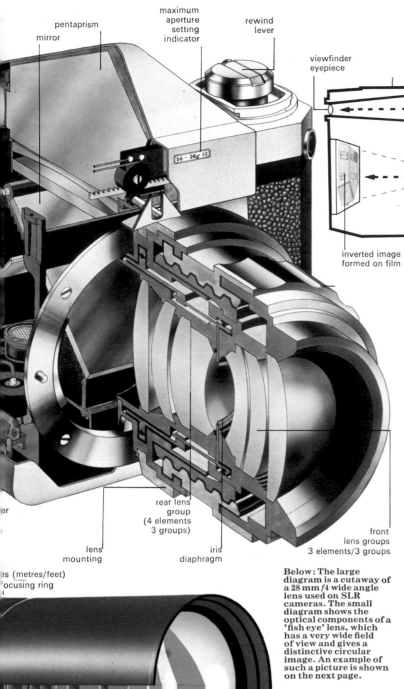

pentaprism

mirror

maximum aperture setting indicator

rewind lever

viewfinder eyepiece

viewfinder lens

light entering viewfinder

shutter

light entering main lens

main lens

inverted image formed on film

iris diaphragm

rear lens group (4 elements 3 groups)

lens mounting

iris diaphragm

front lens groups 3 elements/3 groups

(metres/feet) focusing ring

hragm

light baffles

front lens groups 3 elements/3 groups

oups

sliding lens head

**Above:** This diagram shows how the image is produced within a camera. Light enters the lens, and passes through the diaphragm which controls the amount of light entering the camera. An inverted image is produced on the film when the shutter is opened, usually by a spring mechanism.

**Right:** Two modern 'instant picture' cameras. The Kodak Disc 4000 uses a negative disc which has 15 frames, each measuring 8 by 10 mm. It has fixed exposure and focus which make it easy to use. The Polaroid 660 produces excellent instant prints, each one measures 8 by 8 cm.

Rank Audio Visual Ltd.

**Below:** The large diagram is a cutaway of a 28 mm *f*4 wide angle lens used on SLR cameras. The small diagram shows the optical components of a 'fish eye' lens, which has a very wide field of view and gives a distinctive circular image. An example of such a picture is shown on the next page.

**Right:** This picture of a Rolleiflex SL 86 camera was taken by means of a new technique called *Neutrography*. This process is similar to X-ray photograph, but it uses beams of neutrons instead of X-rays. The image is much more detailed than those produced by X-ray photography.

General Electric Co.

FISHEYE LENS

**Above:** A diagram of a typical telephoto lens design. This one has a focal length of 250 mm and a focal ratio of *f*4, and would be used on a single lens reflex camera. The light baffles within the unit prevent reflections from the inside of the tube, which would lower the contrast of the image.

**Left:** A Nikkormat EL 35 mm SLR made by Nippon Kogaku K.K. (Nikon) of Japan. This camera has an electronic exposure control system, which automatically adjusts the shutter speed to give the correct exposure time for a given aperture setting. The camera shown here is fitted with a 50 mm *f*1.4 lens.

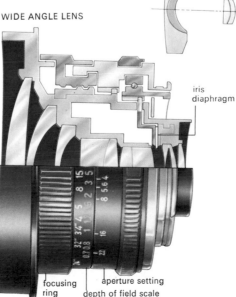

WIDE ANGLE LENS

iris diaphragm

focusing ring

aperture setting

depth of field scale

now available.

There are two factors which the photographer considers when selecting a lens. First, the *focal length*—the distance between the lens and the image it produces. It is not really so much the actual distance that is important as the scale of the image produced. For an ordinary single lens reflex (SLR) camera using 35 mm wide film, a typical standard lens has a focal length of about 45 mm to 55 mm, and produces a field of view suitable for general photography. A longer focal length—up to 400 mm is common, and press photographers may use 1,000 mm—gives a more magnified image, although taking in only a small field of view: these are called *telephoto lenses*. Lenses with shorter than standard focal lengths, say 28 mm, are called *wide angle lenses* since they give a much wider field of view. Extreme versions of these, with focal lengths of 6mm or so, are called *fish eye lenses*.

The second consideration is the *focal*  123

Left: This diagram shows the way in which different colours can be obtained by mixing the *primary additive colours* of light, namely red, blue and green. A mixture of red and green, for example, produces yellow, and white light is obtained by mixing equal amounts of all three primary colours.

Left: The first colour photograph, of a piece of tartan ribbon, which was taken by James Clerk Maxwell (1831-1879) in 1861. The picture was made up of three negatives, each corresponding to one of the primary colours. Projecting these onto a screen, using coloured lights, produced a full colour image.

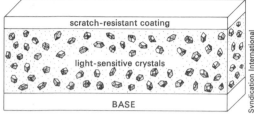

Above left: A black and white film consists basically of a layer of gelatin containing silver halide crystals, known as the emulsion, which is then coated onto a plastic base.

Left: A colour film has three separate emulsions, each sensitive to one of the primary colours.

Above: The Olympic swimming pool, Munich, taken with a fish eye lens.

Below and below left: Two pictures taken from the same position using lenses of different focal lengths. The picture on the left was taken with a normal lens, and the other with a telephoto lens.

*ratio* of the lens. This is the figure given by dividing the focal length by the maximum *aperture*—the clear diameter of the lens. Thus a 40 mm focal length lens with a full aperture of 10 mm has a focal ratio of 4—usually written *f*4. By cutting down the aperture of the lens, using an *iris diaphragm* (an arrangement of metal blades), the focal ratio can be altered, reducing the amount of light passing through the lens. The focal length remains the same, but if the area of the lens has been reduced by half (an aperture of 7.14 mm instead of 10 mm) the focal ratio is now 5.6. The difference between *f*4 and *f*5.6 is called one *stop*—because the ring which controls the iris diaphragm usually has click stops at each halving of the lens area. A full range of stops thus runs 1.4, 2.0, 2.8, 4.0, 5.6, 8, 11, 16, 22 and so on (some of these numbers are rounded off).

The lens' basic *f*-number is when it is wide open, letting in most light. Thus taking pictures in dim light requires a lens with a small basic *f*-number used at full aperture. But at full aperture any imperfections in the lens will be most obvious, so for perfect definition it is best to use a smaller aperture than the maximum possible on any given lens. In addition, the *depth of field* is smallest at full aperture. That is, the range of sharp focus is very small, so that only objects at the exact distance for which the lens is set will be perfectly sharp.

Shutter speeds are also arranged to vary by a factor of 2 between the click stops. So an exposure that was correct at 1/125 sec and *f*8 on a given film can be matched by one at 1/500 at *f*4, trading depth of field for a fast shutter speed which will 'freeze' movement.

If the lenses are to be interchangeable, giving different fields of view in each case, the photographer needs to know how much of the scene is appearing on the film. With non-interchangeable lens cameras, a *viewfinder* is quite adequate—a simple lens system, showing the field of view of the main lens. A development of this is the *twin lens reflex*, in which the viewfinder lens is similar to the main lens and is focused by the same mechanism. Its image is thrown on to a ground glass screen, so that the photographer can both focus up and frame the picture knowing that the main lens is seeing almost exactly the same image.

Many cameras are of the *single lens reflex* (SLR) type, where the image produced by the main lens is reflected by a mirror (placed within the camera, immediately in front of the shutter) up to a ground glass screen. The mirror swings out of the way just before the picture is taken. The photographer views the ground glass screen by means of a *pentaprism*, a prism with a pentagonal cross-section, which reflects the image so that it can be seen the right way round and in the same direction as the view being photographed. The viewfinder thus shows exactly the same scene as the lens.

## Films and emulsions

The image from the lens is recorded by a light-sensitive layer called the *emulsion*, which is coated on to the film or plate material. The word 'emulsion' applies to any mixture consisting of fine particles distributed evenly throughout a liquid. The particles are thus suspended, rather than dissolved, in the liquid. In photographic emulsions, the liquid is gelatin and the particles are crystals or *grains* of silver halide. The emulsion is dried after being coated on to the film or plate, producing a solid coating of gelatin with halide grains dispersed evenly throughout.

Gelatin is made from the hooves and hides of animals. It has the almost unique property of being able to absorb water, so that it swells to several times its original size, and then dries to a solid again. It is also nearly transparent, and has chemical properties which improve the final emulsion.

Silver halides are the *salts* of silver and the *halogen* gases; chlorine, iodine and bromine are the common halogens. The grains are formed chemically in a warm solution of gelatin. The exact rate of addition of the chemicals and the temperature determine the final grain size and emulsion properties.

When a photograph is taken, there is no visible change in the emulsion's appearance. The action of light on a grain is to form a minute speck of metallic silver out of the silver halide. There is a range of sensitivity to light among the grains, so not all will be affected equally and thus subtle gradations of tone are possible. If there is a comparatively large amount of light, then a large number will be affected; if a small amount, only a few will contain the silver specks. Thus an invisible *latent image*, a pattern of halide grains containing silver specks which corresponds to the original pattern of light and shade of the image from the lens, is produced by the exposure in the camera.

This latent image is made visible by a process called *developing*. The developing agent is a chemical, such as *hydroquinone*, which will reduce silver halide to silver. The silver halide grains which have been exposed to light are more susceptible to conversion to silver, and during the carefully timed development process only the grains affected by light are converted to silver, in the form of tangled, fibre-like particles which appear black in colour. The developer is usually diluted with water, which makes the

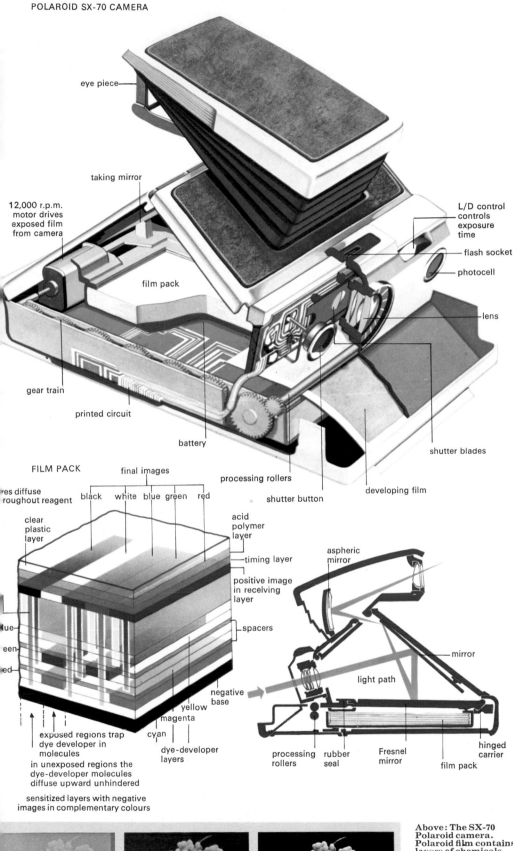

## POLAROID SX-70 CAMERA

eye piece

taking mirror

12,000 r.p.m. motor drives exposed film from camera

L/D control controls exposure time

flash socket

photocell

film pack

lens

gear train

printed circuit

battery

shutter blades

### FILM PACK

final images

processing rollers

shutter button

developing film

…es diffuse …roughout reagent

black white blue green red

acid polymer layer

clear plastic layer

timing layer

positive image in receiving layer

spacers

…lue

…een

…ed

negative base

yellow

magenta

cyan

dye-developer layers

exposed regions trap dye developer in molecules

in unexposed regions the dye-developer molecules diffuse upward unhindered

sensitized layers with negative images in complementary colours

aspheric mirror

mirror

light path

processing rollers

rubber seal

Fresnel mirror

film pack

hinged carrier

Above: The SX-70 Polaroid camera. Polaroid film contains layers of chemicals which develop the exposed film, and the image is chemically transferred onto the print paper. The exposed film is passed between two pressure rollers which burst the envelope containing the chemicals, initiating the developing and printing processes.

Left: This series of pictures shows the gradual development of an image on Polaroid colour film after it leaves the camera.

Polaroid

gelatin swell so that all the suspended grains are accessible to the developing agent.

Once the development has proceeded far enough, the film is washed to remove all traces of the developing agent. The next step is to 'fix' the film by immersing it in a chemical such as *ammonium thiosulphate* or *sodium thiosulphate* ('hypo') which makes the unwanted silver halide (which has not turned black) soluble in water. The developed silver is not affected by this, so after a final wash to remove the dissolved halides the film can be dried.

The result is an image in which the brightest areas of the scene are dark, and the darkest are light—a *negative*. To make a positive print, this must be projected on to photographic paper using an enlarger. The paper is also coated with emulsion, and it is processed in the same way as film.

The sensitivity of an emulsion to light is called its *speed*. Fast films are the most sensitive, and slow films the least. There are two main systems for measuring film speed, ASA (American Standards Association) and DIN (Deutsche Industrie Normen). In the ASA system, a doubling in film sensitivity gives a doubling in the speed figure, while in the DIN system the figure increases by 3 for every stop. Thus a film of speed 200 ASA corresponds to 24 DIN, while one of 400 ASA is 27 DIN.

### Colour and reversal film

A colour film is essentially three black and white emulsions together (a *tripack*), each sensitive to a different colour of light. These colours are usually red, green and blue, since by adding different amounts of these almost any colour can be produced.

An emulsion is normally only sensitive to blue light, but by adding certain dyes which absorb light of other colours, the grains can be made sensitive to other colours as well. Since they are still blue-sensitive, a yellow filter (which cuts out blue light) is deposited in the tripack above the red- and green-sensitive layers.

To make the black and white emulsion yield colour images, dyes have to be substituted for the developed silver. In the case of colour negative films, used for making colour prints, the colours opposite to the layer's sensitivity are used— that is, yellow in the blue layer, magenta (pinkish) in the green layer and cyan (bluish-green) in the red layer. When the negative is enlarged on colour paper, which also produces colours opposite to those it sees, the original colours are produced. The negative film often has an orange 'mask' or overall colouring to correct for colour bias in the printing paper.

This two-stage process is not necessary if a transparency, rather than a negative, is required. The system by which positive transparencies are produced from the original film is called *reversal processing*.

After development and washing, the film carries a developed image consisting of silver, but also a reverse image consisting of undeveloped silver halide—those parts of the image which received little or no exposure. If the negative silver image is first bleached out, these areas can themselves be developed up so as to give a positive image. In the case of colour film this image can be dyed in the original colours—blue in the blue-sensitive layer, and so on.

# Sound Recording

The first recorded sounds, traditionally supposed to have been the words 'Mary had a little lamb', were made in 1877 on the *phonograph* invented by Thomas Edison (1847-1931). This device recorded sound vibrations as indentations in a cylinder covered in tinfoil, although later models used a wax surface. The next significant development was the *gramophone*, invented some 10 years later, which registered the vibrations in a spiral groove on a flat circular disc. Neither of these machines used any method of amplifying the sound before recording it, except for a resonating sound box which acted in the same way as the body of a violin or guitar, and it was mainly for this reason that their performance was relatively poor.

Good quality recorded sound only became possible in the 1920s, when the first electrically assisted recording techniques were developed. The gramophone had by then established its superiority over the phonograph, and for the next 20 years professional organisations such as radio stations recorded entirely on discs.

The possibility of using metal wire or tape to store sounds magnetically had been recognized as early as 1880 by Alexander Bell (1847-1922), the inventor of the telephone. Bell, however, abandoned the idea as impracticable with the technology then available. Then, in 1898, Valdemar Poulsen (1869-1942) demonstrated a working wire recorder which he called the *telegraphone*, and for the next 40 years work proceeded in several countries with the aim of developing a high fidelity magnetic recorder.

The big breakthrough came in Germany during the 1930s with the development of plastic tape coated with iron oxide. The process of recording on magnetic tape involves a series of conversions of the sound energy into different forms. The first of these, performed by a *microphone*, translates the fluctuating sound vibrations into an electric voltage which fluctuates in exactly the same way. Next, this signal is fed to an amplifier, which increases its strength to a level suitable for use by the recording head, which converts it once again, this time into a fluctuating magnetic field. This field aligns particles of iron oxide (or chromium dioxide in the latest tapes) on the surface of the tape (which is driven past it) to produce a pattern of magnetization on the tape which reflects the sound pattern at the microphone.

## Microphones

There are several different types of microphone, each of which has its particular advantages. One of the cheapest and most robust is the *crystal microphone* which relies on the *piezoelectric effect*, whereby certain crystals generate an electric voltage whenever they are bent or twisted. This voltage is proportional to the extent of the bending. The crystal in such a microphone is firmly clamped at one end and attached at the other to a flexible diaphragm.

Sound waves make the diaphragm vibrate and in doing so it bends the crystal back and forth, giving rise to an oscillating voltage which is picked up by leads attached to the crystal surface. The

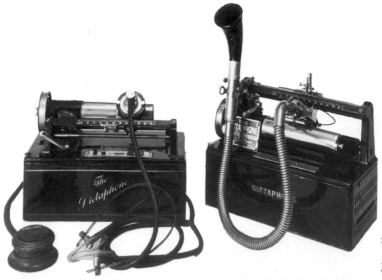

Left: These Dictaphone machines worked on the same principle as Edison's phonograph. The machine on the right is a Type A recorder; when dictating a letter, the user spoke into the tube and the sound vibrations moved a cutting stylus that made impressions on a wax cylinder. When the letter was to be typed, the secretary used the machine on the left, a Type B transcriber, to play the cylinder.

Right: A tape cassette. The tape is contained within the cassette, each end being fixed to a small spool. Tape speed is 4.75 cm/sec (1.875 in/sec), and a pressure pad (bottom) keeps it in contact with the heads.

Right: This recorder, invented by Valdemar Poulsen in 1900, used a steel tape wound around a cylinder. The record/replay head was driven along by the leadscrew as the cylinder was rotated, so that it tracked along the length of the tape. The microphone is on the left, and replay was via the pair of telephone earpieces on the right.

Below: One of the first tape recorders to use a non-metallic tape coated with iron oxide. The first tapes of this kind were made of paper, but were soon replaced by coated plastic tapes. The machine shown here was built by AEG in Germany in 1936, and the tape was made by BASF.

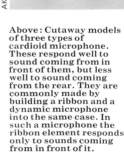

Above: Cutaway models of three types of cardioid microphone. These respond well to sound coming in from front of them, but less well to sound coming from the rear. They are commonly made by building a ribbon and a dynamic microphone into the same case. In such a microphone the ribbon element responds only to sounds coming from in front of it.

Left: A wire recorder of the 1930s. Steel wire is still used as a recording medium today, in aircraft flight recorders which record details such as the airspeed, altitude and control settings. Steel tape and ordinary plastic-based tape are also used in flight recorders.

Philips

response, however, is by no means perfect, treble (high) frequencies responding far better than any other frequencies. It is not consistent either, and tends to vary with changes in temperature and humidity.

The *moving coil microphone*, also called the *dynamic microphone*, is a far superior device. It consists essentially of a coil of wire attached to a diaphragm. As the diaphragm vibrates in response to the sound, the coil slides up and down the centrepiece of an M-shaped permanent magnet. The coil thus cuts through the magnetic field lines, which induce a fluctuating voltage in it. This fluctuating voltage faithfully represents the variations in sound pressure.

Both crystal and moving coil microphones respond equally well to sound from all directions and are consequently called *omnidirectional*, but this may not always be desirable as they tend to pick up unwanted background sounds too clearly. Often a microphone which detects better in one direction than others is more suitable, and this is a characteristic property of the *ribbon microphone*. A thin corrugated aluminium ribbon is suspended in the field of a permanent magnet and the sound arriving at the front or back of the ribbon causes it to move in the magnetic field. This induces a current along its length which is picked up by connecting leads. Sound waves impinging from the sides have little effect because they meet the thin edge of the ribbon. Strictly speaking this is a *bidirectional* microphone because it responds equally well to sound from in front or behind.

If a ribbon is combined in the same case as a moving coil the result is a *cardioid* type microphone which responds well to sound from roughly in front of it but less well to sound which approaches from the rear.

### Recording

The electrical signal from the microphone is boosted by an electronic amplifier and applied to the *record head* of the tape recorder. This is basically an electromagnet, formed by a circular core of magnetic alloy in which is cut a small gap about 0.025 mm (one thousandth of an inch) wide. This is energized by the signal current from the amplifier which passes through a wire coil wrapped around the core.

The magnetic field produced in this coil is channelled around the core and can only escape at the gap. And it is just in the area of this gap that the tape makes contact with the head, so that as the tape moves past the head it cannot avoid the effect of the magnetic field. In consequence the oxide particles of the tape are magnetized either along or against the direction of tape travel according to the direction of the magnetic field when they were passing the gap. The strength of the magnetization also varies with the intensity of the field. So a small area of tape carries a complete magnetic record of the sound pressure at the instant it passed the gap.

Unfortunately the recording produced in this straightforward manner would not satisfy even the least discriminating listener. This is because the tape is not constantly magnetized in simple proportion to the magnetic field in the gap. Although for very small fields it is, as the field increases the magnetization is more nearly proportional to the square of the field. Beyond about half its maximum (or saturation) value the magnetization is once more simply proportional to the field. In short, the tape magnetization is a very poor representation of the field in the recording head gap, and hence it is a poor record of the sound and introduces frequencies which are not present in the original.

Such distortion (a form of *harmonic distortion*) must obviously be prevented and the only way to do this is to ensure that the tape magnetization is always high enough to keep it out of the region where it is not proportional to the field. One solution is to superimpose the amplified microphone signal onto a very high frequency current which is called a *bias signal*. This keeps the tape magnetization out of the danger area but still allows it to be magnetized in both directions, thereby reducing the noise problem.

The tape must of course be completely unmagnetized when it reaches the record head, because any superfluous magnetization appears as noise when the tape is replayed. This is achieved by an *erase head*, which is constructed in the same way as the record head but with a larger gap. The coil of the erase head carries a rapidly varying current of sufficient strength to magnetize the tape to saturation, first in one direction and then in the other, several times as it passes the gap. Any initial magnetization of the tape is thus completely swamped.

The large gap of the erase head allows its field to extend some distance beyond it, so that as the tape leaves the gap it still undergoes cycles of magnetization which become weaker and weaker as it

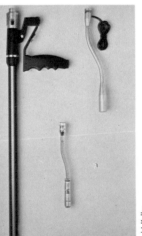

David Kelly

Left: A cardioid microphone (top right), an omnidirectional dynamic microphone (bottom right), and a 'rifle' type of directional microphone. The rifle microphone has a large number of narrow parallel tubes in front of the actual microphone element. Sounds entering the microphone from the front all have the same distance to travel along the tubes, and so they reach the element in phase with each other. Sounds entering from any other angle travel different distances along the tubes, and so reach the element out of phase with each other, effectively cancelling each other out. This makes the microphone highly directional.

EMI Ltd

Ferrograph

Left and above: So sudden and increasingly rapid are the advances in stereophonic tapes and systems that relatively recent breakthroughs can look dated very quickly. Shown left is a standard high quality tape recorder, fitted with the Dolby noise reduction system; it is a half-track recorder and its versatility revolutionized recording. Immediately above is a modern Sony Stowaway, which is so small that you can carry your favourite music around in your pocket – and yet expect to hear it reproduced in exceptionally high quality.

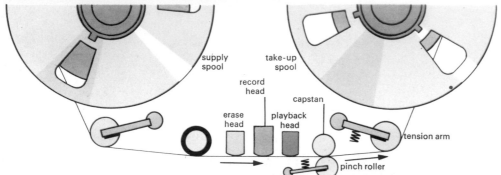

supply spool
take-up spool
record head
erase head
playback head
capstan
tension arm
pinch roller

**Right:** Two different ways of applying the bias signal to the tape. The conventional head arrangement feeds both the bias and the sound signals to the record head. The Akai Crossfield system uses a separate head to apply the bias in order to reduce the possibility of sound distortion.

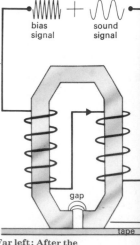

CONVENTIONAL RECORD HEAD

bias signal
sound signal
gap
tape

**Above:** The tape drive and head layout of a high quality reel-to-reel tape recorder. The tape first passes the erase head, which wipes it clean of any previous magnetism, and then passes the record head which records the signal on to it. The playback head picks up this signal during replaying of the tape.

**Right:** The first step in record manufacture is the recording of the music. This picture shows three musicians recording at the EMI studios. Studio tape recorders use tape up to 5.08 cm (2 in) wide, and have 8, 16 or 24 tracks, compared with domestic machines which usually have only two or four tracks.

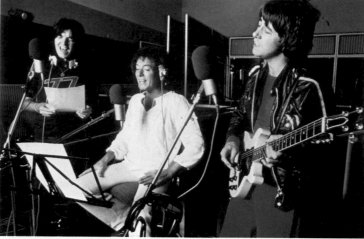

Transworld

EMI Ltd

Decca/Photo:John Goldblatt

**Far left:** After the recording has been completed, the *master tape* is used to drive the cutting lathe (in the background) which produces a lacquer *master disc*. This is the last time the master tape itself will be used in the record manufacturing process. Moulds can now be taken from the master disc, and these will then be used in the record presses.

**Left:** The next step in record manufacture is the production of a *master shell* from the master disc. This picture shows the master disc after it has been given a very thin coating of silver. This silver coating then has 0.625 mm (0.025 in) of nickel deposited on top of it, to form the master shell which is finally separated from the master disc.

**Below:** A master shell about to have a further nickel shell, the *positive shell*, electroplated on to its silver face. The shells are then separated, and the positive shell goes on to the next step in the process.

recedes, vanishing to zero after a short distance to leave the tape completely demagnetized.

When the tape is replayed it is run past a *replay head* (or *playback head*), which is really only a record head operating in reverse—indeed many domestic machines use the same head for both purposes. As the magnetized tape passes the gap in the replay head, the tiny magnetic field which surrounds the tape surface is channelled around the core and hence through the surrounding coil. The alternations in this field, corresponding to the recorded sounds, generate a matching current in the coil (by electromagnetic induction, the same process which on a much larger scale is used to generate current in power stations). The current in the coil is then magnified in an amplifier which is usually the same one used when recording, and fed to a loudspeaker which converts it once again into sound.

### Tape drive

For faithful reproduction of the sound it is essential that the tape is played back at the same speed as it is recorded and that this speed never fluctuates. In the earliest machines one of the two spools on which the tape is wound was directly driven by a motor and dragged the tape past the heads. But this led to unacceptable variations in speed which could be heard as *wow* and *flutter*. These are the sound engineers' names for audible fluctuations in the reproduced sound, wow referring to slow and flutter to rapid fluctuations.

On all modern machines it is the tape itself that is driven, by a spindle (often called the *capstan*) which is rotated by an electric motor. The tape is squeezed between this spindle and a rubber roller and is thus driven along at constant speed. The spools are also electrically driven via friction clutches which are adjusted to slip whenever the tension of the tape rises too high. This ensures that the tape does not break from being pulled too hard onto the spool or spill out of the machine from not being pulled fast enough.

To a large extent, the speed at which the tape moves determines the quality of the recording. If the tape moves too slowly it will not record high frequencies satisfactorily because too short a length of tape passes the head to accommodate the many thousands of oscillations which occur in the space of, for example, one second, when a high-pitched note is recorded. On the other hand, if the tape moves too quickly an inconveniently large reel of tape will be required for a given length of recording. In professional sound studios this does not matter and master recordings are made with the tape moving past the heads at a speed of 79 or 38 centimetres per second (30 or 15 inches per second). For domestic recorders a compromise is sought between quality and bulk so that 19 and 9½ cm/sec (7½ and 3¾ in/sec) are the common speeds.

Decca/John Goldblatt

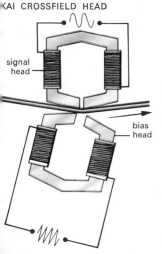

AKAI CROSSFIELD HEAD

signal head

bias head

Decca/Photo: John Goldblatt

Decca/Photo: John Goldblatt

**Above:** One of the later stages of record making is the production of the *matrix shell*, by depositing nickel on to the positive shell. Here, the two shells are being separated. The matrix shell is the one which will be used to press the actual records, having a spiral ridge which forms the groove of the record when it is pressed.

**Right:** Pressing a record. A 'biscuit' of extruded pvc, with the labels in place, is squeezed between two matrix shells (or stampers), one for each side of the record. 7-inch records are usually made by injecting hot plastic under pressure into a mould, instead of by this method which is used for 10 and 12 inch LP records.

**Left:** This machine trims excess plastic from the edges of the records after pressing.

**Below:** This series of diagrams shows some of the main stages involved in the recording and manufacture of long playing records.

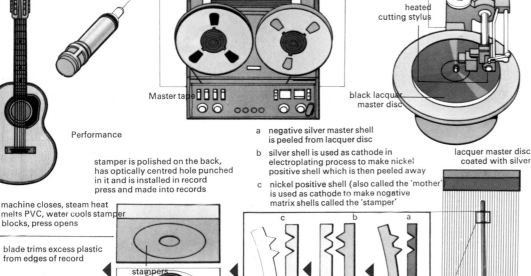

Performance

Master tape

Cutting lathe

heated cutting stylus

black lacquer master disc

lacquer master disc coated with silver

stamper is polished on the back, has optically centred hole punched in it and is installed in record press and made into records

machine closes, steam heat melts PVC, water cools stamper blocks, press opens

blade trims excess plastic from edges of record

a  negative silver master shell is peeled from lacquer disc

b  silver shell is used as cathode in electroplating process to make nickel positive shell which is then peeled away

c  nickel positive shell (also called the 'mother' is used as cathode to make negative matrix shells called the 'stamper'

stampers

'biscuit' & labels

press

## Cassette recorders

The major difference between cassette recorders and normal reel-to-reel machines is that the tape is permanently contained within a plastic box, the cassette, which includes both a storage and a take-up spool. The tape passes through guides along the edge of the box in which there are apertures which allow contact with the erase and record/replay heads.

Irregularities on the tape surface give rise to a slight hissing noise and if the high frequencies are boosted to compensate for loss of high frequencies due to the slow speed (4.75 cm/sec, 1.875 in/sec) of the cassette, this noise is also increased so that it tends to drown out soft passages of music or speech, particularly if they are predominantly low-pitched. There is, however, a method of overcoming this difficulty.

It is known as the *Dolby system*, after its inventor, and relies on sophisticated electronic circuitry to detect low level passages. These are given extra amplification so that they are recorded at as much as ten times their normal intensity and when they are played back they are *attenuated* (reduced in volume) by an equal amount. The result is that these quiet passages replay at their proper level but the tape noise is only a small fraction of the total sound.

Manufacturers have developed the cassette format in other areas — notably in the coatings used on the tapes. The best machines and tapes are now capable of making recordings that are only a little poorer than those made by high-quality professional reel-to-reel recorders — with much greater convenience and at a far lower cost.

129

# Sound Reproduction

Since the 1940s the techniques of sound reproduction have developed at an amazing pace. Today's amateur enthusiast can enjoy a quality of sound which would have astonished even a professional sound engineer before the Second World War.

Sound is usually encoded in one of three forms—in the grooves of a disc, in the magnetized oxide particles on the surface of a tape, or as variations in the amplitude or frequency of a radio wave—and the first stage in reproducing it is to convert it into an electric signal whose variations correspond to those of the original sound signal. The next step is to boost this signal to a more manageable level in a *preamplifier*, which at the same time compensates for any distortion which may have been accidentally or deliberately introduced. Controls for volume and tone are usually incorporated in this section of the equipment.

The signal is then in the right form to operate a loudspeaker, but it lacks strength and must therefore be amplified once again by a *power amplifier*. The loudspeaker is the final link in the chain and serves to convert the amplified electrical signal into vibrations of the air, thus reproducing the original sound.

Most equipment made today reproduces sound *stereophonically*. Stereophonic or stereo recordings and radio programmes are designed to give a more natural effect when replayed by taking into account the ability of our ears to detect the direction as well as the intensity of sounds. If directional information is absent in the reproduced sound it appears somewhat incomplete. When a stereo recording is made, two microphones (or two sets of microphones) are used, one of which receives more sound from the left and the other more from the right. The sounds detected by each are kept entirely separate and are encoded in two completely independent 'channels' of the recording or programme. Stereo reproducing equipment is really only a duplication of ordinary single channel (*monophonic*) equipment, with independent amplifiers and speakers for each channel.

## Record Players

When a disc recording is made, a master disc coated with lacquer is rotated at constant speed on a turntable. A heated cutting stylus travels slowly from the rim to the centre of the disc and cuts a spiral v-shaped groove in the lacquer. The walls of this groove are normally at 90° to each other when no sound is being recorded, as in the run-in and run-out grooves at the start and finish of every record. But the cutting stylus is also moved magnetically in response to electrical signals from the master tape recording. This leads it to cut undulations in the groove walls which encode the sound, with the left channel registered entirely on the inner groove wall and the right entirely on the outer.

The stylus moves much more for a low frequency sound than for a high frequency sound of the same intensity, so much so that it is necessary to deliberately decrease the intensity (or *attenuate*) bass

Left: A turn of the century Edison phonograph. The records were wax cylinders, rotated by a clockwork motor, and as they turned they vibrated a needle connected to a diaphragm within the unit at the bottom of the horn. The sound created by the vibrating diaphragm was amplified by the horn.

Above: The phonograph was eventually replaced by the gramophone, invented by Emile Berliner in 1887. The gramophone used flat discs instead of cylinders, and was the ancestor of today's record players. The first commercial gramophones and records were produced in Germany in 1889.

Right: An HMV Type 12 pick-up cartridge and tone arm, an example of an early magnetic pick-up. The needle was connected to a steel armature, which passed between the pole pieces of the magnet and through the centre of the coil. As the armature was vibrated by the needle, it created changes in the magnetic field which induced tiny electric currents within the coil. These were then amplified and fed to a loudspeaker.

Below right: The tone arm of a Pioneer PL-71 record deck. The small weight hanging to the right of the pivot is the bias compensation weight, which opposes the inward force on the stylus.

sounds to avoid wide undulations of the stylus which would lead it to cut into adjoining grooves. In the final stage, the master disc is copied and any number of records can be manufactured from it.

Playing a record on a record player attempts to reverse the process by which the master disc was produced, translating the groove wall code back into electrical signals without loss of quality. However, there are two main reasons why this can never, even in the most expensive equipment, be achieved to perfection. The first is that it is not possible to use a stylus of exactly the same shape as the cutting stylus, because it would itself cut and damage the record. So a stylus with a rounded tip must be used and this cannot follow the undulations of the walls with complete accuracy because it cannot penetrate the recesses completely.

The more important difficulty is that the stylus, unlike the cutting stylus, cannot be mechanically driven across the record as it rotates. The reproducing stylus must therefore be pulled along by the forces exerted on it by the groove, and this means that the pressure of the stylus on the groove walls will vary. It is just feasible to suspend the stylus, like a travelling crane, from a rail which it

Below: 1. Ordinary mono records have the grooves cut in such a way that the stylus is moved from side to side by the groove.
2. An alternative to this *lateral* recording is the vertical 'hill and dale' method used originally by Edison, in which the stylus is vibrated up and down within the groove. It was originally suggested that stereo records could combine these two methods, with the left channel recorded laterally and the right vertically.
3. and 4. This led to the introduction of the 45°/45° method where the stylus is moved in two directions, each at 45° to the record surface.

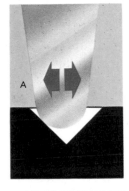
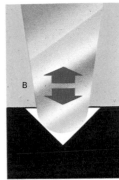
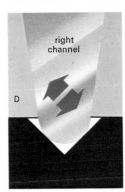
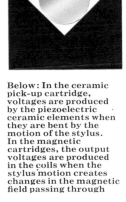

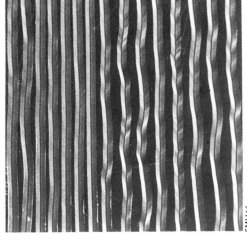

These four close-up photographs show the grooves of mono, stereo and quad records.

Above: The constant-width grooves of a mono record.

Below: A 45°/45° stereo record. The grooves are much more complicated, and their widths vary because the stylus must be moved vertically as well as laterally.

Above right: The grooves of a matrix quadraphonic disc are cut in the same way as those of a stereo disc.

Right: A discrete quadraphonic disc has a high frequency sub-signal cut on each wall of the groove.

Below: In the ceramic pick-up cartridge, voltages are produced by the piezoelectric ceramic elements when they are bent by the motion of the stylus. In the magnetic cartridges, the output voltages are produced in the coils when the stylus motion creates changes in the magnetic field passing through them. This is done by moving the coils within a magnetic field (moving coil), moving an armature which links the field of a fixed magnet with a pair of coils (induced magnet), or by moving a magnet next to fixed coils (moving magnet). The photograph shows a Shure moving magnet cartridge.

CERAMIC

MOVING COIL

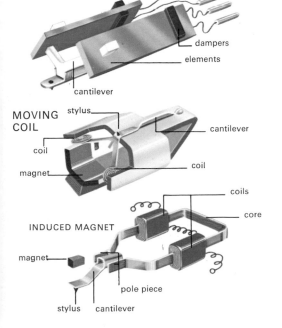

INDUCED MAGNET

MOVING MAGNET

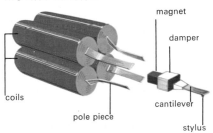

magnet
damper
coils
pole piece
cantilever
stylus

traverses from the rim to the centre of the record. This is the ideal because it ensures that the force pulling the stylus is always directed along the groove, but it is extremely costly to manufacture such a system to be neither so massive that it cannot follow the groove undulations quickly enough nor so weak that it sways and wobbles, introducing worse distortion than that which it was designed to prevent. The usual solution is to mount the stylus on a pivoted arm, known as the *tone arm*. Again, there are problems: however cunningly the tone arm is shaped it can never be exactly parallel to the groove over the whole width of the record. This introduces an unwanted force called *bias* which leads the stylus to press more against the inner than the outer wall. In practice bias can be compensated for by attaching a small weight to the other end of the tone arm in such a way that it tends to pull the stylus towards the rim.

The translation of the motion of the stylus into an electrical signal is accomplished by the *pick-up cartridge* which forms the business end of the tone arm. There are two main types of stereo cartridge, *ceramic* and *magnetic*. In the former, the stylus vibrations are transmitted by a connecting rod to two elements made of a crystalline ceramic material such as barium titanate, one of which is bent or twisted by vibrations in the plane of the inner groove wall and one by those of the outer wall. These elements thus produce, by the *piezoelectric effect*, two electrical signals which represent the left and right sound channels respectively.

In a magnetic *moving coil* cartridge the stylus is attached to two small wire coils, at 90° to each other, each of which

131

vibrates in the field of a permanent magnet. By electromagnetic induction, this produces in each coil a voltage which represents the left or right sound channel. *Moving magnet* cartridges have this arrangement reversed, with the magnet attached to the stylus in such a way that it induces voltages in stationary coils as it moves.

Tape recordings are very easily made in stereo, because all that is necessary is to devote one half of the tape width to each channel of sound. This of course produces a tape which must be rewound after each playing, so it is common to divide the tape width into four, using the first and third quarters for the two channels of one recording and the other two for a second, which is played in the reverse direction. The output from the tape replay heads is, like that from a record player cartridge, in the form of a weak electrical signal.

### Amplification
Although records, tapes and radio programmes are all translated into electrical signals these are not all of the same strength. Consequently, if the same preamplifier is to be used for all three it must be equipped to amplify each signal to a different degree. A preamplifier consists of several transistor amplifier stages in sequence, with the output of each fed to the input of the next in line. Very weak signals like those from a magnetic cartridge are switched through all the stages and the strongest, those from ceramic cartridges, perhaps only through the last stage.

The different types of input also require different degrees of *equalization* to correct for the attenuation of the bass when recording discs or replaying tapes. Radio signals do not need any equalization, nor does the output from a ceramic cartridge because the ceramic elements themselves, when connected to a suitably high impedance, produce a higher output voltage at low frequencies than at higher. Equalization is achieved by taking advantage of the properties of capacitors, which impede low frequencies more than high. If these are inserted in appropriate places in the circuit, either bass or treble can be boosted or attenuated as required.

Capacitors are also used as part of the bass and treble tone controls, which divert a fraction of the signal through a network of capacitances and resistances which attenuates either the bass or the treble. A variable resistance, whose variation is controlled by a knob on the casing, determines what fraction is diverted. Filters are included in the better preamplifiers to eliminate very low-pitched sounds, like the 'rumble' which is caused by mechanical vibrations from the turntable or drive mechanism, and the 'hum' caused by stray radiations at the frequency of the mains supply, and also the very high-pitched noise which sometimes accompanies radio programmes. These filters are like fixed versions of the tone controls, consisting of capacitive networks which effectively cut out all frequencies below about 60 Hz or above about 10,000 Hz. The filters can be switched in or out of the circuit as required.

The power amplifier is often contained in the same case as the preamplifier. Its sole purpose is to amplify the signal from the preamplifier to a level at which it can drive the loudspeakers. It usually has

two or more stages to achieve the necessary amplification, and each stage consists of two transistors because one alone has not enough range to accommodate the large current difference between the peaks and troughs of the signal at these stages.

### Loudspeakers
The final stage of sound reproduction is the conversion of the electrical signal into sound waves by the loudspeaker. There are two main types of loudspeaker, *moving coil* and *electrostatic*. The most common are the moving coil speakers, in which the electrical signal is passed through a wire coil attached to a paper or plastic cone. The coil is free to slide over the centrepiece of an M-shaped permanent magnet which alternately repels and attracts it as the coil becomes magnetized in one direction and then the other. The cone is thus pushed and pulled against the air, creating sound waves.

One such speaker cannot faithfully reproduce the whole spectrum of sound for two reasons. One is that the coil impedes high frequencies more than low; the other is that the cone is mechanically more efficient at producing sound whose wavelength is roughly the same as its

Below: The BSR/ADC Accutrac 4000 can automatically find and play any desired track on an LP record. A tiny unit next to the pick-up shines infra-red light onto the record, and when it is above the unrecorded space between two tracks this light is reflected back up to the unit. As the arm moves across above the record it counts the number of times the light is reflected, and thus the number of tracks, until it reaches the selected track. The machine can be remotely controlled, using the transmitter and receiver units shown in the foreground. The control signals are transmitted by an ultrasonic beam.

BSR Ltd

Right: A Quad 33 stereo control unit or preamplifier. Signals from a sound source, such as a record deck or radio, are fed into the unit. Its output is then passed to a power amplifier which amplifies it to a level which is high enough to drive a pair of loudspeakers. This unit will produce an output of 0.5 V from an input of 2 mV from a magnetic pick-up cartridge.

Below: The unit on the left is a mono valve power amplifier, which has a power output of 15 watts. The other one is a Quad 303 stereo transistor power amplifier, designed for use with the Quad 33 control unit, which produces 45 watts per channel.

Quad

Spectrum

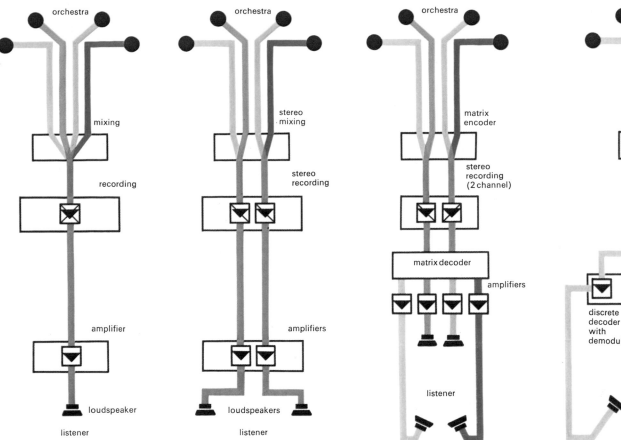
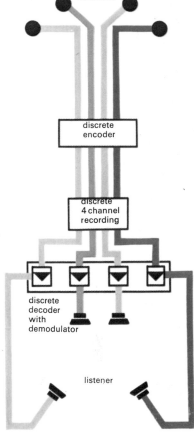

MONO  STEREO  MATRIX QUADRAPHONY  DISCRETE QUADRAPHONY

Below: A Pioneer SA9900 stereo amplifier. This unit, shown with its case removed, is an *integrated* amplifier, containing both the preamplifier and the power amplifier stages. Its power output is 110 watts per channel, and it can handle sounds with frequencies ranging from 10 Hz up to 80 kHz.

Above: This series of diagrams shows how the signals from several microphones can be combined and recorded to produce mono, stereo or quadraphonic records. Mono recordings (1) are the simplest. The microphone signals are combined into a single channel, and reproduced through a single channel. When stereo recordings (2) are being made, the microphone signals are combined into two channels, left and right, and replayed through a two-channel system. Matrix quadraphonic systems (3) encode the four channels into two, which are recorded on disc just like a normal stereo record. When a matrix disc is replayed, the decoder separates the two channels into four. Discrete quadrophonic recordings (4) are encoded together with a high frequency sub-signal, which enables the replay decoder to direct the four channels to their respective amplifiers.

own diameter. A small cone is better for high frequencies and a large cone for low. Thus for good reproduction two or three or sometimes more speakers of different sizes are combined for each channel. An electronic *crossover network* of capacitors, inductors and resistors splits the amplifier signal current into separate frequency ranges and feeds one to each of the appropriately sized speakers. The bass speaker is often called a 'woofer' and the treble a 'tweeter'.

Electrostatic speakers work on a different principle. They move the air by means of a flat flexible diaphragm which is coated with electrically conductive material. This is fixed at a small distance from a metal plate of the same area to which the amplifier signal is applied. A small permanent polarizing voltage is maintained between the two, which induces opposite electric charges on the surface of each (making in fact a parallel plate capacitor). Applying the amplifier signal between the two causes the diaphragm to vibrate as it is alternately attracted and repelled by the plate. This principle is widely used for tweeters and occasionally for full-spectrum speakers, in which case the diaphragm is usually fixed between two perforated plates.

Headphones, which are miniature loud-speakers mounted in a lightweight headset, may also be of the moving coil or the electrostatic type. As is the case with loudspeakers, the majority of headphones in use at present are based on moving coil drive units. Electrostatic headphones, like electrostatic speakers, give a very clean sound, but most types must be connected to the amplifier via an adaptor unit which supplies the polarizing voltage.

PIONEER SA 9900 AMPLIFIER

power transformer
power amplifier
treble controls
bass controls
power supply unit
preamplifier
input sockets
tape duplicate and monitor switches
filter switches
mode switch
balance control
volume control
input selector switch

Left: A high quality loudspeaker system, with the cabinet cut away to show the bass speaker (bottom), mid-range speaker (centre) and treble speaker (top). The electronic crossover network is next to the treble speaker.

Below: A cross-section of a typical dual cone loudspeaker. The signal from the amplifier is fed to the voice coil, and being an alternating signal it magnetizes the coil first in one direction and then the other. This causes it to be alternately attracted and repelled by the magnet, moving the cones with it to produce sounds.

## DUAL CONE LOUDSPEAKER

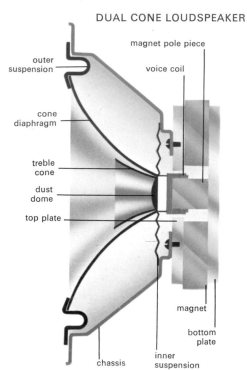

outer suspension

cone diaphragm

treble cone

dust dome

top plate

chassis

magnet pole piece

voice coil

magnet

bottom plate

inner suspension

Left: The back of a Quad electrostatic loudspeaker, showing the perforations in the fixed plates which allow the sound from the moving diaphragms, which are on the other side of the plates, to be radiated from the speaker. This speaker reproduces sound frequencies from 45 Hz to 18 kHz.

Below: This Philips loudspeaker system contains its own power amplifier, mounted within a compartment at the rear of the cabinet. It has bass, mid-range and treble speakers, which give it a frequency response of 35 Hz to 20,000 Hz. The internal volume of the speaker compartment is 9,000 cc (0.32 cu. ft.).

## Digital sound

The sound recording and reproducing methods and equipment described in this and the previous chapter have all been of the *analogue* type. The sound is encoded onto a record disc or a magnetic tape in wave forms that match (or are 'analogous' to) the original sound waves.

Though this system has the beauty of (relative) simplicity, there are many ways in which the analogue wave pattern that is created and reproduced can fall short of exactly matching the original, and there is a limit to how far faults can be corrected.

The way forward is to use computer techniques. During recording, the amplitude (i.e. volume) of the sound waveform is measured or *sampled* many thousands of times a second. Each of those measurements is converted into a number, and those numbers are recorded and stored in the form of a fast-flowing stream of computer *digits* — hence the term digital sound.

The advantage of digital recording is that the various distortions that would have been present on an analogue recording can be corrected for using computer-like techniques to a far higher degree of accuracy — so the sound you hear should be closer to perfect hi-fi than ever before.

The main problem is that the rate at which the digital numbers are produced is far too fast for them to be stored and reproduced using conventional audio equipment. However, *video* tape recorders and players are capable of handling these much faster flows of information, and it is derivatives of these pieces of equipment that are used for digital audio.

Some studios have been using digital tape recorders for some years — often these are simply professional video recorders with a special *analogue to digital converter* unit fitted that takes the (analogue) electrical signal from the recoding amplifiers and turns it into the string of digits that are stored on the recorder. Ordinary black vinyl LPs that are made from these recordings are often called 'digital', in fact they are made in the normal analogue way — the output from the digital recorder being passed through a *digital to analogue converter* first. This can certainly help sound quality, because all the processing, mixing and so on can be done in the studio with the sound in its digital form, and quality can be maintained. But it is only a half-way house.

Compact Discs are unlike conventional LPs because the sound pattern engraved on them is still in digital form. Instead of a wiggly spiral groove cut into the surface of the disc, a Compact Disc has innumerable microscopic metallized pits—each less than one-millionth of a metre in length—etched into its surface. The length and spacing of these pits carries the audio information. A special Compact Disc player is used to read the information off the disc, using a laser beam rather than a conventional stylus. The beam is aimed at the pits, and is reflected off them in varying ways depending on the 'sound' contained within them. And it's only after reading the disc in this way that the information is converted into an analogue form so that it can be amplified and converted back into sound by conventional hi-fi amplifiers and loudspeakers. All the distortions introduced by conventional record players are eliminated, and the resulting sound quality can be much higher.

The Hollywood Bowl has the natural accoustic quality of the amphitheatre. Seating 3,000 people, it is used mainly for musical performances — notably 'Symphonies Under the Stars' in summertime — and has its own orchestra

# Cinema

Draw a little 'matchstick man' on the edge of a page of a book. On subsequent pages, draw similar men with slight differences, so that the movement of arms or legs is split up into individual steps. Now flick the pages so that the individual steps join up into a continuous movement and the man becomes animated.

If your eye and brain were remarkably alert, you would still be able to discriminate each individual step. But this is usually impossible as a result of *persistence of vision*. This is an effect of the eye and brain combined, and means that we do not see separate images if they occur more rapidly than about 12 times per second.

The earliest attempts at making moving pictures, during the second half of the 19th century, used the book page principle, or else consisted of a rotating cylinder with slots, each of which showed for an instant a slightly different picture on the inside of the cylinder. But the real breakthrough came in 1895, when the Lumière brothers in France demonstrated the forerunner of the modern cinema, taking photographs on a long strip of film and projecting each one for a split second.

Because each individual picture, or *frame*, needs an exposure time of about 1/50 sec, the film has to be motionless for a brief period in the film *gate*, to avoid blurring the image produced by the camera's lens. Then it must be moved on very quickly and brought to rest in time for the exposure of the next frame. This *intermittent motion*, first invented by Etienne-Jules Marey in the 1880s, was the secret of the success of the Lumière brothers' technique, and today's cameras work on the same principle. The usual method is to engage a claw in the sprocket holes of the film. This jerks the film along, then extracts itself and moves along to the next set of holes while the film remains stationary as the exposure is made. Meanwhile, a sector cut out of a disc rotating in front of the gate admits light only for a fraction of a second, cutting off the image while the film is being moved.

This procedure occurs at a standard rate. The normal shooting rate for cinema films is 24 frames per second, while amateur films are usually shot at 18 frames per second for greater economy of film.

Professional motion picture cameras generally have a viewfinder which, by a reflex system, shows the image as seen through the camera lens, rather than using a separate viewfinder system. A common way of doing this is to make the rotating shutter disc reflective, viewing the image mirrored in it except when the shutter is open.

There are four main film widths currently in use: 8 mm, 16 mm, 35 mm and 65 mm. The first is mainly for amateur film making, while the others are for professional and feature film work. Most television news or documentary films are on 16 mm film, while feature films for TV and cinema are on 35 mm. The 65 mm film size is used for major cinema films, often wide screen spectaculars, and the image

*Science Museum*

is transferred to 70 mm film for projection to include the soundtrack.

## Sound recording

In some 16 mm movie cameras used for TV news filming, the signals from a microphone are recorded directly on to a strip of magnetic oxide 2.54 mm (0.1 in) wide coated down one edge of the film, a method which ensures that the sound and vision are kept precisely synchronized with each other. Most professional equipment, however, does not use this system. Instead, the sound is recorded separately on a good quality tape recorder and later transferred, along with music and other effects, to the sound track of the finished film.

## Editing

Film scenes are very rarely shot in the same order in which they are shown. For example, all shots made at one particular location will be taken together, even though they may appear in different parts of the finished film. Since only one camera is normally used, many sequences will have to be repeated from different angles —if two people are talking together each actor's part may be filmed separately from over the other's shoulder. For action scenes, however, another camera may be used to provide 'cuts' or alternative views, as it would be difficult to repeat the same events exactly.

The job of putting all this together in the right order, along with titles, special effects and background music, may take several months for a full length film. Much of the work is done using a machine called a *Steenbeck* or *Moviola*, which enables film and soundtrack to be run

Below: An Arriflex 35 mm movie camera, mounted on a tripod. The film is carried in the *magazine* on top of the camera body, and there are three lenses, of different focal lengths, mounted on a *turret* at the front of the camera. The turret is rotated to bring the required lens into position.

Right: A sequence of frames from a cartoon film. The amount of work involved in drawing and then photographing a cartoon film can be considerable; for example, this entire sequence would provide only about one third of a second of viewing time at a speed of 24 frames per second.

The reflex viewfinder of a movie camera uses light reflected from the shutters

1 shutter motor
2 vertical driveshaft
3 helical gear
4 reflective shutter blade
5 stock of film
6 film plane
7 camera lens
8 focussing screen
9 field lens
10 prism
11 viewfinder optics

Below: A cutaway drawing of a professional movie camera. The *matte* box in front of the lenses is used to hold mattes during special effects filming. The small diagram on the left shows the optical components of the reflex viewfinder system used on such a camera.

13 180° mirror shutter at 45° to the film plane
14 Intermittent film claw
15 Mount for lens 3
16 Alternative lens (2nd)
17 Neck strap lug
18 Field lens
19 Focussing levers
20 Prism
21 Film plane
22 Registration pin
23 Filmgate
24 Film stock
25 Lens barrel locks
26 Turret shift tabs
27 Pressure rollers
28 Viewfinder optics (10x)
29 3 lens divergent turret
30 Feed film spool
31 Geared sprockets
32 Take-up film spool
33 Viewfinder focus
34 Eyepiece cup

1 Locknut
2 Matte support bar
3 Front effects stage
4 Front adjustment
5 Matte box
6 Rear adjustment
7 Prime lens
8 Front filter rack
9 Rear filter rack (revolving)
10 Ground glass screen
11 Rear of prime lens
12 Centre turret pivot

Left: An early system for producing optical soundtracks, which could also be used as a sound recorder during location filming. Some of the first 'talking pictures', introduced in the 1920s, had the sound recorded on gramophone records, but these were soon superseded by films with soundtracks.

Right: Special effects man Ray Harryhausen arranging a scene for the Columbia film 'Jason and the Argonauts'. The scene was shot in a large tank of water, using models for the cliffs and for the boat and its occupants. The wave effects in the water were created by a wave-making machine at the edge of the tank.

Science Museum

Grange Calverly/Bob Godfrey Films Ltd

National Film Archive

Picturepoint

Picturepoint

THE BATTLE OF BRITAIN

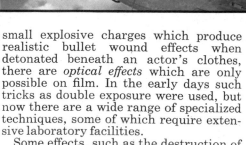

John Toward

John Toward

together, frame by frame, for matching and cutting purposes. The film which is used for preliminary cutting is not the original black and white or colour negative, which is unsuitable for viewing anyway. Instead, prints (positive copies) are made and the original is kept until the editing has been finalized. When the editing is completed, the original negative is cut and the final prints made. This involves *grading* the colour—making sure that the exposure and colour balance are the same from shot to shot.

Music and other sounds can now be added. Quite often it is necessary to match the music to the film, so the musicians perform in a studio with a projector so they can link the two. In many cases extra sounds are added in this *dubbing studio*, such as suitably satisfying cracks, thuds and howls during fight scenes which may well be filmed without the sound being recorded.

Finally a master soundtrack is mixed together, using multitrack facilities similar to those in recording studios. There are two ways of adding sound to a film—by *optical* or by *magnetic* soundtracks. It was the optical system which first came into general use, and is still commonly employed today. Alongside the picture area of the film are two continuous clear lines on a black area, whose width variations correspond to the soundtrack signal like the wiggles in the groove of a record. To play the soundtrack requires a photocell which responds to the variations in the intensity of light passing through the soundtrack, and produces a correspondingly varying electrical signal which is then amplified and passed to the cinema's loudspeakers.

The alternative system uses a stripe of the same type of magnetic oxide as used on recording tape. This is coated down both edges of the film, so that the extra thickness does not cause the film to wind unevenly on the spool.

### Special effects

As well as the wide range of mechanical effects used to make films, such as the small explosive charges which produce realistic bullet wound effects when detonated beneath an actor's clothes, there are *optical effects* which are only possible on film. In the early days such tricks as double exposure were used, but now there are a wide range of specialized techniques, some of which require extensive laboratory facilities.

Some effects, such as the destruction of cities, are carried out using models, with no other illusion than that caused by the lack of scale. Where some monster or mythical creature is required, it will often be made as a model with flexible limbs. These are filmed frame by frame, with slight movements between each frame. Where the model is to be combined with human action, the model can be placed in front of a screen on which is projected, again frame by frame, previously-shot film of the actors. The screen may be translucent with the film projected from behind (back projection) or it may be highly reflective with the film projected from the front. The image from the projector also strikes the model, but as it is not so reflective as the screen it does not show it. These two projection techniques are also widely used at full scale with actors, for example to make it appear that they are in a moving car or perhaps in a desert.

Another method of faking a background is the *glass shot*, which uses a sheet of glass close to the camera on which details are painted. The camera views the scene through the glass, but the aperture is chosen so that both the glass painting and the scene are in focus. This may be used on location to add some landscape details or remove others by obscuring them.

One widely used method of superimposing one scene on another or achieving special effects is by means of the *matte* technique. In its simplest form, this involves masking out part of the scene being photographed by a piece of black card, the matte, right in front of the camera. Then another piece of card, which masks out the rest of the picture but leaves the originally masked area clear, is

This series of pictures shows the main stages involved in making a film.
1. Shooting a scene in a studio. The camera is mounted on a *camera crane*. The picture to the right shows a Panavision camera, mounted in an aircraft, which was used in filming aerial action for the film 'Battle of Britain', and the top picture is a set used in François Truffaut's 'Day for Night'.

2. After shooting, the film is processed in an automatic developing machine.

3. Sound recorded during shooting is transferred from tape to magnetically coated film.

4. The sound and picture are edited.

5. Music and sound effect tracks are added to the dialogue track.

6. These tracks, with the picture, are then played through the dubbing console, where the tone and volume of each track are adjusted to give the correct sound balance.

138

John Toward

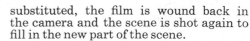

John Toward

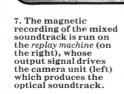

John Toward

7. The magnetic recording of the mixed soundtrack is run on the *replay machine* (on the right), whose output signal drives the camera unit (left) which produces the optical soundtrack.

8. The brightness and colour balance of the picture are adjusted on a *visual colour grader*. The control settings are recorded on punched paper tape, then used to control the machine that produces the final prints.

9. The picture negative and the negative of the optical soundtrack are loaded into this printer, which produces the final combined picture and sound prints that are later distributed to cinemas.

Ian Duff

substituted, the film is wound back in the camera and the scene is shot again to fill in the new part of the scene.

Alternatively, the new piece of action, photographed separately, is added in an *optical printer*, which enables two separate pieces of film to be photographed together on to a third. This allows the use of *travelling mattes*, which can change shape and move. Sometimes the mattes are prepared photographically by lighting the unwanted part of the film set in a hue which affects only the blue-sensitive layer of the colour film. This region can then be turned black by photographic techniques.

Cartoons are made by drawing each frame separately and projecting them in sequence, just as in the matchstick man technique. To save a lot of time the backgrounds are prepared separately and the moving characters are painted on transparent overlays called *cels*. The limbs of cartoon characters are painted on separate cels so that their positions can be changed easily. Usually the soundtrack is recorded first and the drawings made to match it.

## Projectors

Projectors are mechanically quite similar to cameras—in fact, the Lumières used their cameras as projectors by placing a lamp behind the processed film as it passed through the gate. Modern projectors, however, are purpose built.

The light source used in amateur projectors is a tungsten or quartz halogen light bulb. In large cinema projectors, arc lamps, or more recently xenon discharge tubes, are used.

In order to even out the coverage of light across the film, projectors use a *condenser* system. This usually consists of a concave mirror placed behind the light source, to make use of the light given off to the rear of the lamp, and a lens in front of the source which concentrates the light on to the film area. The main projector lens, which beams the film image on to the screen, is situated in front of the film.

In the case of CinemaScope or Pana-

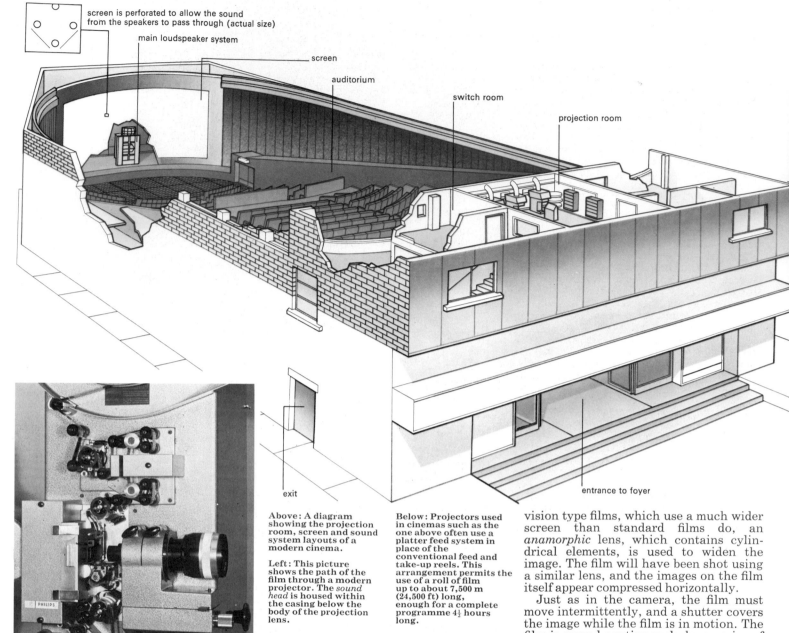

screen is perforated to allow the sound from the speakers to pass through (actual size)

main loudspeaker system

screen

auditorium

switch room

projection room

exit

entrance to foyer

**Above: A diagram showing the projection room, screen and sound system layouts of a modern cinema.**

**Left: This picture shows the path of the film through a modern projector. The *sound head* is housed within the casing below the body of the projection lens.**

**Below: Projectors used in cinemas such as the one above often use a platter feed system in place of the conventional feed and take-up reels. This arrangement permits the use of a roll of film up to about 7,500 m (24,500 ft) long, enough for a complete programme 4½ hours long.**

CINEMA PROJECTOR
WITH PLATTER FEED SYSTEM

EMI

Platter Feed System

lamphouse ventilation flue

projection room window

projection lens

gate

lamphouse

pedestal

feed disc

take-up spool

projector

third disc carries additional programme

vision type films, which use a much wider screen than standard films do, an *anamorphic* lens, which contains cylindrical elements, is used to widen the image. The film will have been shot using a similar lens, and the images on the film itself appear compressed horizontally.

Just as in the camera, the film must move intermittently, and a shutter covers the image while the film is in motion. The film is moved continuously by a series of sprockets; its intermittent motion is made possible by loops of free film above and below the gate. These allow the film to be stopped and started in the gate without interfering with its continuous motion through the rest of the mechanism.

The soundtrack is recorded continuously, and not intermittently like the pictures. For this reason the part of the soundtrack which relates to a particular frame is separated from it by an exact number of frames. At the sound head itself, where the film's movement has to be completely even, it passes round a heavy 'sound drum' whose inertia damps out any remaining ripple in the motion.

The length of film on one reel is limited by bulk—a reel carrying more than about 1,800 m (6,000 ft) of film, lasting about an hour, is difficult to lift up on to the projector. Until the introduction of automated projection equipment, most films had to go on two or more reels, and cinemas needed two projectors for a continuous performance.

Modern cinemas use automated systems, which can often accommodate a whole programme of films over four hours long on a single projector, or on two projectors, operating under automatic control, which can hold about 150 minutes of film each.

# Calculators

One of the most widely-used calculating machines, the *abacus*, is also the most ancient. In one form or another it has been around for thousands of years, and millions are still in use all over Asia and the Soviet Union. The abacus consists of rows of beads, which represent the numbers, strung on rods or wires set in a rectangular frame, and although its operations are limited to basic arithmetic a skilled operator can use it as fast as most people can use a modern electronic calculator.

The first real advances in calculating, after the abacus, came in the seventeenth century. In 1614, John Napier invented the system of calculating by means of *logarithms*. Ordinary logarithms are calculated as *powers* of the number 10, for example $100 = 10^2$, or 10 to the *power* of 2, and so its logarithm (to base 10) is 2.0000. The number 3, on the other hand, is $10^{0.4771}$, and so its logarithm is 0.4771.

Sets of tables, known as *log tables*, have been drawn up for use in calculations, and by using these it is possible to perform complicated multiplication and division by simply adding or subtracting logarithms. As a simple example, to multiply 3 by 4 the logarithms of 3 and 4, which are 0.4771 and 0.6021, are added together. This gives 1.0792, which, by reference to the tables, we find is the logarithm of 12, and so the result is 3 x 4 = 12. Division is carried out by the subtraction of logarithms; 12 divided by 3 would be 1.0792 — 0.4771, which is 0.6021, the logarithm of 4. The adding or subtracting of logarithms to perform multiplication or division is based on the *exponent law*, $10^a.10^b = 10^{a+b}$.

The invention of logarithms led to the development of the *slide rule* by Edmund Gunter and William Oughtred during the first part of the seventeenth century. In its simplest form the slide rule has two scales, one fixed and one moving, which are marked off in distances which are proportional to the logarithms of the numbers they represent. Adding or subtracting these distances, by sliding the moving scale along the fixed one, effectively adds or subtracts the logarithms of the numbers indicated on the scales, and so multiplies or divides them. The modern version of the slide rule is based on a design by Amédée Mannheim in 1859.

## Mechanical calculators

The first mechanical calculating machine was invented by Blaise Pascal in France in 1642. This machine used the rotation of gear wheels to represent the numbers, and its design was subsequently refined by Gottfried Leibniz in 1671. Leibniz was the inventor of the *stepped wheel*, a device which was still used in certain types of mechanical calculator built as recently as the 1960s.

The ideas of Pascal and Leibniz were later bettered by the work of Baldwin, Odhner and Burkhardt in the late nineteenth century, who developed more compact and efficient designs. The design of mechanical calculators was steadily refined during the first half of the twentieth century, and electro-mechanical machines, which used an electric motor

Picturepoint

**Above:** The abacus is a form of calculating machine that has been in use for thousands of years. The original version, which was used in ancient Babylon, was probably a tray or board covered in sand, in which marks were made to perform the calculations. This picture shows a modern Japanese abacus.

**Below:** The first practical mechanical calculator was built by the French mathematician Blaise Pascal (1623-1662) in 1642. It consisted of a system of gears and numbered wheels. Although it could perform addition and subtraction it could not do multiplication or division.

**Right:** The linear slide rule consists of two sets of fixed scales, with a sliding set of scales in between them. The scales are calibrated logarithmically, so that multiplication and division are performed, in effect, by the addition or subtraction of lengths along the scales.

Erich Lessing/John Hillelson Agency

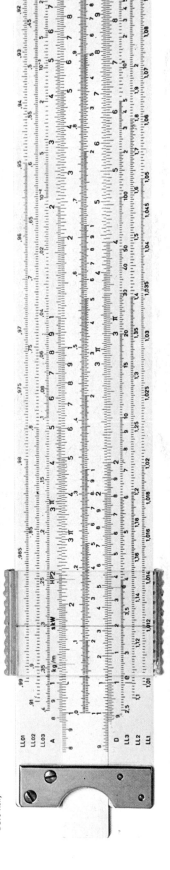

Dave Kelly

Left: A late 19th century adding machine.

Below: The upper two drawings show how a slide rule is used for multiplication. The top drawing shows how a slide rule multiplies 3 by 2; the *unity* ('1') mark on scale C is set at 2 on scale D. The cursor is placed over the 3 on the C scale, and the answer, 6, is where the cursor crosses the D scale. The middle drawing shows 5 x 3, and the way in which the position of the decimal point must be assessed by common sense—the answer is 15, not 1.5 as shown on the scale. The bottom drawing shows how D gives the square root of A, and $C_1$ gives the reciprocals of scale D.

Burroughs

to turn the gears that performed the calculations, were introduced.

## Electronic calculators

The electronic calculator developed as a result of advances in electronic computer technology. The first computers were developed during the 1940s, and were enormous devices containing thousands of electronic valves. However, following the invention of the transistor in 1948, the size and power consumption of computer circuits decreased dramatically while reliability and complexity increased.

The first electronic calculator as such, based on computer circuit technology, was the Bell Punch Anita machine produced in Britain in 1963. It used thousands of discrete transistors in its circuitry, and by today's standards it was a cumbersome machine, but it marked the end of the era of the mechanical calculator based on the gear wheels of Leibniz and Pascal, as well as that of the slide rule based on Napier's logarithms.

With the introduction of integrated circuits by Fairchild and Texas Instruments in the early 1960s, the success of the electronic calculator was assured. An integrated circuit contains the equivalent of many thousands of transistors and their associated components, and is built up from a single chip of silicon which is about 0.3 cm square. The first compact calculator, based on an integrated circuit and using a light-emitting diode (led) readout display, was introduced in 1971, and since then calculator production has expanded enormously. Advances since then have produced calculators little bigger than credit cards, and prices are at almost throwaway levels.

## Basic principles

The actual way in which an electronic calculator works is quite complex, but the basic principles can be explained by reference to the way in which simple calculations are performed.

The operation of a calculator is regulated by a *clock* circuit which, as its name implies, generates timing pulses that are used to synchronize the operations of the other sections of the machine. In a simple calculator the clock may operate at a rate of about 250,000 pulses per second, which would enable it to perform 250,000 operations in one second.

Calculators use a form of binary arithmetic to perform their calculations since, being based on the number 2, all binary numbers can be represented by

Left: A block diagram showing the relationships between the main sections of an electronic calculator. In the latest calculator designs, all the components apart from the keyboard, display and batteries are incorporated into a single integrated circuit chip about 0.3 cm square.

Below: A manually-operated mechanical printing calculator (bottom right) in the foreign exchange dealing room of an international bank. This type of machine has a lever on the right hand side which drives the internal gearing and the printing mechanism when it is pulled.

Syndication International

combinations of '1s' and '0s'. In a calculator, a '1' is present when a circuit is 'on', and a '0' when it is 'off'.

The form of binary arithmetic used by calculators is known as *binary coded decimal* (BCD), and the calculator contains an *encoder* which translates the decimal information from the keyboard into BCD, and a *decoder* which translates the BCD into decimal form to drive the output display.

In ordinary binary coding, the number '1010' represents the decimal number '10'; when read from right to left it represents no '1s', one '2', no '4s' and one '8'—a total of ten. In BCD, however, each *digit* of a decimal number is represented by a four-*bit* (binary digit) binary code, for example '87' would be 0001 1110 in BCD, which is read from left to right.

## Simple calculations

Suppose we wish to do the calculation '5 + 9 = '. On each clock pulse the keyboard is *scanned*, and if there is a valid input present due to a key having been pressed it is sensed by the encoder, which then produces the BCD equivalent of the number.

The first number to be entered, 5, is encoded and then transferred to, and stored in, the *X register*, and it is also shown on the display. The next item to be entered from the keyboard is the *operator*, the '+' in this case, which is sensed by the encoder and sent to the *control ROM* (Read-Only Memory) where it is stored. The control ROM is the 'brain' of the whole calculator, and it controls the operations of the *arithmetic logic unit* which performs the actual calculations.

Left: A calculator assembly line. The girl in the foreground is fitting the integrated circuits to the keyboard assemblies.

Below: The Hewlett-Packard HP-65 is a fully programmable pocket calculator. It can be programmed either via the keyboard or by means of programs pre-recorded on magnetic cards, one of which is shown here, which can store up to 100 program steps each. In addition, 51 scientific and mathematic functions are pre-programmed into its internal storage. The HP-65 has nine storage registers into which data can be entered, and has another four separate working registers.

Below left and centre: The Sinclair Cambridge is a compact, pocket-sized electronic calculator with an 8-digit light-emitting diode display. The centre picture shows the machine with its back cover and batteries removed. The integrated circuit is housed within the rectangular black plastic moulding, and the smaller unit just above it is the rear of the display.

Below right: The CBM/Commodore SR 4148 R scientific calculator, with its top cover removed to show its internal circuits. This machine has two independent storage memories, and is powered by rechargeable batteries.

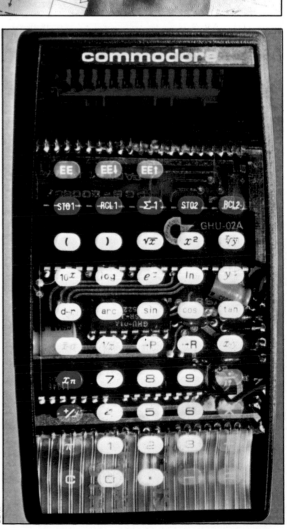

Left: This series of four pictures shows four functions of a miniature electronic calculator/digital wristwatch. From top to bottom, the pictures show: the time in hours and minutes; seconds; the date; and the calculator function.

Below: The Casio Biolator, which contains the additional feature of a program for calculating the state of a person's *biorhythms*, cycles of intellectual, physical and emotional conditions. To find which day of each cycle a person is at involves simply entering the current date and the person's birth date. It can also calculate the number of days since a given date.

Above: The Burroughs C 7200 programmable printing calculator has sixteen storage memories, and its programs are recorded on magnetic cards which each hold up to 408 program steps. Its program storage area can store 816 program steps, and the program cards can also be used for data storage.

The next number, 9, is then entered, and after encoding it is put into the X register, displacing the previous number, 5, into the *Y register*. The number 9 is shown by the display. When the 'equals' key is pressed to complete the calculation, the contents of the X and Y registers are read into the arithmetic logic unit where they are processed according to the operator stored in the control ROM. The answer, 14, is decoded and shown in the display.

Other forms of calculation, such as multiplication, subtraction and division, are carried out in a similar manner, under the control of the pre-programmed instructions of the ROM.

### Complex calculations

When we consider more complex functions of a calculator, such as the calculation of square roots or trigonometrical ratios, the computing power of the calculator becomes apparent. Once again, these are done by addition-type processes, but the numbers may pass through the arithmetic logic unit many times, with intermediate results being stored and recalled as required. These operations are controlled by built-in instruction programs called *algorithms*, the exact details of

which are kept as trade secrets by the manufacturers. The better the algorithms used, the more accurate the calculator.

Simple calculators often have a *memory*, which is just another storage register similar to the X and Y registers, that can be controlled from the keyboard. A *constant* feature is often provided, which acts as a sort of limited memory in that the number is retained automatically in the Y register, and can thus be used for subsequent calculations without having to be re-entered through the keyboard each time it is needed.

On the newer and more advanced 'scientific' calculators, many extra features such as means, standard deviations, linear regression, combinations and factorials are available, in addition to logarithms, trigonometrical ratios and powers. These do not represent the peak of calculator design, however, because programmable machines, into which the user can program his or her own instructions to control the arithmetic logic unit, are also available (though threatened since the advent of 'home' computers).

In the less sophisticated programmables, the manufacturers have provided extra memory spaces so that a sequence of keystrokes for the solution of a particular equation can be 'remembered' and will operate on any number entered. This procedure saves time if the calculation has to be performed repetitively.

Unfortunately, the program is lost once the machine is turned off, and so they must be programmed each time they are used. This drawback may, however, be overcome by the development of new forms of memory circuits which retain their information even when the power supply has been switched off.

The more advanced programmable calculators have the programs retained on a small magnetic card which is put into the machine when required, the information on it being read and stored by the machine. With this type of machine, computer-like techniques can be used since calculation methods such as looping and conditional statements are possible. These pocket-sized machines are so powerful that their computing capacity far exceeds that of the first-generation computers, which occupied whole rooms and consumed tremendous amounts of electrical power.

# Index

Page numbers in *italics* indicate illustrations in addition to text matter on the subject.

## A

abacus *141*
acceleration *102-4*
  gravity effect 104
  Newton's law 48
acoustics *135*
ACV pallets *57-8*
adding machine, 19th century *142*
aeration, water supply 28
aerofoils, lift effect *48-9*
Afgamatic 2000 camera *122-3*
air cushion vehicles (ACV) 56, *57*
air pistol 79
air resistance (drag) 48
air rifle/gun 79
air-launched Cruise missile *92-3*
aircraft *48-51*
  helicopters *52-5*
aircraft carriers 86, *88*
airelons, aircraft 49, *50-1*
airflow
  aircraft wings *48*
  helicopters *54*
Akai crossfield recorder head *128-9*
*Alabama*, USS *85*
*Albion*, HMS *86*
alcoholic beverages *10-13*
Aldrin, Edwin, astronaut 99
ales, production 13
alternating current (ac) 22
aluminium power cables 25
American missiles *90-3*
American Navy warships *85, 88-9*
ammonia refrigerant 20
amplifiers, sound *132-3*
amplitude modulation (AM) 120
anachromic lens 140
angle of attack
  aircraft *49-50*
  helicopters 52
animals, milking 2
anti-aircraft guns *78*
Apollo spacecraft *90, 96-97, 99*
Apollo-Soyuz Test Project *98*
apples, cider production *11*
appliances, domestic *19-21*
aqueducts, Roman *26*
arc welding *109, 110-11*
arched bridges *40-2, 45*
*Ark Royal*, HMS *86, 88*
armour, warships 84
Armstrong, Neil, astronaut 99
Arriflex movie camera 136, *137*
artillery *77-9*
aseptic processing 9
asphalt road surface 34
astronauts *95-9*
Austin car, 1922 *65*
autogyros 52, *55*
automation 106, *108*
automobiles *see* cars

## B

BAC Rapier missile *92-3*
bacteria
  milk 2, *4-5*
  water supplies 26
balers, hay or straw *16*, 17-18
banking control, aircraft *49*
barley
  brewing process *12-13*
  whisky-making *10*, 12
battery powered vehicles 64
battleships, British *84*, 85
Bay Bridge (San Francisco) *44*
beam bridges 40-1, 42

beans, canning process 8-9
Beaumont, Colonel, tunneller 37
Beckmann, Ernst Otto 17
beers 10, *12-13*
Bell, Alexander Graham 58, 114, 126
Bell Punch Anita calculator *142*
Bell X-22A VTO aircraft *55*
Benz, Carl, cars 64, 66
Bernoulli, Daniel, aerofoil 49
bicycles *60*, 62
bikes, racing *62-3*
binary coding, calculators *142-3*
biorhythms calculator *144*
*Birmingham*, USS *86*
bitumen road surface 34, *35*
black top road surfaces 34
Blackbird aircraft *51*
blades, helicopters *52-5*
blasting, tunnel face *36-7*, 38
blasting powder 81
blight, potato *16*
BMW R90 S touring bike *63*
BOD tests, water supply 26
*Boeing Jetfoil* hydrofoils *58-9*
Boeing Sea Knight helicopter *88*
bombs, design *82, 83*
box girder bridges *42-3, 45*
brakes
  motorcycles *61, 63*
  road vehicles 66, *67*
Brand, Vance D., astronaut *98*
brandies, production *12*
Branly, Edouard, radio 118
Braun, Wernher von, rockets 91
*Brave Borderer*, HMS *88*
brazing techniques 110
breech-loading guns *77-8*
brewing process, beers *12-13*
bridges *40-5*
  motorways *32-5*
  resonance effect *105*
Brindley, James, canals 36
*Bristol*, HMS, *85*
Britannia Bridge, Menai Straits 42
Britannia class locomotive *70*
British Rail APT *71*
broadcasting wavelengths *119*, 121
Brown, Samuel, gas car 64
Brunel, Isambard Kingdom 36, 37, 42
Brunel, Mark Isambard 37
BSR/ADC record player *132*
Buick car, 1909 *64*
building construction
  bridges *31-2, 40-5*
  roads *32-5*
  tunnels *36-9*
buildings, bridges *41*
bulldozers, earthmoving *33*
*Bulwark*, HMS *86*
Burroughs calculator *144*
buses 64, *66-7*
butter *3-5*
by-products, beer production *13*

## C

cable systems, telephones *115-17*
cable-spinning bridges *43-5*
cable-stayed bridges 40, *43*
cables, electric power *24-5*
calcium
  milk ingredient 2
  water hardness 28
calculators *141-4*
camber, roads 33, *34*
cameras *122-5, 136-8*

cams, function *105*
canning processes 7, *8, 9*
cannon *74*
cantilever bridges 40, *42, 43*
carbon dioxide refrigerant 20
cardioid microphones *126-7*
cars *64-7*
cartoon movies *136-7, 139*
cartridges
  firearms 76, *77-8*
  recording tape 129
  sound pick-up *130-2*
Casey, Baldwin, hydrofoil 58
Casio Biolator *144*
cassette recorders *127-8*, 129
cattle, dairy breeds *3*
cavitation, hydrofoils 59
Cayley, Sir George, aircraft 52
CEGB control centres 23, *24*
*Célerifère* bicycle 60
Centaur rocket 90
centre of gravity *102-3*
centrifugal force *102, 103*
centripetal force *102, 103*
ceramic pick-up stylus *131*
cereals, whisky sources 12
champagne 10
Channel tunnel projects *37-8, 39*
chassis, road vehicles *64-7*
cheese making *3-5*
Chesapeake Bay tunnel 38
Chevrolet Stingray car *65*
chicken processing *8-9*
chlorine sterilizer, water 27
chunnel *see* Channel tunnel
cider production *11*
cinema *136-40*
cinema theatre *140*
Cinemascope films *139-40*
Cinématographie camera, 1895 136
circuit breakers *22-4*
circuits
  calculators, *143, 144*
  loudspeakers *134*
  pick-up cartridges *131*
  record players *133*
  silicon chips *100-1*
  telephone *113-14*
Citroen car, 1955 *65*
clapper bridges 40
climbing control, helicopters *52*
climbing effect, aircraft 49
clutch mechanisms, cars 66
coagulation, water supply 127
coaxial cable *116*, 117
Cockerall, Christopher 56
coffee, dehydration process 9
cold storage, foods 7
Collins, Michael, astronaut 95
Colorado beetle 16
colour photography *124-5*
Colt automatic pistol *78*
Colt revolver mechanism *76*
combine harvesters 14, *15, 16*
combustion, explosive action 80
commercial vehicles *66-7*
Commodore calculator *143*
compressive stress *102*, 103
Concord aircraft *46-7, 51*
concrete
  bridges *42, 43*
  road-making *33-5*
condensed milk 4
Congreve, Sir William 90
conservation, energy law 104
controls, motorcyles 63
cookers, domestic 19, *20*
copper power cables 25

Coriolis force *103*
Cornu, Paul, helicopter 52, 53
cows, milk breeds *3*
cranks, function *105*
crash barriers, motorways 34, 35
cream *3-5*
crop spraying *16-17*
cruiser type warships *85-6*
crystal sets *118*
Cugnot, Nicolas 64
cutting heads, tunnellers *36, 37*
cutting tools *106-7, 109-11*
Cyclonite explosive (RDX) 82

## D

Daguerre, L. J. M. *122*
Daguerrotype process 122
Daimler, Gottlieb 62, 64, 66
dairy products *2-5*
Darby, Abraham, bridges *41*
*Dat Assawari*, Libyan frigate *87*
Deep Submergence Rescue Vehicles (DSRVs) *85*
deformation and Hooke's law 102
dehydration, foods *8, 9*
delta wing aircraft *49*
demodulation process 117, *118*
derailleur gears *60*, 62
desalination, water supply 28
destroyer type warships *85*, 86
detonation, explosives *80-1*
detonators *82-3*
Deutz, Magirus, engines 67
*Devastation*, HMS, 1873 *84*
developing process, films *124-5*
dialling systems, telephones *114-15*, 117
Dictaphones *126*
Diesel, Rudolf, engines 67
diesel engines
  locomotives 70, *71*
  road vehicles 67
direct current (dc) 22
disc brakes *61, 63*, 66
disease control, plants 16
dishwashers 19
distillation, alcoholic spirits *11-13*
dive procedure, submarines 87
*Dolbadarn* locomotive 69
Dolby system, recorders 127, 129
domestic appliances *19-21*
drag effect
  aircraft *48*
  helicopters *54, 55*
drain laying operation *17*
drainage, roads 33, *34*
Drais de Sauerbrun, Baron von 60
Draisienne, hobby-horse 60
*Dreadnought*, HMS, 1906 *84, 85*
dried foods, methods 9
dried milk *3*, 4
drilling, tunnel face 38
drills, electric 21
drinking water *26-7*
drum brakes 63, 66
Dunlop, J. B., tyres 60
dynamic microphones 127
dynamite 82

## E

Eads, Captain James 41
Earth, radio waves *119*
earthmoving machinery *32-3*
Eastman, George, films 122
Edison, Thomas

special effects
  cinema *137-9*
  radio *128*
speech fequencies 117
speed
  camera shutters 124
  films, photographic *125*
  movie film 136
  sound recording *128*
speed and motion 102, 104
speedway motorcycles *62-3*
spin-dryers, domestic 21
spirits and wines *10-13*
Spuknik I spacecraft 91
SR.N4 hovercraft *56-7*
stall effect, aircraft *48*, 49-50
Stanley brothers, steam cars
  64
steam cars 64
steam locomotives *68-71*
Stephenson, George, railways
  68
Stephenson, Robert, bridges 42
stereo sound systems *131, 132*
stereophonic sound (stereo)
  130
sterilization
  milk 2
  water supply 27
*Stirling* locomotive *68-9*
stones, road-making *32*
strain, definition *102-3*
straw baling 17-18
straw processing 17
stress, definition *102-3*
Strowger, Almon B. 114, 115
studios
  cinema *138, 139*
  radio *120*
  sound recording *128*
styluses, sound pick-up *130-1*
submarine cables 22, *115*
submarines *84-9*
substations, electricity *24-5*
superheterodyne radio *118*
supersonic aircraft *46-7*, 51
surface effect ships (SES) 56
surface piercing hydrofoils 58,
  *59*
Surveyor lunar probes *97*
suspension
  bicycles 60
  cars *65*
  motocycles *62-3*
suspension bridges *40, 42-5*
swing-wing aircraft *51*
switching systems, electric *22-5*

## T

Tacoma Narrows Bridge 45,
  *105*
tail rotor, helicopters *54-5*
Tamar River Bridge, Saltash
  *42*
tape recorders *126-9*
tarmacadam road surface 34
*Tarter,* HMS *86*
tea-picking machinery *17*
telecommunications *112-21*
telegraph, wireless (radio) 118
telegraphone invention 126
telegraphy *113,* 114
telephones, motorways 34, 35
telephony *112-17*
telephoto lenses *122-3*
teleprinters *112*
148  Telford, Thomas    o

bridges 41
  roads 32, 34
temperatures, welding 109-11
tensile stress 102, *103*
tequila (mexian drink) 12
terminal velocity 104
Terront, Charles *60*
Thames river tunnels 37
Thompson, R. W., pneumatic
  tyres 60
Thompson sub-machine gun *77*
Titan launch vehicle *95*
Titan/Centaur rocket *90,* 92
TNT explosive 82
tomato powder process 9
tomatoes, cultivation *18*
topsoil preservation, roads 33
torque effects *104-5*
  helicopters *54-5*
tortion effect, bridges 40
Tower Bridge, London 45
track improvements, railways 71
tractors, design advances 14
trains, railway *68-71*
transformers, electricity *22-5*
transmission, electric power *22-5*
transmission systems, vehicles 65,
  66, 67
transmitters
  microwaves 117, *119,* 121
  radio *120-1*
  telephone *114*
transport
  aircraft *46-7, 48-51*
  helicopters *52-5*
  hovercraft *56-8*
  hydrofoils *58-9*
  railways *68-71*
  road vehicles *64-7*
treatment, water supply *27-8*
Trésaguet, Pierre, roads 32, 34
Trevithick, Richard
  locomotives 68
  tunnelling methods 39
trinitrotoluene explosive 82
Tristar airliner, plan *50-1*
Triumph motorcycle 1903 *62*
trucks *66-7*
trunnions (cannon pivots) 74
Tsar's Great Cannon, Moscow
  74
Tsau River bridge, New Guinea
  *40*
Tsiolokovsky, K. E. *90,* 91 92
tube tunnel designs 37, *38-9*
Tucumcari hydrofoil *58*
tumble-dryers, domestic 21
tuning process, radio 120-1
tunnels *36-9*
Tupolev Tu-144 airliner *51*
turbidity, water supply 26, 27
turboshaft engines 54, 55
turning control, aircraft *49*
twin lens reflex cameras

## U

UHT treatment, foods 2, 8, 9
ultra hih temperature *see* UHT
underground railways *36-7,* 39
underpasses, motorways *34-5*

## V

V-2 missile, World War II 91
vacuum cleaners *19*
*Vanguard,* HMS, 1946 85
vans 67

Vauxhall cars *64, 65*
vectors, meaning 102
vegetable harvesting *16-18*
vegetables, preservation 8-9
vehicles *see also* transport
  lunar landing *96*
Velocifere bicycle 60
velocipede bicycle 60
velocity and motion 102, 104
vertical take-off aircraft *55*
viaducts *see* bridges
Viking spacecraft *90, 97, 99*
*vineyards 10*
virus diseases, potatoes *16*
vitamins, milk 2
viticulture *10*
voltages, electricity supply *22-5*
von Drais ... *see* Drais ...
Vostok spacecraft 95

## W

Wade, General, roads *32*
Wankel-type engines 63
warships *84-9*
washing machines *19, 20-1*
watch calculators *144*
water supply *26-8*
watermills *104-5*
Watt, James, steam engine 106
Watts, Isaac, warships 85
wavelengths, radio 118, *119-21*
weeds, control *16*
welding *109-11*
Westland Wasp helicopter *86*
Westland/Aérospace Lynx
  helicopter *54-5*
Wheatstone, Charles 114
wheel-lock gun mechanisms 74,
  *76*
wheels
  bicycles *60*
  motocycles *61, 62-3*
whisky, production *10-13*
Whitney, Eli, manufacturer 106
wide angle lenses *123*
*Will Rodgers,* USS *89*
Winchester rifle 78
windmills *105*
wines *10-11*
wings
  hydrofoil likeness 58
  lift effect *48-9*
wire sound recorders *126*
wireless telegraphy *see* radio
wiring, telephone *113-16*
work, meaning *103,* 104
wort, brewing liquor 13
Woulfe, P., picric acid 82
wow (record player term) 128
Wright brothers, first flight 48
wristwatch calculators *144*

## X

X-rays, crop sorting use 18

## Y

Yamaha RD 50 motorcycle *61*
yawing control, aircraft *49*
yeasts
  beer brewing *12,* 13
  wine making 10
yogurt *3, 5*
Young, John, astronaut 95
Young's Modulus of Elasticity
  102